The
Curricular Integration
of Ethics

The
Curricular Integration
of Ethics

Theory and Practice

C. David Lisman

Westport, Connecticut
London

Library of Congress Cataloging-in-Publication Data

Lisman, C. David.
    The curricular integration of ethics : theory and practice / C.
David Lisman.
        p.   cm.
    Includes bibliographical references and index.
    ISBN 0–275–95304–1 (alk. paper)
    1. Ethics—Study and teaching (Higher)—United States.
    2. Universities and colleges—United States—Curricula.   I. Title.
BJ66.L57   1996
170—dc20   95–34419

British Library Cataloguing in Publication Data is available.

Library of Congress Catalog Card Number: 95–34419
ISBN: 0–275–95304–1

First published in 1996

Praeger Publishers, 88 Post Road West, Westport, CT 06881
An imprint of Greenwood Publishing Group, Inc.

Printed in the United States of America

The paper used in this book complies with the
Permanent Paper Standard issued by the National
Information Standards Organization (Z39.48–1984).

10 9 8 7 6 5 4 3 2 1

Copyright Acknowledgments

The editor and publisher gratefully acknowledge permission to reprint material from the following
copyrighted sources:

Excerpts reprinted by permission from p. 288 of the Third Edition and from pp. 299, 330–331 of the
Fourth Edition of *Contemporary Moral Problems* by James E. White; Copyright © 1991, 1995 by
West Publishing Company. All rights reserved.

Excerpts from *Research Ethics: Cases & Materials*, edited by Robin Levin Penslar, Indiana University Press, 1995.

Excerpts from *New Choices, New Responsibilities: Ethical Issues in the Life Sciences* by Bruce
Jennings, Kathleen Nolan, Courtney S. Campbell, and Strachan Donnelley. Nutley, New Jersey:
Hoffmann-La Roche Inc., 1990.

To my wife, Vicki, who has supported me in all that I attempt.

To the Community College of Aurora faculty who participated in our curricular integration of ethics project and many of whom supplied case studies in this book.

Contents

1

Introducing Ethics into the Curriculum

The purpose of this book is to provide a theoretical framework for the curricular integration of ethics. This work also will provide examples of how the faculty can integrate ethics in a discipline appropriate way across the curriculum. I successfully directed a three-year program, financially supported by the Fund for the Improvement of Post-Secondary Education (FIPSE) at the Community College of Aurora (CCA). Over the course of three years, approximately eighty-five faculty members integrated ethics in a discipline-appropriate way into selected courses. These faculty members attended a seminar in which they studied ethical theory and ways to infuse the subject into their courses. College students have overwhelmingly found that the project has increased their capacity for ethical understanding and analysis. They believe that they have an improved understanding of interdisciplinary ethical problems, of the relevance of ethics to their academic subjects, and find courses in which ethical issues are raised more interesting. Faculty participants in the ethics project agree with these student perceptions.

I have become aware of a number of ethics-across-the-curriculum projects at colleges and universities across the country. I believe the time is ripe for a book that attempts to draw upon the experiences of these projects and provide curriculum and instructional material for those who are new to this endeavor. Institutional support is essential for the success of such projects. Indeed, many faculty members express a desire to raise ethical issues in their courses. However, they are reluctant to do so because of concerns about diluting the curriculum and vulnerability to student complaints about "teaching values." As this book will document, integrating ethics in a discipline-appropriate way shields ethics discussion from these criticisms. Moreover, I believe this book will convince the reluctant administrator that the curricular integration of ethics has considerable academic value.

WHY DO WE NEED TO DO THIS?

Widespread concern exists about the moral slippage of our society. Former Harvard University President, Derek Bok (1988, 9), observed: "Surveys reveal a wide belief that ethical standards in the society have been declining and suggest that trust in the integrity of those who guide our major institutions has sunk to disturbingly low levels." Wall Street scandals, the S & L failures, the Iran-Contra affair, to name but a few examples of ethical failures in business and government, dislodge our confidence in these institutions. Americans generally believe that family members are more ethical than public figures. However, social critics consider many members of our society to be primarily self-regarding and lacking enthusiasm in their commitment to public life (Bellah et al. 1985). We thus have an emerging profile of a society suspicious of its public leaders, yet unwilling to make public commitments that may be necessary to reform our public life.

Opinions vary concerning the cause of moral slippage. Some cite the deterioration of family values, the waning of religion, and the lack of community as the causes of our civic breakdown. These critics typically call for moral education based on an outlook that locates moral failure in the character of the individual instead of the failure of political and economic structures. They urge parents and schools to improve the moral character of the child as the primary means of moral regeneration.

Others would not disagree that a weakened individual, family, and community support network contribute to moral decline. However, they believe these mediating institutional failures are rooted in a philosophy and political economy that have emphasized individuality and material values at the expense of cultivating the "habits of the heart," that is, the virtues of civic life or concern for the good of all. Dworkin (1990, 7) claims that the attempt to resolve moral lapses through moral education means that our society, or our society's political and educational leaders, have abandoned seeking political solutions to our social problems. Dworkin states, "We have turned to ethics as a substitute for politics. Rather than examining institutional and economic structures, we decide to improve character."

We need not resolve the debate concerning the ultimate source of our crises of moral confidence. Instead, we must recognize that education has a significant role in revitalizing a sense of morality among young people. Families and churches have declined in moral influence over the past few decades, and schools must assume a greater role in providing moral education. Although Dworkin may be right about the reason some people seek "ethical" solutions for our social problems, this insight can become a focal point of an ethics program. We must attempt to get students to understand that the roots of our problems are not solely derived from lapses of individual character but stem from unjust social structures. We cannot expect the media or the business community to provide this form of ethical analysis. These institutions have contributed to the increased tendency to adopt a privatized view of society. If a structural analysis emphasizing justice issues is presented at all, it primarily will be a result of a concerted effort within educational institutions.

There is another important reason why our universities have an important ethical contribution to make. Bok (1988, 9) expresses it very well: "...higher education has assumed a more important social role, and much larger proportions of the population now come in search of advanced instruction." Indeed, virtually every business executive and lawyer, every public servant and physician, every politician and engineer will now pass through our colleges and probably through our professional schools as well. Our colleges and universities can use this strategic position to encourage students to think more deeply about ethical issues and strengthen their powers of moral reasoning.

Historically both public schools and colleges and universities have provided this function. O'Neil (1990, 191) points out that in the nineteenth century a shared sense about the moral order of the universe existed. He observes, "Influenced strongly by the Scottish common sense school of philosophy and mainstream Protestantism, undergraduates received a dose of moral philosophy in their senior year, which provided them not only an understanding of their intellectual and moral heritage, but a systematic way of projecting themselves upon the world they found beyond the college walls." The vision of the school leaders of the nineteenth century and their institutions provided "a theory of action and a public language for those students who matriculated for study." Since that period of history, factors, such as industrialization and corporatization, a decline of the influence of Protestant values, the disintegration of a homogeneous American culture, and the emergence of large research universities and the departmentalization of knowledge, have led to a sense that little common framework of moral values exists.

Although there may be no consensus concerning an issue, considerable agreement exists among disputants concerning fundamental moral values or principles, such as beneficence, non-maleficence, autonomy, and justice. The curricular integration of ethics provides our educational institutions with a framework for reasoned debate and discussion of moral issues integral to the understanding of academic disciplines and professional and social practices.

The objective of providing a framework for ethical discussion can be carried out in several ways. One could do as little as publicize the standard ethics course taught in a philosophy department. Or one could require an ethics course for everyone in a degree program. One also could develop a professional ethics course as a component of an occupational degree. This currently is being done in areas such as business, nursing, paralegal studies, and public policy. However, these approaches may not be practical for many institutions for obvious reasons. Most colleges do not have a required ethics course in the general studies core. Since professional studies programs already have a full curriculum, faculty and administration are reluctant to add yet another course to the degree requirements. The result is that some professional programs either do not include an ethical component or superficially treat the subject.

We need more attention to ethics in higher education. Yet limited opportunities exist to develop special ethics courses. A reasonable alternative is to develop an ethics-across-the-curriculum program, as many schools are doing. It is worthwhile to incorporate ethics into courses across the entire curriculum. Different disciplines, such as paralegal studies and the humanities, approach ethics differently. The aspects of ethics appropriate for these disciplines are not treated in a standard ethics course. For example, literature emphasizes the moral nature of character or deals with questions of the good life. Often these topics are not discussed in an ethics course. Occupational courses may emphasize the problems of an ethics code and those involving the practitioner-client relationship. Such topics are seldom discussed in an ethics course. Moreover, if an instructor does not make the effort to raise a curriculum-appropriate ethical issue, students will have little opportunity to apply what is learned in an ethics course to a sociology or science course. Students seldom delve into an issue more deeply than does the instructor. Students without any background work in ethics cannot be expected to make the connections between subject matter and ethics on their own. Even if students are willing to make the connections, ethics discussions require competent guidance. Faculty members who explore the nature of ethics and the application of ethics to their discipline can guide students in effective analysis and discussion of ethical issues.

To effectively integrate ethics into the curriculum, faculty members need some background. While faculty members frequently report they have been "raising" ethical questions in their courses for years, they may be doing little more than raising questions. They may not be guiding student analysis and discussion. Too often faculty members may insert ethics questions at several points in their courses, as business texts do at the end of each chapter. However, this superficial treatment is not very successful. What is needed instead of touching lightly on a variety of questions, is an in-depth analysis of one or two ethical issues that pertain to a course. Also, research undertaken in the CCA project suggests that faculty will have a greater impact on the moral development of students if they provide guided discussion of ethical case studies or situations where the students come to a decision concerning the right thing to do in a particular situation.

Effectively guiding ethics discussions requires several competencies: knowing how to integrate ethics into a course, being able to articulate a common moral framework in terms of which ethical issues are analyzed, and a grasp of some of the essentials of moral theory that will help an instructor feel confident in guiding ethics discussions. A suggestive report states that teachers are reluctant to introduce ethics in their courses because of concerns about how the students will react (Cunningham 1992). One instructor claims that students have a distaste for thinking. Other students, either out of respect for pluralism or out of a relativistic perspective, consider it wrong to disparage or even openly disagree with another's moral point of view. A cluster of problems must be addressed: absolutism, individual and cultural relativism, and how an instructor might deal effectively with students in terms of these perspectives. I give attention to these and related issues in later chapters.

HOW DO WE DO IT?

At nearly every conference on moral education I have attended, someone announces that he or she is attempting to develop a moral education component in their curriculum, school, or college. They want to know how to do this and especially how to measure whether people become morally better themselves because of moral instruction. Other attenders impatiently point out that measuring moral improvement is extremely difficult because of the complexity of the moral life. Moreover, it is argued that what we should be about is to help people think more critically about moral issues. We assume that if people sharpen their analytical thinking skills about ethics, they will presumably make better moral decisions. Of course, we want people to be moral. In some cases, especially with younger children, direct moral instruction is the appropriate pedagogy. However, as young people become more mature, they develop a greater sense of independence. Developing moral independence not only is necessary for maturity, but it is a moral virtue. In our zeal to mold moral beings through direct moral instruction, we can jeopardize independence of character. As most parents know, the art of parenting involves balancing the responsibilities of forming moral character and of promoting independence of character. At times we need to direct moral instruction. There is a time to make clear to young people or young adults that we are on the side of honesty, compassion, and justice. However, many ethical issues of the day involve conflicts, not over whether or not one should be moral, but over how to apply these moral norms or principles in concrete situations. Students need guidance in accomplishing this task.

Assuming young people have developed some of the virtues of the moral person, they need assistance in developing the ability to think critically about ethical issues. Moral education should promote the critical agency of students (Brookfield 1991). Being able to critically analyze ethical issues and make effective ethical decisions is as important as the will to be moral. I comment more about these issues in a later chapter. For now I shall simply state that at the high school and college level, the core of moral instruction should be critical. We should help students understand moral ideas and teach them to apply these ideas and principles in concrete situations.

My approach to infusing ethics into the curriculum presupposes that we have some fundamental agreement over moral norms, such as honesty, justice, and autonomy. I assume that we want to deepen students' understanding of and commitment to these norms. This should provide some comfort to conservative critics of moral education who fear that if we do not engage in direct moral instruction, the effect will be to weaken or undermine the student's commitment to moral principles. At worst, it is feared that such an approach may promote moral relativism. But as Carr (1991) states, who can be against honesty and fairness? Reinforcing one's commitment and deepening one's understanding of these fundamental moral values is an important aspect of the goal of the curricular integration of ethics.

Based on my experience of working with approximately eighty-five faculty members, I recommend that participating faculty members focus on discipline-based case studies. I define a case study broadly as a personalized and contextualized account of an ethical issue. The nature of these accounts varies with the academic discipline. I shall discuss these differences in more detail in the following chapters. However, for the present I simply suggest that case studies are highly effective tools for presenting ethical issues. In a separate chapter I will discuss teaching techniques, including how to effectively present a case study.

In light of the current service learning movement, I would like to touch upon the relevance of the curricular integration of ethics to promoting service learning. Service learning is generally defined as the inclusion of community service as an optional assignment in a course. The service experience is expected to be tied to the course objectives, and there should be an opportunity for structured, critical reflection on the service experience. One of the main reasons for promoting service learning is very similar to encouraging the curricular integration of ethics to promote a greater sense of civic responsibility. At the heart of being civically responsible is being committed to working for the good of all, or the common good. This, we shall see is also at the heart of what it is to be a moral being. Of course, being civically responsible involves more than being committed to working for the good of all, but that is at least a part of the meaning of the concept of civic responsibility.

Another linkage exists between the curricular integration of ethics and service learning. Conducting ethics discussions of issues related to course objectives and the service experience is an excellent way to promote an increased sense of civic responsibility. A sense of civic responsibility simply does not come out of the service experience; it requires guided reflection. Providing ethical discussion in a course, related to course objectives and the service experience, is one way to structure the critical reflection component in such a way as to help achieve what for many is the overall objective of service learning, namely, promoting a greater sense of civic responsibility.

EVALUATION

It is important for a college or university division or for the school itself to assess the effectiveness of the curricular integration of ethics. This can help in showing the effectiveness of this venture and can be useful in seeking outside funding.

Impact on Students

One of our instruments evaluated the extent to which integrating ethics into courses had enriched ethical understanding. This instrument showed that most students have a significantly increased understanding of ethical issues in society and in the related disciplines.

Impact on the Faculty

As one evaluation of the project, faculty members provided a year-end report, including a summary of how they carried out the teaching of ethics in their courses. These are included in the *Project Reports: A resource handbook for integrating ethics into the curriculum* (1992). Several themes emerged in the faculty assessments. The faculty participants believed that the integration of the teaching of ethics into their disciplines has had the following effects on both students and faculty members:

- Promoted a heightened awareness of ethics and ethical issues.
- Promoted a sense of the classroom as a moral learning community and fostered better interaction between students and instructors.
- Enabled instructors and students to better clarify their own values.
- Empowered faculty members and students to integrate, understand, and apply the practical and the theoretical aspects of their disciplines.

Most faculty members participating in the project continued to conduct ethics discussions in their courses. Over fifty percent of the previous ethics project participants still teaching at CCA responded to a questionnaire concerning whether they were still implementing ethics into their courses. Out of forty responses, only two said they were not implementing ethics. Based on this response, I conclude that the curricular integration of ethics has become a permanent part of the instructor's repertoire at CCA.

Some results from the project I had not anticipated. For example, ethics discussions promote a greater sense of community in the classroom. As the students wrestled with important ethical dilemmas and case studies, they realized that they could respectfully engage in reasoned arguments with their fellow students. Finally, in course after course, students found new relevance in much of their academic material. They have found that discussing discipline-appropriate ethical issues has made their courses more relevant. They realize that effectively analyzing and thinking about ethical issues requires mastering some of their course material because ethical issues are at the heart of this material.

The CCA ethics project has had a significant impact on students. Students display an increased understanding of ethical issues in society and in their disciplines. They exhibit an ability to identify ethical issues and dilemmas and have an increased understanding of how to analyze ethical problems. Finally, the students have displayed increased skills as critical thinkers with increased ability to make principled, moral decisions.

Similar results have been duplicated elsewhere. Ashmore and Starr (1991) report that faculty members who participated in their curricular integration of ethics project made ethics a serious component of their courses and developed new pedagogical strategies. Marquette University's project was so successful that they obtained a dissemination grant from the National Endowment of the Humanities to help twenty other colleges and universities develop similar programs.

Encouraged by these successes, I shall offer a discussion of the key ingredients of a curricular integration of an ethics program, including a basic discussion of the elements of moral theory, ways to deal with challenges to accomplish this pedagogical effort, and discipline-specific examples.

HOW TO APPROACH READING THIS BOOK

Not everyone will be interested in reading some of the theoretical parts of this book. The main purpose of these chapters is to provide the reader with a deeper understanding of the framework of ethical reasoning. I would not anticipate that an instructor integrating ethics case studies in a course would spend any time discussing ethical theory. Hopefully, this material will help an instructor detect the positions students take with respect to ethical issues. Some of these theoretical issues crop up in discussions, especially virtue theory, ethics of caring, religious ethics and multicultural relativism. However, some readers may wish to browse through these chapters and spend more time on the discipline-specific chapters.

Part I

The Moral Framework

2

The Elements of Ethics

RECOGNIZING ETHICAL SITUATIONS

"Morality" refers to a set of principles or rules that guides us in our actions. "Ethical theory" and "moral philosophy" refer to reflection on the nature of morality. This definition of morality provides us with a guideline for distinguishing an ethical from a nonethical situation. Guided by this conception of morality, let us first consider an example of an ethical situation and then contrast this with a nonethical situation.

An Ethical Situation

Read the following story as a possible example of an ethical situation. As you read the story, ask yourself what features of the story make this an example of an ethical situation.

Case Study: The Fate of Baby Amy

Lynne Vuillemot, a former obstetrical nurse practitioner, told the agonizing story of the decision she and her husband, John, made not to allow intervention surgery for their daughter, Amy (Vuillemot 1992). Amy suffered from hypoplastic left-heart syndrome (HLHS), a malformation of the aorta, and an undeveloped left ventricle, the main pumping chamber of the heart.

The Vuillemots initially believed their daughter was healthy. But shortly after her birth, Amy began to experience difficulty breathing. They took the baby to the Oakland, California, Children's Hospital. There the attending physician told the Vuillemots that Amy had HLHS, a syndrome that occurs in about one of 5,000 births.

The Vuillemots faced three choices. One was to do nothing and allow the baby to die. No legal obstacles prevented them from refusing further intervention, because the recommended surgical procedures were unproved and carried high mortality rates. Second, their daughter could await a heart transplant. Ten of the thirteen babies who had transplants at that hospital they were considering were alive, but half the babies had died waiting for a suitable donor. Also, anti-rejection drugs used for heart transplant patients can cause major health problems, especially in infants. The third option was for Amy to have two open-heart surgeries in her first two years to correct her problem. Amy's chances for surviving both operations were less than fifty percent. The doctors said that if Amy survived the operations, her life could be somewhat normal.

The Vuillemots wrestled with whether they should allow the surgery. As they learned about the complications of the surgeries, such as blood clots, infection, and hemorrhage, they began to doubt that Amy would be able to live a healthy life even if she survived surgery. What were her actual chances of health and happiness?

The Vuillemots finally admitted surgery was not the best idea. However, they felt guilty about such thoughts. To make matters worse, the physicians would not give them a clear opinion. The Vuillemots painfully realized that they must make the decision. They worried about the long periods of hospitalization during the first year of life, at a time when a child should learn to trust the surrounding world. No one would predict what the life expectancy was for children who survived this surgery. The Vuillemots wondered if it was selfish to think of preserving their marriage, and hoping for future children? What was in Amy's best interest?

An older cardiologist told them that in Europe HLHS is not treated. This strengthened their growing resolve not to go through with the surgery. They told Amy's pediatrician their decision.

The next day the hospital chaplain performed a short service at Amy's bedside. Amy had received a scheduled dose of morphine and was comfortable. The Vuillemots helped their pediatrician disconnect Amy from the medical tubes that kept her alive. Amy died in the intensive care unit, bundled up in her receiving blanket, with her loving parents beside her.

Characteristics of an Ethical Situation

Why does this story present an ethical situation? What if one were to say that it is an ethical situation because it is a highly emotional one? It is that. The realization that their daughter was suffering from HLHS was devastating for the Vuillemots.

However, not all emotional situations are ethical situations. For example, someone might be upset over a broken television set. Being angry with the television set is not an ethical situation. Moreover, not all ethical situations are emotional. Consider a person who makes a promise to meet a friend at a given hour, and when the appointed time nears, proceeds indifferently and without further deliberation to keep the appointment. Although this is an emotionally neutral situation, it is nevertheless an ethical situation because the person has made a promise.

Perhaps the Vuillemots' story is about an ethical situation because it is a value situation. It is important to recognize, however, that not all value situations are moral situations. For example, a decision concerning whether one wants to eat apple pie or ice cream for dessert or buy a Ford or a Toyota automobile may represent value situations. These situations would not ordinarily represent ethical situations. There are many different kinds of values—aesthetics, personal values, religious values, etc. Of course, these present norms may be implicitly involved in an ethical decision.

The controversy surrounding the initial 1990 decision by the National Endowment for the Arts to withdraw a $10,000 grant supporting "Witnesses: Against Our Vanishing," a planned New York City art exhibition inspired by the AIDS crisis, illustrates a connection between aesthetics and ethics. Following a storm of criticism from the art world and the decision by Leonard Bernstein to refuse a 1990 National Medal of Arts, John E. Frohnmayer, the chairperson of the National Endowment, reversed his decision. There are two separate issues here, one moral, the other aesthetic. The aesthetic issue concerns whether the controversial works of art had artistic merit. The other issue concerns the moral justification of the Endowment's decision to withdraw funding of controversial projects.

To continue, one might suggest that an ethical situation is one in which we use ethical language, such as "ought," "ought not," "right," and "wrong." Sometimes, however, we use these words in nonethical senses. For example, consider a situation where some person is trying to decide whether to get off welfare and go back to work. If you were to say that this person ought to get a job, you may not be expressing an ethical judgment. Using the word "ought" in a sentence does not necessarily make a situation an ethical one. Although you may be rendering a moral judgment, it is possible that you are not. Here you only may be prescribing a certain course of action as desirable if one wants a job. This is a hypothetical prescription. The obligations implied by hypothetical prescriptions are conditioned upon someone's interest. For example, if I were to say to my friend that to become an anthropologist, she must go to college, I am recommending a given course of action as a means to some desirable end. In contrast, as we shall see in later detail, we use ethical concepts to make prescriptive claims, such as, "You ought to keep your promise." Claiming that one ought to do something from the moral point of view implies that the obligation is not conditional upon someone's interest. The distinction between these two kinds of prescriptions will be discussed in greater detail later.

Finally, there is the possibility that the Vuillemots' situation was ethical because they confronted a dilemma. Their dilemma was whether to let their daughter have surgery or to let her die. The Vuillemots indeed confronted an ethical dilemma, but that is not what makes this an ethical situation. Many ethical situations involve no dilemmas. Again, suppose that someone makes a promise to meet someone at a restaurant later in the evening. As the time for the promised meeting approaches, the person remembers the promise and proceeds to the restaurant. Here there is no apparent dilemma. The person who made the promise does not face compelling alternatives characteristic of dilemmas. This person has incurred a duty because of having made a promise.

Although an ethical situation does not necessarily contain a dilemma, the dilemma-like features of the Vuillemots' story may serve to bring into focus what makes this an ethical situation. The Vuillemots had to decide whether to let their daughter die or to allow risky intervention surgery. They had to make a decision that affected the prospects of their daughter's life. Ethical situations are those that affect the potential well-being or interests of other persons. If our decision had no effect on others, then it would not be an ethical decision or a decision with ethical implications. To give, perhaps, a highly unlikely example, consider a person lost in the jungle, far from civilization with little or no hope of any human contact. This person has cut his leg and has developed gangrene and is experiencing great pain. He realizes that he can go no further and decides to take his life. His decision is not an ethical decision, because it involves only his interests. Of course, this example might involve religious factors. However, that does not represent an ethical consideration, at least from the perspective of secular ethics.

This is a rare situation, because most decisions have ethical implications, or at least have background ethical considerations. For example, trying to decide whether or not to go on a diet primarily concerns one's own well-being. Nevertheless, it is a health decision and, as such, may affect others. If it affects others, this decision has an ethical dimension. This observation should not be construed to imply that, as ethical beings, we must dredge up all the ethical implications of our decisions. That would be self-defeating; we would be so busy thinking about ethical implications that we would never get anything done. We recognize that we must deal with the relevant ethical dimensions of our decisions. For example, a physician tells a parent that she has emphysema and that if she continues smoking, she will become seriously ill. Here the parent must consider the potential effect on the family of the decision of whether to quit smoking.

There is yet another factor that makes the Vuillemots' situation an ethical one, and that is they are not only confronted by a decision involving the well-being of someone else, but they realize that their decision is a decision of principle. They recognize that they need to think about the situation, to search for appropriate information to help them in their decision, and to base their decision on certain general rule-like considerations. They recognize an obligation to do whatever is in the best interest of Amy. They want to help prolong Amy's life. They also do not want to contribute to further suffering. They must decide which course of action to pursue: to risk the potential suffering that Amy might incur in the hopes of providing her with the opportunity to continue living, or not to allow her to continue living in the belief that there is a far greater possibility that Amy will suffer or eventually die than that she will be healthy. Two principles are in conflict in their situation: (1) one ought to promote the good, including not taking an innocent life; and (2) one ought not to inflict suffering on innocent victims. At the very least, identifying the moral principles implicit in an ethical situation helps one understand the morally relevant features of a circumstance and to reflect on possible choices.

To summarize, a moral situation is any situation in which the interests or needs of another must be considered and in which one faces a decision of principle concerning whether one's own needs or interests deserve precedence over those of others.

Although we usually use ethical language to discuss ethical situations, it is not necessary to use these terms for a situation to be a moral one. For example, suppose you confront a dilemma concerning whether to report a mistake in your favor to your credit card company. Although you may not use ethical language to characterize your situation (you may think of it in terms of what you get out of it or wonder if the risk of getting caught is worth it), this is a moral situation. It is so because you are considering whose interests should prevail, yours or your credit company's.

To take another example, consider a business situation in which someone is trying to make a decision concerning whether to change jobs based on a cost-benefit analysis. If the decision turned solely on whether the person would find the new job more satisfying, the moral aspect might well be minimal. Let us suppose, however, that the job change would have a serious impact on one's family. Here a moral element comes to the fore as central to the decision.

As ethical beings, we usually manage to do the right thing without much deliberation. For example, when you see someone ahead of you drop his or her wallet, you call out to the person without considering keeping the wallet. This is a moral situation in which you recognize that the interests of someone else have a prior moral claim. You feel obligated to call out to the person who has dropped the wallet.

THE MORAL POINT OF VIEW

Having developed an understanding of what a moral situation is, we need to consider what is implied by adopting the moral point of view. Since a moral situation is, by definition, any situation in which consideration of the interests of others is appropriate, we adopt the moral point of view when we acknowledge the appropriateness of taking these interests into consideration in making a decision. To adopt the moral point of view, then, is to consider impartially the interest of each individual involved in the moral situation (Rachels 1986). We also recognize that moral decisions or judgments must be supported by good reasoning. I want to elaborate on both points.

First, an unwillingness to make a rational decision is to fail to follow through seriously in fully considering the interests of others. The Vuillemots considered the interest of all affected persons. In their deliberations they wondered if they were putting their own interests ahead of Amy's. Were they being selfish in "hoping for happier times with future children," or in wanting a child so much that they were willing to approve risky intervention surgery? The Vuillemots were trying to be as impartial as possible. They wanted to be sure that they were not giving more weight to their own needs than should be given and that they were acting in Amy's best interest. This commitment to impartiality is the hallmark of the moral point of view.

This case also illustrates a couple who made a rational decision, even though it was very painful. They attempted to base their decision on the best available evidence concerning Amy's prospects. They were, of course, frustrated because they could not get the physicians to give them solid advice. Gradually, they began to accumulate enough evidence to become convinced that there was not much liklihood that Amy would survive the second surgery or have an opportunity to live a healthy life. They realized that if they permitted the surgery, they would in all likelihood be condemning their child to a couple of years of prolonged suffering, which the child certainly would not be able to understand, only to be followed by her death. Keeping their daughter alive was paying too great a cost of human suffering.

MORAL PRINCIPLES

Adopting the moral point of view involves not only the willingness to consider the interests of others as they may make claims upon us, but also the willingness to justify our ethical decisions by an appeal to reason. What counts as reason in these situations? Let us consider an example of an ethical situation and examine how reason comes into play.

A Rape in New Bedford

At approximately 9:00 p.m. on March 6, 1983, Jane walked into Big Dan's, a small dilapidated bar on the fringes of the North End of New Bedford, Massachusetts, a part of town where people of mainly Portuguese origin live (Whitley 1987). The twenty-one-year-old woman, Jane, had grown up in New Bedford, and although not Portuguese, moved recently to the North End with her two daughters. Big Dan's, a hangout for Portuguese men, had a reputation of being a trouble spot. The bar was located on a street with brightly painted three-story houses, grimy factory outlet stores, and a few cafes.

Jane came into the bar to buy a pack of cigarettes but saw a female acquaintance, and the two women had a drink together. The friend finished her drink and left the bar, leaving Jane the only woman in the bar. When Jane headed for the door, a bar patron prevented her from leaving.

The man threw Jane on the floor, stripped her from the waist down, lifted her up onto a pool table, and raped her. When he finished, another man raped her. She was raped by four men. Two other men held her down and forced her to perform oral sex. She was threatened with a knife held to her throat. The dozen or so customers circled the pool table and watched like spectators at a sporting event. They ordered drinks and joked among themselves. While Jane cried out for help, the customers shouted, "Go for it, go for it!" Others entered the bar during the attack, saw what was happening, and walked out. No one telephoned for the police, and no one attempted to prevent what was happening.

Around midnight, when one of the attackers let go of Jane so another could take his place, she ran screaming into the street and flagged down a passing car. She was driven to a phone where she called the police.

She met a patrol car at Big Dan's. The officers went into the tavern where they found business as usual. The officers picked up Jane's clothes and sealed off the bar. She dressed in the back of the patrol car, then went into the bar and identified two of the attackers who were still there. The officers arrested them and took Jane to the hospital where she was treated and sent home. The police tracked down the other suspects and witnesses. One witness said that he didn't intervene because he didn't consider it any of his business. The bartender said a man prevented him from calling for help. Another man said he was afraid to do anything to stop it. Four men were charged with aggravated rape and jailed.

All four suspects were Portuguese immigrants, a large number of whom lived in New Bedford. They were either unemployed or were working at odd jobs. Three had arrest records, although none had been previously charged with rape. The episode created a controversy in the community over the behavior of the Portuguese population. Some accused Jane of being a prostitute. Spokespersons for the Portuguese community, stunned by the crime and national attention it was generating, issued statements in which they deplored the incident and accused the media of bias.

A week after the incident, several thousand people in New Bedford participated in a candlelight march to show support for Jane and to protest the witnesses' involvement. Some had posters saying, "Rape Is Not a Spectator Sport." Jane's attorney filed a ten million dollar lawsuit against the owners of Big Dan's on Jane's behalf. The four men were eventually convicted of their crime against Jane.

Here is an example of a scandalous and traumatic moral situation, involving the gang rape of a woman. I have chosen this example because it illustrates a moral situation about which little disagreement exists regarding who was wronged. There is such widespread agreement that it is wrong to sexually abuse others, that the word "rape" is a pejorative term, that is, it connotes a morally disapproving attitude. If we were pressed to say why we thought that sexually abusing another in this way is wrong, what sort of reason would we give?

Most of us probably would say that this is an example of imposing or forcing our own demands on another person, treating people in a degrading way, or inflicting pain on another person. Let us suppose that we are in basic agreement that what makes the New Bedford incident wrong is that someone was sexually degraded and hurt. The consideration of pain and suffering involves an appeal to a general rule or principle to support our specific judgment that it was wrong for these men to rape Jane. This is a typical example of moral reasoning in which, along with considerations of certain appropriate substantiating facts establishing that the rule applies in the given situation, a general rule justifies a specific rule. The logical form of this argument is:

It is generally wrong to do X (X = Harm Others) or One ought not to X
(X = Harm Others).
This is a situation in which Y occurred (Y = Rape) and Y is an instance of X.
Therefore, Y is wrong.

Although we encounter many ethical dilemmas in which we may not be sure what is the right thing to do, we are clear about what is the right thing or the wrong thing to do in many ethical situations, as this above example serves to illustrate. Moreover, we hold in common general moral principles. Some principles that we probably agree upon are the following:

- One ought not to take another human life.
- One ought not to willfully injure or inflict suffering on harmless victims. (Principle of non malfeasance).
- One ought to alleviate suffering.
- One ought to keep promises.
- One ought not to lie.
- One ought to be free to say and do what one wants. (Principle of Autonomy)
- One ought to treat others fairly. (Principle of Justice)

While this is far from an exhaustive list of general principles that we might agree upon, nevertheless, it represents a core of shared moral agreement. We often encounter very little difficulty in applying these principles to specific situations.

MORAL DILEMMAS REPRESENTING A CONFLICT OF PRINCIPLES

However, we do encounter difficulties making moral decisions in situations where moral principles are in conflict. These are *moral dilemmas*. Most of us manage to resolve some moral dilemmas without much difficulty. For example, suppose you have made a promise to meet a friend at a given time, and while you are en route to keep your appointment, you come across an accident in which someone is injured. Let us further suppose that you are the only one who has arrived at the accident and you happen to be a nurse and can render aid to this victim. You realize, however, that taking time to stop and help this victim means that you will not be able to keep your promise to meet your friend. This represents a moral dilemma, because the decision you confront involves a conflict of two moral principles to which you subscribe: (1) you ought to keep your promises, and (2) you ought to help alleviate suffering. This dilemma is not very difficult for most of us to resolve, because most of us intuitively sense that generally our duty to alleviate suffering in situations like this should take priority over our duty to keep promises.

However, not all dilemmas are so easily resolved. Most of the major moral controversies that we encounter professionally and societally involve such dilemmas.

It might be helpful to examine an example of a more complicated dilemma to see what else might be involved in attempting to resolve it. Consider the following example.

Protest Spawns Ethical Fight

In 1983, Cecil Andrews, a thirty-seven-year-old unemployed roofer with a history of alcohol and personal problems, phoned WHMA-TV in his hometown, Anniston, Alabama, and said that he planned to set himself on fire in the town square of nearby Jacksonville, Alabama. He said he was doing this to protest unemployment in America (Earley 1987).

Two television crew members appeared on the scene and videotaped Cecil Andrews lighting matches and catching his knee on fire. They taped for a half a minute before one of the crew members, Gary Harris, yelled, "We can't let this happen." They tried to put out the flames with a small notebook.

As Andrews, on fire, ran across the town square, the other crew member, Ronald Simmons, continued videotaping. A fireman arrived on the scene and extinguished the flames with a portable fire extinguisher. The victim was transported to the University Hospital in Birmingham. He sustained second- and third-degree burns over more than half his body.

Although the television station did not broadcast the 82 seconds of the videotape, the episode raised questions about the standards and practices of journalism and the problems unique to television reporting. Various media commentators contended that the crew acted unethically. First WHMA and its news director should not have dispatched the crew, because in doing so the station may have contributed to the man's igniting himself. One television station said that they did not cover suicides, unless it was a public person or it occurred in a public place. And if it was in a public place, they might cover the story, but would not videotape the actual suicide.

Some critics pointed out that even if the presence of the crew was necessary, they should have acted to prevent the man's immolation. Organizations expect their staffs to report under great stress, such as in wartime gunfire, weather, and natural disasters, but they are not expected to report when their reportage might contribute to the risk of other human life. The incident set off a number of responses by the national network and media criticism. CBS provided fire footage, stopping when Andrew's knee caught fire. ABC showed the man igniting himself, stopping the fire footage after the man's thigh began to burn. NBC showed Andrews, a ball of fire, racing across the town square.

In their defense, WHMA claimed that there were mitigating circumstances. The station said that they notified the police before dispatching the crew. They further claimed that the police were unable to locate the man and had asked the crew to come, hoping their presence would lure Andrews into sight. The two crew members believed that the police were hiding when they arrived, and that they were going to grab Andrews when he appeared.

This situation involves a conflict over at least two principles: (1) we ought not to harm others, and (2) we ought generally to be free to say and do what we please. Taking up the first principle, while the television station contended that the reporters believed that they were aiding the police in preventing the victim from igniting himself, it could be argued that when they were filming the man, they were not trying to prevent him from harming himself. One also could contend that because they had the camera going before the man ignited himself, they were contributing to the act. That is, it is likely that the man might not have ignited himself if, once the TV crew realized the police were not going to show up, they had made it clear that they were not going to film him.

Turning to the second principle, generally the press has the right, even the duty, to report the news. Freedom of the press is not only an important constitutional right, but, as an application of the second general principle, it is an important moral right. However, does freedom of expression include the right to do and say what we want when doing so causes harm to others? Most of us probably would agree that our right to do as we please does not include the right to harm others. Here the principle of nonmalfeasance overrides or limits the principle of autonomy. This limitation of our liberty has been expressed by John Stuart Mill as the "harm principle." This principle states that *we are free to say and do what we please, unless in so doing we harm others*. The adage that we do not have the right to stand up and yell "fire" in a theater illustrates this principle. Although we may agree with this principle, disagreement exists over what counts as "harm."

For example, the controversies concerning the censorship of pornography illustrate our difficulties in applying the harm principle. People debate whether reading pornographic literature or viewing pornographic films causes males to harm women sexually. A minister publicized a videotape of an interview with the serial murderer,

Ted Bundy, who confessed that pornographic literature and films precipitated his violent acts. Some argue that the Bundy confession illustrates that the accessibility of pornography causes men to harm women sexually. Others reply that viewing pornography is only a weak contributing factor. Indeed, one might claim that "normal" people who indulge in pornography are not criminally affected, while people like Bundy would criminally assault women despite the inaccessibility of pornography. Although there are serious dilemmas, nevertheless, we still have some basic agreement over the "harm principle."

The dilemmas of the person faced with a decision whether to break a promise to render assistance to an accident victim and the television coverage incident illustrate that in situations of conflict we need to arrange our principles in order of importance. While we intuitively manage situations such as that of the accident victim, we need to find some procedure for prioritizing our basic principles in more complicated situations. Another way of putting this is to say that we recognize that moral principles are not absolute, they include exceptions. How do we decide when to include exceptions?

Usually, moral principles include exceptions when a more weighty moral rule overrides the general principle. How do we decide that? The situation would be simpler if it turned out that our moral principles were always weighted the same. One might be tempted to think that the rule of nonmalfeasance overrides our right to do as we please. Yet, as the current moral dilemmas of euthanasia and abortion illustrate, there are many people who believe that we are justified in taking the lives of others in certain situations. Some also would argue that in times of war, we should draft young men into the armed services to risk their lives in the service of their country. How can we make any headway in dealing with these and many other dilemmas?

THE ROLE OF MORAL THEORY

These problems illustrate the need for moral theory. Moral theory, as Beauchamp and Walters (1982, 11) suggest, is the advancement of "bodies of principles and rules that are more or less systematically related." Moral theory provides a basis for justifying fundamental moral principles or rules and a procedure for arranging conflicting principles in order of importance. In upcoming chapters we will examine consequentialism, non-consequentialism, and virtue theory, the most widely used theories in the current discussion of ethical issues. We also will consider difficulties of these theories.

3

The Role of Moral Theory in Ethical Decision Making

The kind of conflict that we encounter in dilemmas, as we have seen, involves a conflict of moral rules or principles. We need some procedure for ranking our rules, that is, for deciding which rule should take precedence over another rule in a situation. Perhaps in these situations we should abandon the rules altogether. If we should not, then why should we not?

In ranking rules, we could adopt the strategy of determining an abstract principle from which we could derive these rules. We then could use the principle in deciding which rule or norm takes precedence in various circumstances. This is a search for an ethical theory. As Beauchamp and Walters (1982, 12) says, "A structured normative ethical theory is a system of principles used to determine moral obligations." A good moral theory should accomplish two purposes. One, it should provide us with an account of the source or grounds of moral value, that is, it should supply us with an answer concerning as to why we should be moral. Second, a theory should provide us with a framework or strategy for ranking moral norms when we confront a dilemma. While historically there are several important moral theories, recent work in applied ethics has come to feature two theoretical approaches—*utilitarian* and *deontological*, or *consequentialism* and *non-consequentialism*. I focus on these two theories. Following this, I discuss another popular theory, *contractarianism*. I discuss this third theory in conjunction with a presentation of John Rawls' theory of justice.

UTILITARIANISM

Utilitarianism is the view that an action or practice is right if it leads to the greatest possible balance of good consequences or to the least possible balance of bad consequences for all involved. David Hume (1711-1776) first proposed this theory, but Jeremy Bentham (1748-1832) and John Stuart Mill (1806-1873) definitively formulated it. Bentham and Mill were social reformers who viewed morality as promoting human welfare by minimizing harms and maximizing benefits. They believed that there was no point in having moral codes unless they served this purpose. For Bentham and Mill, the Good is the greatest amount of happiness for the greatest amount of people. Bentham argued that morality was nothing more than the attempt to cause as much happiness as possible in this world. There are two versions of utilitarianism, act and rule-utilitarianism, associated with Bentham and Mill, respectively.

Act Utilitarianism

According to this view, we are to evaluate each specific moral situation and adopt that course of action that contributes to the greatest balance of pleasure over pain. Bentham expresses his view as follows:

By the Principle of Utility is meant that principle which approves or disapproves of every action whatsoever, according to the tendency which it appears to have to augment or diminish the happiness of the party whose interest is in question; or what is the same thing in other words, to promote or to oppose that happiness. (Mill 1967, 17)

Let us take an example to illustrate how one would apply act utilitarianism.

AIDS

Richard Restak, in an article, "The AIDS Virus Has No 'Civil Rights,'" contends that we should quarantine AIDS victims (1987). Restak illustrates the seriousness of the disease for society. As of 1985, 13,000 Americans had confirmed cases of the disease and probably more than one million Americans were infected. The number of confirmed cases could double every year. Restak says that although we should treat those who have the disease with care and compassion, merciful treatment should not be confused with a refusal to keep this disease from spreading further.

Historically, plagues such as syphilis, bubonic plague, tuberculosis, and polio have resulted in quarantining the victims. However, quarantining those who test HIV positive is unpopular. Instead, many are advocating that we should accept the AIDS victim in our schools and place little or no restrictions on employment or housing.

According to Restak, quarantines have been very effective in defeating outbreaks of scarlet fever, smallpox, and typhoid. It is a means of protecting society from the spread of this disease. Restak objects to city and state laws that have given AIDS victims legal rights not to be discriminated against in seeking employment, housing, and health care, and to allow children with AIDS to continue to attend school.

Here we have a very good example of a utilitarian argument. Protecting our society from AIDS is so urgent that we must override the "rights" of the AIDS victims and isolate them from the rest of society. Let us leave aside the issue of whether it is feasible to attempt to quarantine the thousands of people with this disease. Some would reply that it is wrong to ignore or override the rights of these people. Nevertheless, in advancing a utilitarian argument, Restak contends that considerations of the welfare of our society as a whole demand that we ignore these rights.

Act utilitarianism, then, is the view that we are to pursue the action or policy that will produce the greatest amount of happiness for all concerned. The appeal of this theory resides in offering a practical way to calculate what we should do. We must weigh the costs and the benefits of our decisions and pursue that course of action that will produce more benefits than costs.

Restak's view brings to fore the most serious criticism of this theory, namely that utilitarianism seems to justify acting in the name of expediency. The civil rights of AIDS victims should be weighed against the utility to society of virtually imprisoning these people. However, as we can see from Restak's position, for the act utilitarian, rights are never absolute. We only need to respect the rights of people if it is expedient for society to do so.

Let us consider rule utilitarianism to see if it has a way out of this problem.

Rule Utilitarianism

Mill maintained that the standard of morality is the "rules and precepts for human conduct, by the observance of which an existence such as has been described (happiness) might, to the greatest extent possible, be secured to all mankind, and not to them only, but so far as the nature of things admits, to the whole of sentiment creation" (Mill 1967, 412-13). According to Mill, we need to appeal to the general principle of utility in two circumstances. One is when we justify moral rules or principles, such as the principles of nonmalfeasance, liberty, or autonomy. The other circumstances are those situations where rules are in conflict. We apply the principle of utility to determine which rule will promote the greatest amount of happiness for all concerned. For example, the principle of utility justifies promise keeping, not because keeping a promise is the right thing to do in a specific situation, but because promise keeping is a kind of action that if practiced generally contributes to the welfare of the entire society. Upholding promise keeping contributes to the good of all parties concerned through upholding promise keeping as a moral institution for the entire society.

The following story illustrates the importance of upholding fundamental norms of decency and justice. The Argentinean writer Julio Cortazar (1989) relates a true story from a newspaper clipping. In this clipping Laura Beatriz Bonaparte Bruchstein wrote that on the morning of December 24, 1975, the day after a battle between the Argentine army and Argentine citizens, her daughter, Bruchstein Bonaparte, age twenty-four, was arrested in the Monte Chingolo slum, which was where the previous day's uprising had occurred. She was taken to the military headquarters of the 601st Battalion and, along with others, was arrested, tortured and shot to death that same Christmas Eve.

Authorities notified Laura Bonaparte of her daughter's death and took her to the police station. After three hours of interrogation, they told her where her daughter was buried. They showed her hands cut from the daughter's body, which had been placed in a jar. The following day she went to the cemetery where her daughter was buried in a common grave. More than a hundred people were murdered and buried, among them her daughter.

Laura Bonaparte brought charges of murder against the Argentine army. Because of the accusations, her daughter's fiancé was murdered on a street in Buenos Aires and her husband, a doctor of biochemistry, who was an invalid because of a heart attack and with a prognosis of three months to live, was dragged from his bed and taken away by the military. They questioned him about Laura Bonaparte. They abused and tortured him until he died (Cortazar 1989, 251-53).

Here we see an example of a society where fundamental rules of due process and respect for human life have broken down. Individuals who challenge the government are jailed without due process and systematically tortured and executed. This graphic story illustrates the importance of upholding fundamental moral principles, such as guaranteeing due process and rules prohibiting the indiscriminant torture and murder of a society's members. Without upholding these principles, civilized society is virtually impossible.

Second, in terms of rule utilitarianism, the principle of utility enables us to determine which moral norm or principle to follow in situations where moral principles are in conflict. For example, in euthanasia cases, two moral principles or norms are in conflict, mercy against the protection of life. A utilitarian would say that one should act on the principle that promotes the greatest amount of happiness for all concerned.

Proponents of rule utilitarianism have defended themselves against the charge that they would sacrifice justice to expediency by insisting that in the long run it would be unwise to make such a sacrifice. For example, while it might be expedient in the short run to institute slavery, in the long run such a policy, because it is unjust, would prove socially disruptive. The slaves would eventually revolt against their unjust treatment. Thus the utilitarian, with a view toward promoting social stability in the end, would refrain from advocating unjust expedient policies.

However, does this theory adequately deal with this problem? In the first place, if, as a society, we are committed to securing the greatest amount of happiness for all concerned, utilitarianism appears to be unable to rule out the possibility of instituting repressive measures. A perverse utilitarian might argue that in a society, such as Argentina, where civil unrest exists, the government must deal efficiently and harshly with dissidents. While people, such as Ms. Bonaparte, will be upset by the torture and executions of the members of her family, our perverse utilitarian might argue that such measures are necessary for creating the political stability that is required for sustaining the welfare and happiness of the majority of the members of society.

One might reply that irrespective of the contentedness of the majority of the members of a society, any society that engages in the systematic torture and execution of dissidents is immoral. Unfortunately, utilitarianism cannot justify this ethical defense. The only ploy available is to argue that we need to make a distinction between supporting the "immediate happiness or good of a society" versus "securing happiness or good in the end." The utilitarian may claim that it is not expedient in the long run to engage in acts of brutality, including the execution of dissidents. Yet, how can we be confident that the unjust regime will crumble under its own acts of injustice? Perhaps this is a lesson we might learn from history, but there is no guarantee that a repressive regime will always fall. As Orwell's *1984* (1949) and Margaret Atwood's *The Handmaid's Tale* (1988) illustrate, if a regime engages in sufficiently systematic and persuasive repression, it might be virtually impossible to bring the government down.

Still, this point does not get at the basic criticism of utilitarianism. We instinctively believe that systematic torture of people is wrong, despite the fact that engaging in the torture of a few will promote the happiness of the majority. Utilitarianism maintains that the right-making feature of an action is its contribution to human happiness. Surely, doing the right thing is connected to the contribution those actions bring to happiness.

We generally believe that supporting right conduct will contribute to the welfare of all, but we also believe that there are other right-making features of actions.

DEONTOLOGICAL THEORIES

The Prussian philosopher Immanuel Kant (1724-1804) advanced a deontological theory that has been enormously influential. While some of his ideas remain extremely useful, some are not. I want to dispense with his problematic ideas first and then take up the more fruitful aspect of his theory.

Kant drew the distinction, which I have already commented upon, between hypothetical and categorical prescriptions or imperatives. Hypothetical imperatives are conditional imperatives that require us to adopt the means that enable us to attain the ends we set for ourselves. For example, suppose I say to you that you ought to take out a bank loan if you want to buy a car. In saying this I am prescribing that you take out a loan to attain the goal you have presumably set for yourself.

The other type of imperative, the categorical imperative, is the imperative of morality. These imperatives are not conditional upon our needs and desires, but binding upon us as rational agents because we are rational. For Kant, our moral rules, expressed in the form, "One ought to do X," e.g., keep promises, repay our debts, tell the truth, etc., are binding upon us as rational moral agents. Kant attempted to show how moral principles can be derived by autonomous moral agents and have the kind of authority in our lives characteristic of an authoritarian ethic, such as the command theory, i.e., that what makes an act right is that it is willed by God. (I discuss this theory below.) For Kant the authority of justified moral rules resides in their inherent rationality. We, as rational moral agents, derive and justify our rules as satisfying the conditions of rationality. How, one might ask, can we know when our rules are rationally justified?

The Categorical Imperative

According to Kant, our rules are justified when they satisfy the requirements of what he calls the categorical imperative. The imperative states: "Act only on that maxim through which you can at the same time will that it should become a universal law" (Kant 1964, 88). Kant is claiming that moral principles or maxims must be universalizable. We must recognize, as rational agents, that if we advocate a moral principle, it must be applicable to everyone, not just to those for whom we are expressing the principle. For example, if I were to say that my rule is that I ought to reward honest work, I am not being fully rational unless I acknowledge this should be a rule for everyone (regardless of whether others would agree to abide by it). So the test for any putative moral rule is its universalizability, namely its application to everyone. For Kant, if we choose to be as fully rational as possible, we would recognize that moral principles must be universalizable because universalizability is a template of thinking rationally.

Kant illustrates the categorical imperative with several examples. One of his examples is that of a person who is considering whether are not to make a false promise. Let us suppose that someone is trying to borrow money from another without intending to repay the loan. Kant says that if a person is attempting to be fully rational, the person must ask himself whether his rule here, namely, that "Whenever one needs a loan, promise to repay it, although realizing that he cannot do so," can be universalized? That is, can we imagine everyone adopting this as their rule? Kant thinks not. Such a rule would be self-defeating. For if this rule were universally adopted, no one would believe anyone else when they asked to borrow money and promised to repay the loan.

In his examples of the categorical imperative it becomes clear enough that, according to Kant, moral principles have another characteristic besides universalizability, namely reversibility. Moral principles apply to everyone, including the person advocating the moral principle. For example, suppose I have a relative who is terminally ill and is suffering greatly. I am the guardian, and it is legally permissible to remove the life-support system. The physician in charge asks me what he should do. Should he remove the life support system and allow my relative to die in dignity, or should he prolong this terrible suffering? I reply that my relative must stay on the life support system because euthanasia is wrong under any circumstance. If this principle applies to everyone, it also must apply to me. Would I consider it wrong to have my death eased and hastened, were I experiencing unbearable suffering? The concept of reversibility is captured by the Golden Rule which states that we should "Do unto others as we would have them do unto us." We should subject our moral recommendations for others to the test of reversibility to be sure that we really are being consistent.

Difficulties with the Categorical Imperative

The problem with Kant's categorical imperative is that it is merely a formal requirement. While Kant thought that this imperative was sufficient to derive moral principles, it is not. This imperative would suffice to derive many rules that are not moral rules. For example, suppose I am considering whether to take my umbrella with me on a sunny day. What if I asked myself, is it possible for everyone to adopt a rule, namely that on a sunny day everyone should take their umbrella with them wherever they go? It does not seem self-defeating for everyone to walk around with umbrellas. As silly as it might be, we can imagine a society in which people walk around every day carrying their umbrellas. So this rule is universalizable; it satisfies Kant's formal condition of universalizability. Yet this rule strikes us as silly. It is not a moral rule that we would expect a society to have. Something has gone wrong here. What has gone wrong is that the categorical imperative is only a formal requirement. It cannot provide moral content. Moral rules, I would agree, must be universalizable. However, this is an insufficient basis for generating moral principles. We need another way to derive moral rules.

Kant regarded moral rules, once derived (and justified) as absolute; that is, they admit of no exceptions. In one of Kant's celebrated examples, which James Rachels (1986) calls the Case of the Inquiring Murderer, Kant maintained that we have an absolute obligation not to lie. For example, suppose a friend asks me to hide him from a murderer who is after him. I do so. The murderer knocks on my door and asks me if I am hiding my friend. According to Kant, I have an obligation to tell the truth, although it may mean that the murderer will kill my friend. This seems ridiculous. We do not believe that we should sacrifice the life of a friend to avoid telling a lie. That Kant considered moral rules to be absolute represents a problem with his theory. Kant apparently thought that moral rules were absolute because he believed that, as rational agents, we must be consistent in our moral judgments. That is, if I am considering adopting a moral rule or basing my action as a rational agent upon a rule, I must acknowledge that it must be possible for everyone to act in this way. This is a requirement of consistency. Kant seems to have thought that consistency in this matter implies that there can be no exceptions to moral rules. However, is this true?

All that is required by Kant's fundamental notion is that when we violate a rule, we do so for a reason that we would be willing for anyone to accept, were they in our position. The reason Kant may have thought that consistency of this sort implied that moral rules were absolute was because he believed the categorical imperative not only stipulated a formal requirement that moral rules must satisfy, but it provided a requirement of content. That is, if the categorical imperative could not only require us to be consistent in our moral reasoning, but if it also could tell us what we ought to do and not do, then the categorical imperative itself would generate moral rules. These rules would be justified by the categorical imperative, which did not provide us with a procedure for deciding whether rules admitted of exceptions. This becomes particularly problematic in situations where there are conflicts of rules, presumably justified by the categorical imperative. For example, in the situation of the Inquiring Murderer, I have already incurred the duty to tell the truth, but also the duty not to cause the death of innocent victims. Which duty should prevail? Most of us would say that we have a greater duty to protect the life of our friend than to tell the truth to the murderer. Unfortunately, the categorical imperative, even if it could generate moral rules, does not provide a procedure for resolving dilemmas. In a dilemma the categorical imperative cannot pick out which rule has greater weight.

Principle of Respect for Persons

Kant states another imperative that is central to moral theory. He regarded this as another formulation of the categorical imperative. I call this imperative *the Principle of Respect for Persons*. Kant stated it (1964, 96) as follows: "Act in such a way that you always treat humanity, whether in your own person or in the person of any other, never simply as a means, but always at the same time as an end."

Leaving aside a discussion of why Kant considered the Principle of Respect for Persons to be another formulation of the categorical imperative, we can see that this principle provides us with moral content. The principle does not provide, as does the categorical imperative, merely a formal requirement. It stipulates that when we are considering whether to adopt a rule, we need to ask whether the rule we adopt includes treating persons, not merely as a means, but also as an end. The Principle of Respect for Persons enables us to see, I think, why we would reject the rule that everyone ought always to carry umbrellas. While the umbrella rule satisfies the categorical imperative, i.e., the principle of universalizability, it does not satisfy the Principle of Respect for Persons. To expect everyone always to carry their umbrellas, no matter what they are doing or where they are, seems arbitrary and demeaning. Thus the Principle of Respect of Persons enables us to rule out rules inconsistent with treating people with respect as ends.

Since this book is not a work on moral theory, I believe it would take us too far afield to discuss further the merits of utilitarianism and Kant's duty theory. I also do not believe that either theory provides us with an adequate framework for moral decision making. However, each theory appears to provide a fundamental component for effective moral decision making. In many ethical situations we find it appropriate to consider which course of action will promote the greatest amount of good for all concerned. We also find it appropriate in many situations to ask which course of action is compatible with promoting the dignity or respect of persons.

A STRATEGY FOR ETHICAL DECISION MAKING

Bearing this in mind, as a general strategy in decision making, I recommend that both criteria be combined in the following way:

"WE SHOULD ACT ON THAT PRINCIPLE OR ADOPT THAT COURSE OF ACTION OR POLICY THAT IS UNIVERSALIZABLE, RESPECTS THE DIGNITY OF PERSONS, AND WHICH PROMOTES THE GREATEST AMOUNT OF GOOD FOR ALL CONCERNED" (Brown 1990).

Let us apply this strategy to an ethics case study.

Case Study: Surveillance at Work

"Report Says Computers Spy on 7 Million Workers in the U.S." read the *New York Times* headline on September 28, 1987 (DesJardins & McCall 1990). According to a report prepared by the Congressional Office of Technology Assessment for Rep. Don Edwards (D-Calif.), over seven million American workers are being monitored at work by computers. For many of these workers, this surveillance occurs without their knowledge.

Computers monitor such things as rest breaks, use of telephones, presence at work stations, and frequency of errors. Some computers count individual typewriter keystrokes, eavesdrop on customer service calls, and count the number of incoming phone calls. The computers can then be programmed to evaluate job performance against a norm established by monitoring other workers.

If you were a manager and you were offered this service, would you take advantage of it? Would the decision of whether to use the service depend on the type of workers that you were supervising? Would it make any difference if most of your workers were in the secretarial pool, or were professionals such as accountants or loan officers? How is this any different from more traditional methods of monitoring employees? Would it make any difference if the employees were informed about these procedures beforehand (DesJardins & McCall 1990)?

Applying our decision strategy to "Surveillance at Work" we might ask the following questions:

Adopting a Policy

1. What is our organizational purpose? Will permitting surveillance at work serve that purpose?
2. Does pursuing our purpose violate any principles? Promote respect for persons?
3. What are the consequences of surveillance? Will these consequences cause more harm than good?

Thus in facing an ethical decision, we might ask the following:

1. Does the projected course of action respect the dignity of persons?
2. Does the projected course of action promote the greatest amount of good for all concerned?

THEORIES OF JUSTICE

A complicated moral notion involved in discussing ethical issues is the principle of justice or fairness. Accordingly, I briefly want to discuss this and related issues. The formal principle of justice states that people should be treated equally unless there is justification for treating them differently. This principle is involved in the discussion of many ethical issues across curricula especially in the social sciences. The difficulty confronting the formal principle of justice arises in determining the justificatory grounds for differential treatment. For example, is gender a relevant factor in determining whether someone should be hired for a job? Differential treatment in hiring practices is only justified when that treatment can be shown to be job-relevant. For example, if being able to lift seventy pounds is critical for a job, an employer would be justified in not hiring those who are unable to lift this amount of weight.

The most difficult justice issues have to do with economic and social arrangements. What is fair treatment in the workplace? Are significant inequities between the wealthy and poor morally justified? Theories of justice vary in terms of the justificatory procedure, for example, whether a theory is consequentialist, non-consequentialist, or contractarian. They also differ in terms of the human or social qualities that serve as the benchmarks of justice. For example, the libertarian conception of justice holds that individual liberty is to be maximized. For a libertarian, social goods are distributed unfairly if they are done in a way that robs an individual of his basic liberty, such as the right to own property or the right to earn as great an income as one wants. Extreme liberals, on the other hand, make absolute social equality the ideal. For example, a socialist usually subscribes to the right of the government to ensure that everyone has fundamental social and economic equality with respect to food, shelter, and health care. More moderate liberal views of justice agree with socialists in believing that everyone has the right to minimal economic security. However, unlike socialists, liberals emphasize the importance of certain individual rights, such as freedom of speech. Liberals disagree among themselves concerning the degree of social inequalities that should be corrected. For example, a utilitarian liberal might hold that "inequalities are justified to the extent that allowing them maximizes the total amount of good in a society" (Mapes & Zembaty 1992, 351). If increased productivity depends on providing workers a larger income than those on welfare, and if doing this increases the total amount of good in a society, then the inequalities between the assembly-line worker and the welfare recipient would be justified for the utilitarian. John Rawls, as we shall see, offers a different view. He maintains that only those inequalities of social good are justified as will increase the advantages of the least advantaged. Recently, communitarian theories have been critical of Rawls' view and have advocated a view similar to the utilitarian view of justice mentioned above, insisting that the common good takes precedence over the rights of individuals.

Although there are a number of theories of justice, the most prominent of these is John Rawls' (1971) theory. Accordingly, I provide a brief discussion of his theories and some of the difficulties he confronts. I hope this discussion will provide a philosophical framework for discussing justice-related issues.

John Rawls' Theory of Justice

Rawls (1971, 83) theory is expressed in two principles. These are:

First Principle - Each person is to have an equal right to the most extensive total system of equal basic liberties compatible with a similar system of liberty for all.

Second Principle - Social and economic inequalities are to be arranged so that they are both: (a) to the greatest benefit of the least advantaged (difference principle), and (b) attached to offices and positions open to all under conditions of fair and equal opportunity (principle of fair equality of opportunity).

Rawls maintains that the two principles are a special case of a more general conception of justice that can be expressed as follows: "All social values (primary goods)—liberty and opportunity, income and wealth, and the bases of self-respect—are to be distributed equally unless an unequal distribution of any, or all, of these values is to everyone's advantage" (Rawls 1971, 62).

The basic notion is that everyone is to be assured an equal liberty to pursue whatever plan of life one pleases as long as it does not violate what justice demands. Justice attempts to secure a scheme of cooperation that enables individuals to pursue their own interests or to pursue the primary goods of life (liberties, opportunities, powers income, wealth, and self-respect).

The First Principle: Liberty

The first principle distributes basic liberties, which include political liberties, such as the right to vote, free speech and assembly, and liberty of conscience and thought (Rawls 1971, 61). "These liberties are to be equal and as extensive as possible consistent with an equal liberty for everyone" (Strike 1990a, 32).

The Second Principle: Difference and Equality of Opportunity

The second principle governs the distribution of social goods and resources, including economic resources. The first part of the second principle is called the *difference principle*. The difference principle assumes that an equal distribution of basic social goods and resources is required, unless it can be shown that an unequal distribution is to everyone's advantage. According to Rawls, showing that a given distribution is to the advantage of the least advantaged person in society constitutes an unequal distribution that is to everyone's advantage.

The difference principle not only governs government policy with regard to the economy, but it also governs other institutional arrangements of goods and resources, especially education. Rawls (1971, 101) says that "the difference principle would allocate resources in education ... so as to improve the longer-term expectation of the least favored." For example, the difference principle would uphold developing remedial education programs, to the extent that the learning deficiencies of "at risk students," are due not to lack of natural abilities but to class-related or socio-economic background. Rawls would not necessarily rule out programs that benefit those who show greater intellectual or creative aptitudes, for example, programs for the gifted and talented. Rawls only stipulates that giving more attention to the better endowed is only justified if it can be shown to improve the long-term expectation of the least favored.

Let me illustrate the difference principle in terms of the plight of females. There is evidence that in the early years of schooling females outperform males in math. However, the situation is reversed in later years. Historically, mathematics and the sciences have been male-dominated, and females and teachers discourage females from taking math seriously. Because of this state of affairs, developing a special math program for females to encourage them to overcome gender discrimination in this area might be justified.

However, treating females preferentially in the classroom is different from having a special math program for females. This has to do with the dissimilarity between the *difference principle* and the *principle of fair equality of opportunity*, the second part of the second principle.

The Principle of Fair Equality of Opportunity

While the difference principle governs the distribution of benefits and burdens, or resources and goods, the principle of fair equality of opportunity governs, among other things, accessibility to resources. Access to jobs and other opportunities is to be equally available to everyone. Hiring, for example, should be based on relevant criteria, such as ability to do the work, rather than on irrelevant criteria such as race or sex. The principle of fair equality of opportunity captures the formal principle of justice, namely, that persons who are alike in morally relevant respects ought to be treated alike, and that persons who differ in morally relevant respects ought to be treated differently in proportion to the differences between them.

Lexical Priority

According to Rawls, the principles of justice have lexical priority. This means that the first principle of greatest equal liberty has priority over the second principle of differences of fair equality. Thus the first principle of basic liberties cannot be overridden in satisfying the demands of the rules of the second principle. For example, if we consider having the right to private property a basic liberty, then attempting to distribute social benefits to the advantage of the least advantaged cannot include seizing personal property. Also, for Rawls, the principle of fair equality cannot be overridden in satisfying the demands of the principle of difference. For example, although under the principle of difference, preference could be given to hiring a person from a previously disadvantaged group, the preferential treatment must be conducted in a way that does not systematically exclude people outside of the preferential group from a fair opportunity for employment.

The Contractarian View

Rawls' contractarian theory is part of a general framework of moral justification originating with John Hobbes (1588-1679) and John Locke (1632-1704). Hobbes maintained that life outside of social arrangements was "nasty, brutish and short." People discover that it is in their self-interest to enter into a contact to form a society with laws regulating human conduct. Individuals thus renounce their right to do whatever they believe to be in their self-interest in the state of nature and agree to obey an authority they establish (Barclow, 1994). Locke pondered the problem confronting individuals who find themselves living in society and not having ever explicitly agreed to form a social contract. He contended that as long as people partake of the advantages of society, they have implicitly given their consent to the "contract." Rawls takes the issue one step further, by arguing that there never was any original social contract. It is only that there is a "hypothetical contract" reflecting the justification for principles of justice and other aspects of morality.

Rawls (1985) attempts to justify these principles of justice in terms of appealing to the concept of enlightened egoism, i.e., individuals as predominately motivated by considerations of seeking their own self-interest. Rawls offers a hypothetical argument, called the original position, in which he attempts to show that arranging a society in terms of the two principles of justice is the rational thing to do. His argument suggests that we imagine that we are living in a pre-moral society in which everyone is motivated by self-interest. In such a society, we assume that individuals are operating from a "veil of ignorance" in which they do not know what will happen to them in the future after the society implements principles of justice. Rawls assumes that individuals in such a position would find his principles of justice to be the most rational principles to accept, particularly the principle of difference. If an individual did not know whether he or she would be wealthy or poor, for example, presumably this individual would opt for a system of justice that gives the greatest advantage to the least advantaged. This is because an individual might end up among the disadvantaged.

There are difficulties with this theory. For example, as Strike (1990b) points out, the argument assumes people are more risk avoidant than they really are. Recent communitarian critics of Rawls also have claimed that his argument presupposes the ideology of individualism, i.e., individuals are a sole reality who enter a contract, as opposed to recognizing that individuals are social beings essentially. Sandel (1982, 62) argues that Rawls' account "rules out the possibility of what we might call 'intersubjective' or 'intrasubjective' forms of self-understanding, ways of conceiving the subject that do not assume its bounds to be given in advance." Similarly, Sullivan (1982, 115) claims that Rawls is a part of liberalism's individualist and utilitarian vision of human nature that has "compelled contractarian thinkers to base their social contract upon a moral will that is discontinuous with the desiring nature of the human self." Distributing social goods based on what is to everyone's mutual benefit may not always result in providing an advantage to the least advantaged. For example, while it may not be to the advantage of the least advantaged in our society to have a work-fare program in which welfare recipients are given a couple of years to get off welfare or be required to do public work, it might ultimately be in the best interest of society as a whole to have such a policy.

There is some evidence that Rawls (1985) has begun to abandon the contractarian argument of ethics in favor of an appeal to the fundamental concept of personhood , which he believes is given within our Western intellectual tradition. That approach either assumes that the concept of personhood is derived from a particular cultural tradition, or the Kantian view that respect for persons is entailed by rational activity. In the first case, this leads to cultural relativism. In the second case, a deeper analysis suggests that "personhood" is rooted in our essential sociality. Unfortunately, I cannot explore this intriguing notion further.

Going further into the communitarian/liberal debate concerning the principle of justice would take me too far afield. Suffice it to say, whether one agrees with Rawls' (1971) contractarian perspective or with his principle of difference, he has made an enormous contribution to justice theory. Leaving aside the principle of difference, Rawls' (1971, 62) more general formulation of the principle of justice, namely that all "social values (primary goods)—liberty and opportunity, income and wealth, and the bases of self-respect—are to be distributed equally unless an unequal distribution of any, or all, of these values is to everyone's advantage" is a useful place to begin discussing justice issues.

Part II

Teaching Ethics

4

Deontological and Virtue Theory

A theoretical challenge to developing a framework to ethics is the current debate between a deontological theory of ethics, emphasizing the role of moral principles as a framework for ethical decision making, and advocates of virtue ethics. This latter approach, rooted in Aristotle, maintains that the most important enterprise of ethics is to help develop moral individuals. The basis for deciding right from wrong in terms of this theory is considering what a virtuous person would do in a given situation. Rather than discussing and analyzing moral principles, virtue theorists discuss and analyze the virtues of good people.

The overarching goal of the curricular integration of ethics is to help students learn how to think more critically about ethical situations and make better ethical decisions. The secondary goal of the curricular integration of ethics is, of course, to promote moral growth. As I stated in the opening chapter, I have found that providing students with the opportunity to critically discuss ethical issues contributes to the moral growth of individuals in a variety of ways. Being able to think more carefully and clearly about ethical situations is itself a form of moral growth. Also, young people become more conscious of their moral responsibilities as a result of deliberating over ethical issues. Literature, as a curricular integration of ethics, has the capacity to promote moral growth in interesting ways. I shall explore this topic in the chapter on the humanities and ethics. However, as I suggested in my opening chapter, I believe there is a limit to the extent that one can "directly" instill virtues in young people in the school setting. Clearly, the attempt to directly promote moral growth is more appropriate when dealing with younger students. Elementary schools typically attempt to accomplish this in a variety of ways, such as by enforcing rules of fairness and sharing, etc. But as students grow older, in the interest of promoting the virtue of autonomy, we refrain from such direct moral instruction. Instead we try to engage students in critical discussions about ethical issues out of the conviction that this process will help them come to see the value in making the right moral decisions and becoming moral persons. The curricular integration of ethics can further this cause. But a couple of issues need to be dealt with at this point because of the debate between deontological, or principle-based, ethical theory and virtue ethical theory. The first issue concerns the general view that there are "two" approaches to ethics. Are there two ethical approaches, or is it that we can see these two approaches to ethics represent two different ways of perceiving ethical situations?

Second, this issue has been clouded by the view that there are gender differences in the way males and females approach ethics. It is alleged that females adopt a virtue approach to ethics, emphasizing caring, whereas males tend to adopt a principled-based approach to ethics. I shall explore this issue in the next chapter.

PRINCIPLE-BASED ETHICS THEORY AND PROMOTING MORAL GROWTH

As previously stated, the underlying assumption of the curricular integration of ethics is that one of the most effective ways to promote moral growth among older students is by providing them with opportunities to engage in critical reflection over ethical situations and dilemmas. I also have stated above that providing moral education, or promoting moral growth, clearly involves activities besides critical discussion. We can see what is missing in an approach to moral education that limits itself to reliance on critical discussions of ethical dilemmas by briefly examining Kohlberg's (1971) theory.

Drawing upon Piaget's developmental theory of psychology, Kohlberg (1971) claims that all children, despite their culture, possess the capacity to pass through three levels of moral growth (pre-conventional, conventional, and post-conventional) consisting of a sequence of six stages of moral development. These range from morality based on hedonistic consideration and group loyalty to the highest level of Rawlsian principles of justice and fairness and the belief in universal moral principles. Kohlberg used the Heinz dilemma in his research with both young and older children. Heinz confronted a dilemma concerning a critically ill wife who needed a drug that was more expensive than Heinz could afford. Kohlberg and his associates presented this dilemma to young people. The researchers asked their subjects what Heinz should do in this situation.

The student's responses revealed their level of moral development. For example, if a student maintained that Heinz should not steal the drug because "he will get in trouble if he breaks the law," the student's level of moral development is at the most primitive stage, "punishment and obedience orientation," characterized by sticking to rules backed by punishment. If the student's response involved a defense of Heinz putting his own immediate interests first, the student is at stage two, "instrumental relativist orientation," following rules only when in one's immediate interest. If the student's response refers to being loyal to his wife, the student may be at stage three, "mutual interpersonal concordance orientation," doing what people close to you expect, or doing what people expect of a good son, brother, or friend. A student is at stage four, "law and order orientation," if he or she insists on upholding laws unless one is in conflict with other fixed social duties, or if he or she insists that people should contribute to the "good of society." Stage five, "social-contract or legalistic orientation," involves utilitarian defenses, such as insisting that we should abide by the law because of our "social contract" to make and abide by laws for the welfare of all and for the protection of everyone's rights. Stage six, "Universal ethical principle orientation" is the highest one and it is that of insisting on universal ethical principles, such as Heinz's wife's right to live.

Carr (1991, 167) contends that the problem with Kohlberg's attempt "to cut moral reasoning loose from any substantive conception of moral life as exhibited in a particular range of moral virtues or qualities of character is that the relationship of moral thought to feeling and conduct becomes rather obscure if not totally mysterious." Carr also claims that an account of morality that focuses exclusively on moral reason and judgment does not encompass the scope of what we normally consider to be important in our moral deliberations and actions. For example, although truly virtuous acts are those that a person of sound practical wisdom would perform, a small child who performs an act of kindness in the absence of having a worked out set of universalized prescriptions, by Kohlberg's standards, would not have behaved in a morally commendable way. Moreover, someone who has a consistent system of moral principles may fail to act ethically due to weakness of will or failure of nerve. Kohlberg's theory does not seem to provide for any explanation of this. Carr concludes that Kohlberg does not do sufficient justice to the motivational and affective dimensions of moral conduct.

I might summarize the basic problem for a theory of moral education that advocates promoting moral growth mainly through ethical reflection. It fails to recognize the Aristotelian point that there is a difference between knowing the right thing to do and doing the right thing. As Carr points out, we may understand what we ought to do and still not possess the moral will to do it. Moreover, there are levels of moral understanding that Kohlberg fails to capture. A child may have some sense of justice and not be able to clearly explain the meaning of the concept. Children are often quick to recognize when they are being treated unfairly, and this recognition is not linked to a Kohlbergian early stage of moral development, such as a hedonistic or relativistic viewpoint. Children in some situations exhibit a clear understanding when an injustice has been done to them. This insight squares with virtue theory's notion that when people, young or old, begin to acquire virtuous qualities of character, they not only will tend to act morally, but they also will be able to understand how virtue requires them act. A person who has developed a sense of fairness, or who strives to be a fair person, understands what fairness or justice requires in many situations.

The difficulty with virtue theory lies in the over reliance on the notion that instilling virtue does not involve developing critical reflection on moral principles. The theory also assumes that the virtuous person will intuitively know what to do in most ethical situations. I turn to the first point.

Parents can and do instill moral virtue in their children by their own moral example. However, there is a limit to training by moral example. Children need to develop moral discernment, that is, the ability to recognize what to do in unfamiliar situations. For example, a child may clearly recognize that he or she should not hurt other people, but fail to recognize that it may be all right to defend oneself if attacked by others. Or a child may fail to recognize that he or she may be hurting someone in an unfamiliar way, such as telling an adult, "you are a very fat person."

Second, a child may have a difficult time in deciding what to do when confronted with a dilemma, where virtue requires conflicting responses. The child may have been taught to always tell the truth and to always be kind. But what does the child do (to use the Kantian example) when he or she is hiding a friend from a bully who wants to harm the friend, if the bully asks where the friend is? In some basic sense, the child may realize that in situations like this it is more important to be kind than truthful. However, virtue theory does not provide us with a very coherent analysis of why this is the case. Moreover, there may be situations where truth should prevail over kindness. Suppose the child is trying to restrain her brother from climbing a tree. She knows that her little brother wants to do this more than anything, but fears that he may harm himself. Her little brother starts climbing the tree and asks her not to tell on him. Unable to stop her brother, she decides to run into the house and get her father. So she tells on her brother at the expense of her brother's happiness because she does not want her brother to be hurt. How does virtue theory distinguish when truth comes before mercy and when mercy comes before truth?

Instead of being two "ethics," a consideration of both principles and virtue are two indispensable aspects of the moral-point-of-view. We discuss moral considerations in terms of different discourses, i.e., a virtue discourse and a discourse of moral rules and principles. However, the "discourse" we adopt depends on our purposes. When we discuss moral issues, we emphasize principles. When we discuss moral education, virtue language often is the appropriate one. I explain this point in more detail below.

COMBINING DEONTOLOGICAL AND VIRTUE THEORIES

A comprehensive moral theory should incorporate both approaches to ethics. Virtue theory is useful as we think about how to promote moral growth among people. A principle-based ethics theory is important as we attempt to help people develop the ability to reason more clearly about ethical dilemmas and situations. While Kohlberg may have overemphasized the role of moral reason in moral growth, clearly we want people who can do the right thing from an understanding of what to do. This is what we mean by moral wisdom, someone who can discern what to do, and also possesses the will to do it. I shall briefly sketch the role of virtue in the moral life and suggest how one can better understand the relationship of principle-based ethics and virtue theory.

Virtues are settled states of character, or if one prefers, dispositions to feel, think, and act in certain predictably moral ways. If one has cultivated the quality of justice, one will be disposed to treat others with respect. Moreover, if one is a just person, one will be angry in the face of unjust treatment. Acquiring a virtue means that one has moral emotions and is disposed to act in moral ways.

One mark of the moral person is the possession of other regarding virtues, such as unselfishness, consideration, sympathy, benevolence, kindness, generosity, courtesy, respect, charity, patience, and tolerance. The moral person also will possess self-regarding virtues, such as modesty and humility. Other self-regarding virtues include our sense of autonomy; our ability to take care of ourselves, including our mental and physical development; and the ability to be prudent, that is, to make wise choices concerning our life goals and the means to attain them. In the chapter seven I comment on several of these virtues in the context of education. Virtues are the acquired character traits that enable us to achieve the goods associated with cooperative human activity, to make principled moral decisions, and to achieve a fulfilled life.

Contrary to Carr (1991), who argues that moral rules are to be evaluated in terms of their contribution to the virtuous life, I suggest in agreement with MacIntyre (1981) that we come to an understanding of the nature and meaning of virtues in relation to the moral practices and rules of a given society. We believe that cultivating virtuous persons produces members of a society who uphold fundamental moral norms and rules. Carr (1991,47) agrees with the Aristotelian notion that "man is essentially a social animal whose ultimate good even as an individual person can only be realized in the context of some sort of human society." In this respect, I consider Carr to be a communitarian acknowledging that human beings are essentially social beings. Unfortunately, Carr maintains that the ideals of the virtuous person become the criteria for assessing moral rules. The truth is the very opposite.

Virtuous ideals are to be assessed in terms of their contribution to upholding moral rules, that express our essential sociality. We only indirectly come to see the virtuous life as intrinsically worthwhile. Although that is how we may "experience" the virtuous life, such a life is ultimately justified by reference to upholding the social good. For example, courage is a virtue because courageous people uphold causes and concerns critical to our society's practices, such as promoting equality and liberty, maintaining domestic tranquillity, and protecting our society from assault by other societies. We also define ourselves by reference to standards of truthfulness and trust and justice.

The virtuous person in the acquirement of specific moral habits of character has developed a moral conscience, including a fundamental sense of self-respect and respect for others. Acquiring self-respect means one recognizes one's own self-worth as equal to the value of others. Fundamentally, respect for others consists of being willing to enter into personal relationships based on reciprocal agreements in which the bonds between people derive from their own appraisals and decisions, rather than from any social role or institution. Such persons voluntarily share in the development of the public life of their society. The mutually accepted obligations that sustain relationships are considered to be binding just because they are voluntarily undertaken and enable the parties to base their judgments on the moral probabilities of others.

Since our moral actions and beliefs are defended by reference to the interests of others, the morally educated or virtuous person must be aware of those interests. This in turn implies that ignorance of the feelings and interests of other people, including the failure to act on moral principles based on those feelings and interests, is another mark of the morally uneducated. The awareness of other people's feelings is conceptually and in practice connected to the awareness of our personal emotions. Suppressing or failing to acknowledge our own feelings leaves us unable to recognize them in other people. Consequently, we may have distorted perceptions of others. Similarly, we are unable to learn more sophisticated and accurate descriptions of feeling unless we can match these descriptions to our own experience. This involves understanding our own feelings to match them with the descriptions. Some people exist with a minimal awareness of themselves as person. They fail to recognize the moral claims others make upon them.

Virtue requires that we maintain physical and mental health and to make prudential decisions. One also attempts to balance a sense of personal freedom with responsible action. One recognizes that it is important to be free to do as one pleases, but our freedom is limited by the demands of self-respect and respect for others. As a part of a sense of responsible selfhood, we are aware of our possibilities and limitations. While we may be influenced by our physical needs or by the interests of the groups to which we belong, our actions are not completely determined by these needs and interests. And while we may take into account the advice of others, ultimately we must be the one to make the decision, not someone else. No group or authority can legislate for us how we must live our life, except in so far as we are legally constrained. Even that constraint is subject to our willingness to obey laws. In acting autonomously, we are also responsible for our decisions. We will suffer the consequences of bad decisions, and ultimately we can not blame others for our mistakes.

We are also aware of our limitations. We are confronted with our own fallibility, which includes our awareness of the reality of death and of our dependency upon the world and uncertainty of the future. We are aware of our dependency upon external forces that may prevent or impede us from doing what we want. The morally mature person manages to come to terms with nature as unaffected by human whims and wishes.

It is often difficult to accept responsibility for our actions, especially given the brevity and finality of life. We are anxious to make the most of our life and impatient with burdensome restraints. We also realize we must make our moral decisions without ever being certain we have made the right ones. Unanticipated consequences or knowledge can subsequently reveal that a decision was bad one, but this comes too late because we have already acted.

Moral education should foster the development of moral virtue. Helping young people to analyze moral dilemmas may be an important step in the inordinately complicated process of moral education, but emphasizing only the analysis of moral dilemmas, typical of the Kohlbergian approach, neglects the promotion of the development of moral virtue. We want people who are not merely rational but who are affectively engaged in moral matters (which, of course, implies rational engagement as well). We want people to care about justice and honesty, and so forth, not merely be able to analyze dilemmas that involve these norms.

5

Counter-Ethical Theories

Instructors who present ethics case studies in the class room will discover that some students resist an open and reflective approach to discussing ethical issues. They may do so in terms of conflicting points of view, absolutism, subjectivism, and relativism. I first look at religious absolutism, because it is the primary form of absolutist resistance. I then turn to subjectivism and to two forms of relativism, individual and multicultural.

RELIGION AND ETHICS

Many young students, reflecting their home environment, adopt an absolutist point of view, maintaining that moral principles are absolute and admit of no exceptions. Instructors will be disappointed if they expect to change such students' opinions through an initial discussion. Counter-arguments really do not change the viewpoint of the most entrenched. Nonetheless, providing them with an understanding of opposing viewpoints might eventually result in their coming around to a more moderate way of looking at issues. This attitude permeates the discussion of life and death issues, especially euthanasia and abortion. Typically, an absolutist will maintain that it is always wrong to take an innocent life, despite the circumstances. Clearly issues, such as euthanasia and abortion, are dilemma topics because major norms or principles are in conflict. For euthanasia, the norm of mercy is in opposition to the right to life, and for abortion the right to privacy or choice is pitted against the right to life. One might respond to this blanket generalization by citing examples in which the absolutist may see that even he or she may not believe that it is always wrong to take an innocent life. One might ask the student if he or she considers it wrong for the United States to have killed innocent civilians in Iraq during Desert Storm, assuming that many Iraqians did not want to have anything to do with Sadam Hussein and the U.S. war. This student might say, "This is an exception."

Turning to abortion, Judith Jarvis Thompson (Olen & Barry 1989) offers a counter-example to try to get the reader to realize that at least in the case of a pregnant rape victim, abortion may be justified. In her example, Thompson has you imagine that you awake after being drugged and discover that your circulatory system is plugged into another person. You are told that the other person is a famous violinist whose kidneys have failed, and only you have the matching blood type. The violinist will need the use of your kidneys for dialysis for about nine months, and you will be involuntarily medically linked to this person in bed for the duration. If you sever the connecting medical tubes, the patient will die. Taking Thompson's example a step further, let us suppose that you discover a knife and have the opportunity to escape from your involuntary assignment as a living dialysis machine by severing the circulatory tubes. Would it be morally justified for you to sever the tubes and escape? If you are inclined to think that you would be justified in escaping, this illustrates a case where it is not immoral to take an "innocent life."

Often the anti-abortionist takes the position that a fetus is a "human being," claiming that all human beings are sacred. Mary Ann Warren (Rachels 1989) claims that the anti-abortionist fails to understand that "human being" is being used equivocally. "Human being" can mean "person," or it can mean "a biological form of life." If the term is being used in the second sense, no moral obligations immediately follow. Many biological forms of life generally are not accorded any "rights." On the other hand, if one means by "human being" a "person," it must be noted that we do not ordinarily use the term "person" to refer to a fetus. Generally, we use the term "person" to refer to a being that, at the very least, has characteristics associated with human beings who have been born, such as having consciousness and having some degree of biological independence.

Even if we agree that fetuses in the early stages of development are not "persons," it may not be morally right to commit an abortion. We might, for example, consider it wrong for a woman to have an abortion simply for the sake of convenience in the third trimester. Just because a fetus is not a person, it does not necessarily follow that it has no moral rights. For example, we consider it immoral for someone to abuse or sadistically kill their pet dog or cat. The extent to which a being is included in the web of the human community or, in the case of late fetal development, is sufficiently person-like, we consider it immoral to mistreat such beings or take their life.

Turning to issues of euthanasia, the case of Nancy Cruzan illustrates a circumstance where many people believe that it is morally justified to allow a patient to die. Nancy had existed in a persistent vegetative state for more than five years, following a near fatal car accident that left her with no functioning brain cortex and with only a brain core (the part of her brain that kept her basic bodily functions operating). In this state, Nancy, like other similar victims, could not think or even feel pain. She was conscious but totally oblivious to herself and her surroundings. Her condition was irreversible.

In 1989, the U.S. Supreme Court determined that there was not clear and sufficient evidence concerning Nancy's wishes, and that her nutrition and hydration tube could not be removed. However, several months later, friends of Nancy Cruzan testified that she had said that if she were ever seriously mentally disabled, she would not want to live. The district judge subsequently accepted this evidence and ordered the hospital to remove the feeding nutrition and hydration tube that had kept her alive. Many believe that in these circumstances mercy should overrule the right to life, and that we should assume that such a victim would not want to be alive under such circumstances.

Despite strong counter-examples to the absolutist claim that it is always wrong to take a life, the absolutist may retreat to a religious perspective. This person may claim that it is always wrong to take a life because it is the will of God. This viewpoint is called the *Divine Command Theory*. The obvious question that comes to mind for this theory, is: "How do we know what God's commands are?" The orthodox believer may be able to offer a couple of reasons in support of the theory. According to this view, one can know God's commands by reading (in the case of Christianity) the Bible. The second ground is an appeal to personal discernment of God's will through prayer and meditation.

This viewpoint is subject to several difficulties, which I will only briefly discuss. Taking the Biblical command first, one might ask what does one do when the Bible offers contradictory recommendations? The Old Testament seems to uphold a more retributive God, but in the New Testament we find Jesus suggesting that we should turn swords into plowshares. Additionally, the Bible does not provide very helpful ethical guidelines for technological and environmental ethical issues.

This point of view is opposed by many nonorthodox believers who do not accept the Bible as the inerrant "Word of God," but instead see the Bible as a historical record of the Israelites and the early Christian Church. In this context, the Bible incorporates the myths and legends of the people of the times and must be read in a mythological context. The most famous Biblical theologian who wrote on this topic is Rudolf Bultmann (1961). In his famous work, *Kerygma and Myth,* Bultmann wrote that the New Testament stories should be interpreted in terms of the prevailing prescientific mythological view of the time, which involved a three-storied universe and the belief in angels and demons. Bultmann maintained that these stories needed to be demythologized, that is, extracting their existential truths. Sheehan (1986) provides a good critical approach to understanding the life of Jesus in these terms. Thus a more critical reading of the Bible exposes serious difficulties to the absolutist appeal to the "inspired Word of God."

Despite these difficulties, an orthodox believer may claim that he can discern the will of God through prayer and meditation. But how does one decide among contrary views? Which is "truly" God's will? Suppose someone says that it is God's will that Nancy Cruzan die, and someone else says it is against the will of God. Who is right? Surely, if we are going to make any headway in ethical decisions, we must have a more rational framework than this.

Another problem with this point of view is the ineffectiveness of it in dealing with people who do not believe in God. Many agnostics and atheists consider themselves ethical persons and hold ethical opinions. The person operating from the perspective of the divine command theory has little to say to such people.

Plato offered the classic critique of the Divine Command Theory. It has been expressed in terms of the question, "Is an act right because God commands it, or does God command it, because it is right?" Surely, the orthodox believer intends the first interpretation. But this interpretation means that there is nothing, as such, that is virtuous, good, right or non-virtuous, bad or wrong. Therefore, whatever God wants is *ipso facto* good. Suppose that God wants people to suffer in all sorts of terrible ways? Would we then say that it is good for people to suffer? Moreover, the very idea of a "good God" makes little sense, given that good, means "whatever God wills." To say that "God is good" amounts to saying that "God wills whatever God wills." This is far from what we mean by the concept of a "good and loving God."

On the other hand, if we accept that God wills an act because it is right, this implies that grounds exist outside the will of God that makes the act right. Then we do not need to consult the will of God to decide what is right; we only need to discover the right-making and wrong-making properties of moral acts. In this case, we need a non-theistic foundation of ethics.

Although I have discussed the Divine Command Theory critically, it does not follow that religion has nothing to do with ethics. I cannot go into an extended discussion of this subject, but it bears stating that being an ethical person may be a necessary condition for being religious. That is, unless we are ethical beings, we cannot lay claim to being religious. A person who is selfish and abusive of others may be wrong in considering himself or herself "religious." Second, although people may be ethical without being religious, being a religious person may provide powerful motives for being ethical. If a person believes that not only is it good to be moral, but that God wills that one be good, he or she may be more inclined than a nonreligious person to be ethical.

When students lose their absolutism, they often swing to the other extreme and embrace either *ethical egoism, subjectivism* or *relativism*. I turn next to these viewpoints.

ETHICAL EGOISM

Ethical egoism is the view that one ought to maximize one's own self-interest. An advocate of this view is Ayn Rand (Rachels 1989). This is an anti-ethical theory because it abandons the moral point of view, namely the view that in a moral situation we should base our decision on a consideration of what is in the best interests of all parties concerned. In assessing this viewpoint, two standards of self-interest need to be distinguished. The first, cruder viewpoint, would allege that one need only base one's decision on which course of action maximizes individual self-interest. For example, suppose I unobtrusively pick up a wallet that I have seen someone drop. In trying to determine whether I ought to return the wallet to the owner, I need only consider which course of action maximizes my own self-interest. If I am economically the better off for keeping the wallet and nobody will know the difference, then I may determine that it is in my self-interest to keep the wallet.

The problem with this viewpoint is that it obviously provides no guidance for resolving ethical dilemmas that involve conflicts of interest. Suppose two students want to be selected to represent their school in an activity. If both were ethical egoists, they more than likely could not resolve the difficulty on the assumption that both saw it as in their own individual self-interest to represent the school.

The other viewpoint is akin to the contractarian theory of ethics, which maintains that it is in an individual's enlightened self-interest to base one's decisions on standards of morality that do not necessarily advance one's immediate self-interest. For example, if I found the wallet in the above circumstances, I might decide to return the wallet to the rightful owner even though it will make me unhappy in the short run. I would do so because I believe that it is in my enlightened self-interest to uphold the principle of honesty. The problem with this justification, as with the contractarian theory, is that not only does it fail to capture the right making characteristics of actions, but the appeal to enlightened self-interests breaks down in situations where we observe other people failing to uphold moral norms. If I feel that others are indulging their own self-interests, I will be tempted to forgo the moral high road in favor of maximizing my own self-interest.

Ethical egoism is appealing to people who are breaking away from an authoritarian ethical background. Young people who were always told what to do by their parents are attracted to this viewpoint as they attempt to create their own sense of independence in the maturation process. On a less positive note, this viewpoint is symptomatic of people living in a society that is experiencing a legitimization crisis. Such a crisis exists when people are unwilling to assume the responsibilities and burdens necessary to sustain such a society. Some thinkers, such as Taylor (1991), believe that the United States is experiencing such a crisis.

SUBJECTIVISM

Subjectivism is the view that moral opinions are merely expressions of feelings. According to this view, when I say that some action is right or wrong, I am only giving expression to my feelings of approval or disapproval of the action in question. Moreover, it is alleged that feelings are non-rational, that is, they are like our taste for food; we simply find ourselves, perhaps as a result of our upbringing or of the society in which we live, simply having certain feelings of approval or disapproval.

Historically, this viewpoint is grounded in the empirical tradition of philosophy that maintains that the only kind of claims about the world that could be rationally appraised are statements of mathematics (analytic statements) and statements about the physical world (empirical statements). We decide the truth value of mathematical statements by reference to mathematical rules, and we decide the truth value of empirical statements by an appeal to our perceptions. For example, the mathematical statement, "2+2=4" is true by virtue of the rules of math. The statement is analytically true. The statement that "the book is on the table," in the case where the person who is making the statement is looking at a book on a table, is empirically true. Subjectivists argue that moral claims are neither analytic nor empirical. They are nothing but expressions or statements of our feelings of approval or disapproval. If this viewpoint were true, the consequence is devastating for moral philosophy and ethics. No rational grounds exist for moral discussion. All we could do is lapse into expressing our feelings of approval or disapproval. We might hope that someone would feel differently, but no rational ground exists for attempting to change the other person's mind.

Although once a popular moral theory during the 1950s and 1960s, it is now widely rejected among moral philosophers. There are two important reasons for rejecting this view. In the first place, it is now recognized that "feelings," far from being nonrational, represent highly self-involved appraisals (Solomon 1976). I discuss this view further in the chapter on feminist ethics. Second, rather than being expressions of feeling, many philosophers consider moral judgments, such as "It is wrong steal that car," to be prescriptive claims that owe their validity to general moral rules, such as "It is wrong to steal," which is in turn validated by the claim that "It is wrong to harm others." Moral theory, as I have claimed previously, should provide us with a justification of more general moral rules, but specific moral claims of this sort are justified by reference to moral principles themselves. Similarly, moral claims, such as "Mary is a good person," are considered to be general statements of commendation, which in turn are justified by reference to the qualities implied by the kind of commendation one makes. In a nonmoral example, if I say, "Fords are good automobiles," I imply that there are some good-making characteristics that apply to these kinds of automobiles, such as "runs well," "gets good gas mileage," and "mechanically dependable." In a moral example, when I say, "Mary is a good person," I presumably mean that she possesses certain moral qualities, namely, virtues, such as "kindness" and "honesty."

Sometimes, when one states that ethics is merely a matter of feeling, what one really has in mind is relativism, which is a more formidable position.

INDIVIDUAL ETHICAL RELATIVISM

According to this view, what is right for one person is not necessarily right for another person. For example, one person may contend that "keeping a promise is the right thing for me to do, but I can see how someone else may feel differently, and it may not be right for them." This statement is an expression of individual ethical relativism.

This version of relativism is defended on the grounds that ethical relativism is entailed by the principle of equal respect for each person's opinion: to respect the right of each individual to entertain his or her opinion, we must be relativists. I will call this the Argument from the Principle of Equal Respect. The argument can be summarized as follows:

1. Each individual is entitled to one's own opinion about anything, including morality.
2. Therefore, what any individual believes is right or wrong is as valid as what anybody believes.

As we shall see, this argument is mistaken.

In the first place, individual ethical relativism, leads to inconsistencies. As Bloom (1987) points out, many people express this point of view out of a spirit of respect for the right of each person to develop one's own moral viewpoint. That is as it should be. We are rightly anti-authoritarian. We do not believe that others should impose their moral values on us. In this spirit, we also recognize that someone confronting a moral decision is usually in the best position to decide the relevant factors that need to be considered in making a decision. For example, a pregnant woman who is trying to decide whether or not to have an abortion probably is best able to decide what is best. I recently saw a bumper sticker that said: "If you are opposed to abortion, don't have one."

However, it does not follow from these considerations that people never make wrong moral decisions. To take an extreme example, suppose that a man, confronted for sadistically beating his children, says, "I see nothing wrong with beating my children; after all, spare the rod and spoil the child!" Are we to assume that this is right for him, just because he believes that it is right?

Second, the statement, "What is right for one person may not be right for another," is ambiguous. Let us examine the possible meanings that this statement may express. In the first place, one may be asserting something logically similar to the notion that what is true for one person or society may not be true for another person or society. "True" in this context is ambiguous. If "true" means "what is believed to be true," then the claim that "truth is relative" amounts to the claim that our beliefs vary from individual to individual. This is correct, but it is a trivial claim. On the other hand, if by the claim that truth is relative one means that "what is fact" varies from individual to individual, then this is incorrect. For example, our beliefs concerning the shape of the earth have varied in the past few centuries, but the earth remains a sphere despite our beliefs about its shape.

Let us apply this line of analysis to the claim that "what is right for one person may not be right for another." If one means by this that someone may believe that a course of action is right, while someone else may believe that it is wrong, this is hardly disputable. Beliefs about what is right regarding many issues vary from person to person. Some people believe that abortion is wrong, some believe that it is right. However, if in asserting that "what is right for me may not be right for you," one means that one's belief about a particular matter may not be the same as somebody else's belief, one should simply say this.

On the other hand, if by asserting that what is right varies from individual to individual, one means that what is in fact right varies from individual to individual, one may be saying something that is simply incorrect. For example, if it is wrong for some individual, Sam, to have raped a woman, Brenda, at night on a jogging path, it follows that such an act is wrong for any relatively similar person in any relatively similar circumstances. This is called the *generalization principle*. This principle states that what is right or wrong for someone is right for wrong for any relatively similar person in relatively similar circumstances. The generalization principle is derived from an analysis of the meaning of moral concepts, such as "right" and "wrong."

Of course, in claiming that moral values are relative to each individual, one may mean that what may be right for one individual may not be right for another because the individual circumstances may vary significantly. For example, a pro-choicer might claim that while it may be morally permissible for a rape victim to seek an abortion, it may not be equally permissible for a pregnant woman in her second trimester to get an abortion because her pregnancy is interfering with her plans for a trip to Europe. Individual circumstances do vary, and in this sense what may be right for one person may not be right for another just because their circumstances are significantly different. However, this consideration is fully compatible with the generalization principle. This principle only asserts that what is right for one person is not necessarily right for any other person, provided the persons and the circumstances are relatively similar.

Finally, individual ethical relativism may trivialize moral arguments and disputants. In proposing the Argument from the Principle of Equal Respect, one may be guilty of the fallacious assumption that retreating into ethical relativism is a way to minimize ethical conflict. For example, one may say to a potential disputant, "My moral decision is right for me but it may not be right for you," from a belief that he or she is avoiding an argument. Perhaps argument can be avoided, but it may be avoided at the price of undermining serious moral discussion between the two disputants. Moreover, in agreeing to disagree, instead of engaging in a serious discussion regarding the disagreements, neither person is really taking the other seriously.

Thus, while individual ethical relativism may be prompted by a spirit of equal respect for the autonomy of individuals, this view actually may undermine this respect. Part of what it is to be a person is to be a rational being who bases one's decisions on reason and principle. To advocate ethical relativism is, in effect, to claim that our opinions about some important aspects of life are without solid foundation and are credible only by virtue of being believed. Insisting upon this kind of relativism may result in not taking people seriously and not treating them with respect for their beliefs. Suppose that having spent much time soul-searching and thinking through a complex ethical situation, you finally arrive at a decision. You tell me about your decision, and I disagree, but respond, "I disagree, but I can see you think you are doing the right thing. Well, that is right for you but not right for me." My comment may leave the impression that I did not take you seriously enough. I may undermine your own sense of credibility. After all, as an ethical relativist, I would have no need to challenge any other person's moral belief; whatever the person says is all right.

Let us return to the issue of abortion again. From the perspective of individual relativism it makes no difference whether that person is for abortion or against abortion. Whatever that person believes is right, is right for that person. However, we do believe that our opinions matter, and we want to have our opinions respected. One way of showing respect for the opinions of others is to acknowledge the full moral status of those opinions. They are not merely whims or expressions of personal taste; they are principled moral beliefs and decisions. We should strive to create a climate of mutual respect in which we can treat each others' opinions in this way.

One might reply that ethical conflict is belittling or serves to undermine respect for the opinions of one another. However, why should we assume this? To the contrary, serious moral disagreement can be confronted in ways that include and promote mutual respect. Fostering mutual respect is a moral requirement for ethical discussion. We have seen that adopting the moral point of view involves the willingness to base one's ethical decisions on reason. So long as ethical disagreement is conducted in a reasonable way, this is compatible with expressing respect. Engaging in reasonable discussion is the primary way that we show respect for others in such discussions, because that is what it means to "respect others as persons."

The generalization principle supports the principle of equal respect for the opinion of others. The generalization principle recognizes that as persons we are sufficiently similar that what is obligatory or permissible for one person is obligatory or permissible for all others in similar circumstances, because we are similar as rational beings, or as persons, or as moral agents.

There is another point that bears considering. Retreating into a shell of individual ethical relativism, by saying that "What is right for me may not be right for you," may be a way of refusing to engage in serious ethical discussion. It may reflect our fear or unwillingness to be reasonable or to have our views challenged. While individuals have the right to withdraw into their own shell of moral rectitude, doing this is adopting an irrational attitude toward ethical discussion. It is to abandon the moral point of view. Adopting the moral point of view implies recognizing that we owe equal respect to others. In refusing to engage with others to take them seriously, are we not in some sense giving more weight to our own individual shell of moral rectitude and thereby not treating the interests of others impartially?

MULTICULTURAL ETHICS

Many of us are aware of the current controversy on college campuses between the multiculturalists and the traditionalists. Multiculturalists, in attempting to promote multicultural diversity, have advocated diversifying the college curriculum, instituting speech codes, and enforcement of affirmative action programs to attract minorities to prestigious colleges and universities. The traditionalists, on the other hand, denounce dilution of the "literary canon," politically correct efforts to enact speech codes, and claim that affirmative action policies are exacerbating charges of reverse discrimination. An additional complicating factor is emerging, an outgrowth of multiculturalism, *multicultural ethical relativism*. This is the view that it is not possible to develop universal ethics, because moral rules that characterize mainstream ethics discussions, such as the principles of benevolence, non malfeasance, autonomy, and justice, are merely oppressive Western technocratic norms.

Anthony Cortese (1990,107) claims that "ethnic groups have different moral structures, each adequate to the reproduction of the social life-world found in each ethnic group." Cortese's view represents a multicultural version of cultural relativism (phrased in phenomonological terms) and is subject to the same kinds of criticisms applicable to cultural relativism. In passing, I might mention that there is not surprisingly a parallel viewpoint among some feminist advocates of *gender differentiated ethics*. For example, Seigfried (1989, 67) states: "Universalizability as a criterion of ethics or value systems should be unmasked for the drive for domination which it is. It should be replaced with a recognition of the diversity of values that have been developed to answer to different needs and a search for what is required for a harmonious community based on cooperation rather than coaptation and domination." As previously indicated, I take up the issue of gender-specific ethics in the following chapter.

Before turning to the specifics of Cortese's view, let me briefly discuss *cultural relativism*. This is the view that there are no universal or cross-cultural ethical norms; rather ethical norms are derived from specific cultures. Now, no one would deny that moral values are cultural-specific, that is, expressed in culturally specific terms. For example, one culture's concept of honesty may differ from another culture's concept. Benedict (1959) states that the Dobu considered it dishonest to take something from someone without warning. Otherwise, as long as the victim is warned, taking their property is not considered to be dishonest. This view of dishonesty differs from that of our own society. What is important for a view advocating that there are cross-cultural norms, such as honesty, is that even though our culture and the Dobus may have had two different interpretations of honesty, both societies adhere to a norm of honesty.

There are two standard criticisms of cultural relativism. First, cultural relativism renders meaningless any cross-cultural moral comparisons. We could no longer condemn other societies just because they are different. This difficulty could be construed as a strength of cultural relativism. This calls into question our tendency toward ethnocentrism, that is, to judge other societies by our own standards. However, the inability to criticize other societies presents some problems. For example, suppose a society went to war with a neighboring country to take slaves, or a society or minority group was anti-Semitic and attempted to destroy its Jewish residents. Relativism would not allow us to say that either of these practices was wrong. We believe intuitively that despite the beliefs or mores of a society, enslaving others or systematically exterminating a group of people because of their ethnicity or race is immoral. One might attempt to defend relativism against this criticism by claiming that a racist ethnic group or society is guilty of ethnocentrism. However, if the ethnic group contends that racism is a part of their life-world or their value system, how can we condemn them for this without violating the relativistic framework?

Second, in terms of relativism, we would always have to decide whether actions are right or wrong by consulting the standards of the society or the ethnic group in question. What happens when members of the same society or ethnic group disagree over standards in a given society? Perhaps one segment advocates abortion, for example, and another is against abortion. On what grounds can we decide who is right? Do we do this by a majority vote, believing that the majority really represents the life-world of a given society? As an example of this problem applied to African-Americans, consider that there is some disagreement over affirmative action between professional Blacks and political leaders of the Black underclass. Members of the Black professional class believe affirmative action hiring policies stigmatize Blacks, but Black political leaders of the underclass argue that affirmative action policies are essential to counteract racist hiring practices. What does multicultural relativism say to this issue? Does the multiculturalist say that we have two distinct racial groups and that each viewpoint is as valid as the other? I comment further on the value of a universalistic theory against relativism following my discussion of Cortese.

Cortese appears to defend multicultural relativism. With some qualifications, he wishes to maintain that ethnic groups, such as Hispanics, have evolved a *sui generis* ethical framework, epitomized by a caring orientation, and that an ethics of principle is a product of Western culture and counter to ethnic ethical traditions.

Taking up his first point concerning the non-transferable and ethical uniqueness of ethnic traditions, Cortese acknowledges that Hispanic culture has been significantly affected by class stratification. Yet, he appears to claim that despite the alteration of the Hispanic culture brought about by class assimilation or adaptation, a remnant of an indigenous moral culture continues to exist.

For example, he notes that there are attitudinal differences between African-Americans and Whites at lower income levels. Cortese (1990, 93) says that for attitudinal and value testing, African-Americans score lower on "trusting people," "future orientation," and "individual responsibility for poverty." Cortese does not find much difference between middle-class minorities and Whites. Cortese's study of moral judgment finds that there is not much difference between Chicano, Black, and White young adults. Cortese (1990, 93) states: "Ethnicity is less powerful in the middle-class than in the lower classes." He believes that this is because as lower-class people move into the mainstream of economic life, they take on the values of the upper-middle class life style.

Cortese (1990, 93) qualifies the above remarks with the observation that upwardly mobile Chicanos do not give up their ethnic identification significantly. "It seems to be the shedding of lower-class culture rather than ethnicity which is related to upward mobility." Cortese does not cite many examples to support this observation. One example of ethnic values that presumably survives upward mobility is child-rearing practices. Cortese claims that Chicano parents, like African-American parents, "expected their child to assume earlier responsibility for their behavior than did Anglos." This expectation contradicts the fathers' authoritarian attitude. As another example, perhaps, of persistent values, Cortese (1990, 93-94) states, "A moral judgment scale for Chicanos must respond to a Chicano value orientation that strongly emphasizes interpersonal relations rather than individual rights, abstract principles, law and order, or self-chosen principles."

In a questionable conclusion, Cortese states that what is needed in moral education is an emphasis on a caring focus because this relates to ethnically persistent values. Cortese sees a similarity between the way Chicanos respond to moral issues and the way Carol Gilligan and other feminists believe that females generally think about ethical situations, namely with a caring orientation. Promoting moral development or growth among Hispanics, according to Cortese, involves couching moral issues in "caring" language.

Although there are ethnic differences in moral judgment between children, Cortese (1990, 106) suggests that there is not much disparity in stages of moral development between ethnic categories in the adult sample. As children mature, their self-identity exceeds ethnic boundaries. Ethnic minority young adults become more middle-class, "cognitively, if not behaviorally. " In the process of acculturation, ethnic minorities tend give up their native culture and acquire the dominant American culture.

Cortese (1990) is so intent on rejecting an emphasis on principled moral reasoning as hegemonic—similar to some feminist advocates of the ethics of caring—he fails to notice that a caring orientation among the lower-classes may be a product of hegemony, that is, the dominant ideology or system of beliefs serving to perpetuate the political economy of great economic and social inequity. If Chicanos are more "caring" than Anglos, this may signify something Anglos are missing or have lost in their own process of modernization. However, as I show in the chapter on feminist ethics, a caring orientation may be as much a product of oppression as an overemphasis of an ethics of principles. Puka (1989) suggests that a caring orientation represents a coping strategy for dealing with oppression. Let me briefly suggest an account of how an interpersonal orientation may come about because of class-stratification.

It should not be surprising that an oppressed people would rationalize their predicament in moral terms that makes a virtue out of necessity. A powerless ethnic group understandably may cultivate a caring orientation much as the early Christians emphasized an ethics of compassion. A caring focus is considered to be virtuous, because one is not allowed to do anything else or conceive of oneself in terms other than as a caring person, that is, in terms of resignation and acceptance of one's plight of powerlessness.

In attempting to appeal to moral grounds as a basis for political empowerment and liberation, the moralist must recognize that the goodness as self-sacrifice orientation of the oppressed make it difficult for the "moral message" to be heard by the oppressed. Telling the oppressed that they are being treated unjustly, for example, may not take hold simply because they blame themselves for their plight, and even if they agree that they are being treated unjustly, they may remain unconvinced that they should protest their condition. The oppressed may resist working for social change, feeling that they are to blame for their own misfortune and that it is better to turn the other cheek than to agitate for social change. They engage in acts of self-denial and self-abnegation and thus become unwitting participants in their own oppression.

Although caring may be an important normative concept of Hispanics, probably the more significant norm of minorities, at least of poor minority students, is resistance to the dominant culture. Cortese overlooks this coping strategy. Such a norm requires a cross-cultural analysis. Ogbu (1988) claims that minorities react to their subordination and exploitation by forming oppositional identities and oppositional cultural frames of reference. That is, minorities develop an identity system that they perceive and experience not merely as different but as in opposition to the social identity system of their dominators, or in the case of African-Americans, "White oppressors." Racial minorities consider mainstream attitudes and ways of acting, such as being studious, as not appropriate because these are attitudes and ways of members of the dominant group, the "White ways." Minorities consider opposing attitudes and behaviors, such as resisting learning, as more appropriate for themselves. I conclude that the value structure of ethnic groups, such as Hispanics in our own society, should be understood partly as a product of the ethnic group's position of subordination. Failing to acknowledge the contribution of subordination in the formation of the ethnic "lifeworld" will result in seriously misunderstanding the nature of the ethnic group's values.

Moral education that emphasizes a caring orientation may be useful in reaching oppressed minorities with a view toward promoting moral growth in a way that enables the economically subordinated to understand the nature of their oppression. Cortese (1990, 120) forcefully states, "The dialectal relationship between the self and systems of production holds the potential for changing the oppressive character of the relations of production." If some ethnically oriented individuals exemplify a caring orientation, we must communicate with these people in their moral terms. It is the way to reach them. Moreover, a caring orientation is as much a part of universalistic ethics as are formal principles. We want people to care about being moral itself, that is, actively promoting the interests of others. We want people to care about justice and honesty. Moral education that only emphasizes the cultivation of moral reasoning and fails to nourish and develop our moral emotions is seriously deficient. It is through a caring attitude that we articulate the concrete interests to be taken into consideration in a moral decision.

We must be careful that appeals to caring are not used oppressively and in a manner that disguises social relationships of exploitation. Houston's (1989) criticism of an ethics of caring, notes that all too often appealing for one to be caring amounts to encouraging acts of self-abnegation in which one complies with one's own exploitation.

In this same vein, identifying Hispanics as having a caring orientation can be used as a tool of exploitation or unfair treatment. In an ethnographic study, Ortiz (1988) found that a caring orientation was appealed to in discriminating against Hispanic children. Rather than seeing this as a moral virtue, teachers' references to these children as caring served to reinforce the perception that Hispanic children did not possess abilities and capacities for success. In Ortiz's study, physical ability of Hispanic students was more readily acknowledged than intellectual capacity. Ortiz observed that if a class was short a textbook, a puzzle, a desk, or something else, the child to be left out will be Hispanic. One teacher explained: "Well, you see, Hispanics are cooperative children. They don't mind sharing things. These other students like to work alone and independently. With Hispanics it is all right to have students work together." (Ortiz, 1988, 79)

Second, Cortese claims that an ethics of principle is a product of Western culture and counter to ethnic ethical traditions. Cortese's comments occur in a context of criticizing Lawrence Kohlberg's view of moral development. He contends that Kohlberg's invariant stage sequence is culturally biased and ethnocentric. Cortese (1990, 104) claims that the focus on core values of "fairness defined as reciprocity, equality, and individuality" are "appropriate for people with a Western European background but not for Chicanos or African Americans." I agree that Kohlberg's claim to universal, sequential stages of moral development is seriously questionable.

The undertone of Cortese's view is not merely that Kohlberg's theory of moral development is wrong, but that the moral principle of justice, constituting the highest stage of moral development for Kohlberg, is also a relativistic value, namely a value merely of Western culture. Another feature typifying this undertone of criticism is captured by Seigfried (1989) in claiming that Western values are not merely relativistic but are "tools of exploitation."

Cortese offers powerful insights into the effects of oppression and exploitation on the moral development and moral outlook of the lower classes. He mainly provides examples of the ways in which minorities have been treated unfairly or unjustly. He claims that the structures of a morally inconsistent society needs to be eliminated before an autonomous self is possible. He further states that when one sells one's labor in the work force, one sells one's moral character. Minorities and members of the lower class are excluded from the construction of social knowledge. Morality is not produced by situated and interacting individuals. It is mass-produced by bureaucratic organization, the media, and technical experts. Cortese believes that relations of production is the foundation of the structure of culture, consciousness, and moral development. The relationship between the self and systems of production contains the potential for changing the oppressive character of the relations of production. Cortese (1990, 120) concludes: "People forced into menial work by the structures of race, class, and gender privilege may have low self-esteem. This, in turn, may subvert self-control, self-determination, and a view of oneself as a moral agent."

No doubt material principles of justice, such as a libertarian concept, are very Western. They are in fact capitalistic, and indeed may be tools of capitalistic exploitation. However, I would argue that the formal conception of justice, namely that we should not treat people differently unless there is justification for doing so, is no more Western than are our powerful scientific concepts. Just because the theory of relativity has emerged in the

West, it does not follow that it is without universal application. The same point applies for the concept of justice. While I agree with Cortese's view that oppression has seriously negative moral effects and that moral education often is used hegemonically, this fails to establish his basic claim that justice is a relativistic concept. Quite to the contrary, Cortese begs the question because his critique of the dominant culture presupposes the very concept of justice that he is attempting to debunk in terms of his critique.

The question begging nature of his argument illustrates the value of the concept of justice as a moral tool for underrepresented groups and the serious consequences of trying to dispense with that concept. To attempt to relativize the concept of justice is to deprive marginalized classes of their most powerful tool for combating oppression. These groups have been treated economically unjustly. Contending that the problem of minorities is a matter of class stratification assumes that justice is a cross-cultural concept, implying a universal ethics.

Why would anyone in the name of advancing the interests of minorities erect a moral theory that would appear to deprive these minorities of one of their most powerful ethical concepts? One reason might be that minorities within the professional class are uneasy with a viewpoint that characterizes poor minorities as oppressed. It seems to stigmatize minorities as not having the ability to rise above their circumstances and detracts from the achievements of economically successful minorities. Unfortunately, the consequence of a refusal to acknowledge the oppressed status of minorities, instead of creating a positive image of minorities, has the unintended and opposite result of blaming the victim. It should be obvious why this happens. If one is attempting to understand why minorities are so disproportionally poor without the concept of economic oppression as a basis for explanation, what is left but the notion of blaming the victim? This viewpoint has the hegemonic consequence of reinforcing the conservative notions that the poor remain poor out of choice or due to welfare dependency.

A related hegemonic view popular among multiculturalists is to maintain that minorities are victims primarily of racism and ethnocentrism instead of economic injustice. The multiculturalists seek educational solutions that mainly emphasize encouraging respect and appreciation for cultural differences. Certainly, it is important to promote multicultural appreciation and to combat racism. These are probably necessary steps to helping minorities gain more equitable opportunities in our society. However, focusing on multicultural appreciation without acknowledging that the plight of minorities is primarily due to economic injustice will unfortunately only compound the problem. While this brand of multicultural ethics appears to cultivate an appreciation for the cultural heritage of minorities, it accomplishes this at the expense of depriving minorities of the tools of ethical empowerment. There is great value in cultivating an appreciation for cultural differences. Promoting moral growth among individuals in our society, where there is an intersection of ethnic groups, including Blacks, Hispanics, and Native Americans, involves appreciating the culturally laden ways that people respond to ethical issues, and other issues as well.

I hasten to add that universal ethics and multicultural appreciation are not mutually exclusive notions. As James Rachels argues, group survival itself requires that certain fundamental values prevail in any culture or society. A group could not survive if it did not value its young. Rachels contends that similar reasoning shows that other fundamental values must be shared cross-culturally. Rachels (1986, 21) says: "Imagine what it would be like for a society to place no value at all on truth telling. When one person spoke to another, there would be no presumption at all that he was telling the truth—for he could just as easily be speaking falsely. In that society, there would be no reason to pay attention to what anyone says."

On the assumption that in some sense fundamental ethical norms of groups represent survival values, we need to acknowledge that values such as respect for life, truth, autonomy, and justice are such values. Any society or group that attempts to function in disregard of these norms imperils its own survival. Again, I insist that we must respect the culturally diverse ways these norms are expressed, and we must be careful not to condemn a moral practice of another group or society just because it is different from our own. For example, while we may be tempted to criticize the Eskimo practice of infanticide, we need to ask why the Eskimos did this. They did not do this because they had less affection for their children or less respect for human life. An Eskimo family always protected its babies if conditions permitted. However, they lived in a harsh environment where food was often scarce. A family may have wanted to nourish its babies but were unable to do so. Many Eskimo mothers nursed their infants over a much longer period than mothers in our culture, often for four years, perhaps longer. Even in the best of times there were limits to the number of infants that one mother could sustain. The Eskimos were also a nomadic people; they had to move about in search of food. Infants had to be carried, and a mother could carry only one baby in her parka as she traveled and did her outdoor work. Other family members could help but this was not always possible. Infant girls were more readily disposed of, because they were not as necessary to the economy of the society. The males, as hunters, were the primary food providers. It was important to maintain a sufficient supply of males. Also because the hunters suffered a high casualty rate, more adult men died prematurely than women. Therefore, if male and female infants survived in equal numbers, the female adult population would soon greatly outnumber the male adult population. Once we consider the role that infanticide played in ensuring the survival of the tribe itself, we realize that this moral practice was not as cruel and barbarous as we might have imagined. It may even have been less cruel than our own society's practice of subjecting infants born prematurely to an array of painful medical treatments.

In conclusion, I contend that multicultural ethical relativism, instead of advancing the cause of promoting appreciation of racial and ethnic minorities, will in all likelihood have the opposite effect of reinforcing the conditions that primarily contribute to prejudice and racism, namely economic subordination. It is imperative that minorities have available the cross-cultural and universal concept of justice as a tool of their own empowerment.

APPLICATION

Exercise in Understanding the Moral Point-of-View

"What Should You Do?"

Purpose: To stimulate awareness and enable analysis of a problem from a moral perspective involving the recognition that we must consider the interests of others equally and that we need to base our moral decisions on moral principles.

Assumptions: We often fail to see problems from an ethical perspective. The research of Lawrence Kohlberg demonstrates that there are various levels of moral development, ranging from concern for one's own self-interest to decisions of moral principles. While this exercise does not assume the validity of the Kohlbergian model, it is based on the belief that people do reflect different perspectives about ethics. This exercise assumes, in contrast to Kohlberg, that one has not attained the moral-point-of-view until one comes to recognize that one must be willing to consider impartially each person's interests. This role playing exercise depicts an individual's exhibiting various levels of moral development, from a self-centered perspective to a rule-based approach to ethics.

Time: 1 hour, approximately.

Materials: room with movable chairs and tables; copies of suggested problems; copies of the role-play directions; 3 x 5 cards; and newsprint and marker.

Procedure:

1. Ask for five volunteers to play one each of the following roles as "ethical experts" or "moral problem solvers."
   a. A person who is only looking out for his or her own self-interests in everything he or she does. Example: "I will help him because he may help me in return."
   b. A person who is mainly concerned about doing what pleases others or is socially approved of by others. Example: "I will go along with you, because I want you to like me."
   c. A person who is concerned about doing that which complies with authority and upholding social order. Right conduct is "doing one's duty," as defined by those in leadership positions. Example: "I will comply with the order because it is wrong to disobey."
   d. A person who is concerned about doing that which shows tolerance for individual views. When there is a conflict between individual and group interests, the majority rules. Example: "Although I disagree with his views, I will uphold his right to have them."
   e. A person who is concerned about doing that which involves a fundamental respect for the dignity of others. This person considers that his own interests should not take precedence over others. This person usually will either base his or her moral decision on moral principles or on the basis of empathetic concern for others where his or her own self-interests is given equal recognition. Example: "We can't do that, because it is unfair to everyone."

2. Ask for two or more observers who will distinguish the differences between the ways problems are perceived.
3. Give to each of the other group members one 3 x 5 card with a suggested moral dilemma on it. As them to consult the "ethical experts" to get their opinion about the dilemmas.
4. Each person with a moral dilemma goes to each of the five volunteers in turn. The moral problem solver asks each person, "What's your dilemma?" The dilemma is stated, an analysis is offered, and the player goes to the next moral expert. Have the person seeking help make a brief note of the advice he gets from each expert.
5. In plenary session observers report distinctions between each response. These are recorded on newsprint. Those with dilemmas should also comment on distinctions they observed. The role players should have an opportunity to express how they felt in their role. (30 minutes)
6. Wrap up. Review one of the dilemmas, explaining how the various moral perspectives reflect different levels of moral reasoning.

6

Feminist Ethics of Caring

One of the most controversial versions of virtue theory is the "ethics of caring" approach adopted by some feminists, especially Gilligan (1982) and Noddings (1984). They maintain that females frequently have a different orientation toward ethics. Females frequently are concerned more about how decisions and actions will affect other people and whether actions are done in a caring spirit than they are about any moral principles involved in decisions.

A constellation of issues ultimately requires examination, whether caring is gender-specific, whether a theory of moral obligation can be elaborated in terms of caring, and whether a rules-based approach to ethics and a caring approach can be reconciled. Finally, while no one would seriously disagree that our objective in moral education is to help develop moral beings, we need to consider in relation to the ethics of caring, whether this goal can be attained without considering the role of moral principles in ethical decision making. I first take up Noddings' theory and then consider the issue of gender differences in ethics.

NODDINGS' THEORY OF THE ETHICS OF CARING

Noddings has subsequently elaborated an ethical theory based on the concept of *care*. According to Noddings (1984, 4-5), ethical caring has the following characteristics: "Ethical caring, the relation in which we do meet the other morally, will be described as arising out of natural caring—that relation in which we respond as one—caring out of love or natural inclination."

Noddings claims that caring requires some action in behalf of the cared-for; caring involves the displacement of interest from my own reality to the reality of the other; a caring person is present in acts of caring; a caring person acts to "enhance the welfare of the cared-for."

The above statements characterize the natural attitude of caring, which Noddings distinguishes from ethical caring. According to Noddings, ethical caring is based on natural caring. She maintains that women—and men to a lesser extent—care quite naturally without any ethical effort. Sometimes situations arise in which women recognize that they must care for others in ways that they may not be inclined to do so. Noddings

(1984, 83) characterizes ethical caring as follows: "... the genuine moral sentiment (our second sentiment) arises from an evaluation of the caring relation as good, as better than, superior to, the other forms or relatedness. I feel the moral 'I must' when I recognize that my response will either enhance or diminish my ethical ideal. It will serve either to increase or decrease the likelihood of genuine caring." Women, then, are guided by the ideal of ethical caring when they recognize that their natural sentiment of caring is inadequate to provide decisional guidance. They are ethically obliged when they recognize that a given course of action will enhance their ethical ideal of themselves as a caring person or when failure to act will diminish their ethical ideal.

Noddings (1984, 88) uses the abortion issue to illustrate the difference between nonethical caring and ethical caring. Consider a married woman who accidentally becomes pregnant. She finds herself unable to "destroy this known and potentially loved person-to-be." However, someone else who presumably gets pregnant by someone she does not love, may have serious reservations about bringing a child into the world. Given the lack of relationship with the male, this woman, we will suppose, considers abortion. However, given the growing potential of relationship of the fetus, the woman who does not care naturally, "must summon ethical caring to support her as one-caring." Noddings (89) adds that she "may not ethically ignore the child's cry to live."

Noddings' Theory of Obligation

First, we might consider how Noddings attempts to derive ethical caring from natural caring. Natural caring, according to Noddings (1984, 81), is a natural sentiment. "We just do care; no ethical effort is required." Caring requires one to respond to an initial impulse with an act of commitment speaking for the cared-for. Noddings (82-83) observes: "When my infant cries in the night, I not only feel that I must do something but I want to do something. Because I love this child, because I am bonded to him, I want to remove his pain as I would want to remove my own. The 'I must' is not a dutiful imperative but one that accompanies the 'I want.' ... However, this 'must' is not yet the moral or ethical 'ought.' It is a 'must' born of desire."

Noddings (1984, 79), following Hume, states that caring is a "natural sentiment," that is an inner feeling or an inner episode, not involving any form of appraisal. The Humean notion of natural sentiment has been widely criticized in favor of the cognitive theory of the emotions (CTE) (Solomon 1976), the view that emotions have an appraisal or evaluation component. I shall explain the relevance of the CTE shortly.

Noddings attempts to establish the view that caring is a merely an inner feeling or episode by citing the example of joy, as an effect of being a caring person. She claims that joy refers to an experience that is not analyzable in terms of the appraisal view of emotions. She says that joy is unlike emotions in two essential respects: (1) joy is objectless; (2) it has an element of reflectiveness. But even if this is an accurate analysis of joy, this does not establish that caring has these same properties. Caring, for example, unlike joy, seems to involve an object. Solomon distinguishes between moods and emotions. It is characteristic of moods that they are objectless. Joy would seem to be a mood rather than an emotion, and caring seems to be more like an emotion than a mood.

In sum, Noddings does not appear to realize the implications of the cognitive theory of the emotions for her conception of nonethical caring as a natural sentiment.

Let me briefly review the critique of the Humean view, so that we may fully understand the implication here. Kenny (1963) discusses Hume's view of the passions. For Hume the passions are particular kinds of experiences consisting of impressions. The passions are secondary impressions, or impressions of reflection, that result from original impressions of the senses, and bodily pains and pleasures or our ideas of those impressions. The passions may be divided into calm passions, such as aesthetic emotions, and violent passions, such as anger and love.

Hume distinguishes between the cause of a passion and the object of a passion. He discusses pride in relation to desiring a suit of clothes. The cause of pride is the perception of the suit of clothes exciting the passion of pride and affecting our self-image. The self is the object of pride. The important point here is that the association of impressions and ideas produce passions. Kenny (1963, 25) observes: "Love, for instance, is an agreeable sensation which calls up the idea of some other person; it may be produced by the beauty of that person. This is because love, being a pleasant sensation, is associated by resemblance with the pleasant sensation which is caused by beauty, while the idea of this beauty is related to the idea of the person whose beauty it is, which idea represents the object of the passion of love." According to the Humean conception of the passions, the objects of our passions are contingently related to our passions. That is, for Hume the objects of the passions are causally—instead of logically or noncontingently—connected to the passions. Second, the passions are internal episodes made up of impressions and ideas.

The cognitive theory of the emotions (CTE) rejects both claims about the emotions. According to the CTE, the emotions are highly self-involved appraisals. For example, the emotion of anger involves a highly self-involved appraisal that someone has wronged the angry person. In terms of this view the objects of the emotions are noncontingently connected to emotion. A notable defender of this view, Solomon (1976, 177) claims: "An emotion is not distinct or separable from its object; the object as an object of this emotion has no existence apart from the emotion. The object of my being angry with John for stealing my car is not the alleged fact that John stole my car (for he may not have), nor is it simply John. The object is irreducibly that-John-stole-my-car."

The CTE also denies that emotions are labels for episodic feelings. Solomon (1976, 187) says: "Emotions are self-involved and relatively intense evaluative judgments. They are always, whether implicitly or explicitly, judgments involving oneself as well as whatever else—disputes, cantaloupes, movies, other people or situations." Sensations are associated with but do not constitute the emotions. When I am angry with someone, I may feel flushed or upset. However, these sensations do not form the emotion of anger. The emotion of anger is the more encompassing self-involved appraisal of being wronged by someone. One can be angry with someone, without "feeling" anger, that is, without experiencing the sensations associated with anger.

Considering the CTE, I suggest that caring, in the sense of "S cares about X," where S is a person and X is an object of care, although not an emotion, could be classified as an attitude, and thus is a species of passion. Although I cannot here offer a taxonomy of the passions, caring shares with other species of the passions the feature of being a self-involved appraisal of another person or thing as worthy or desirable in some sense. As a rough analysis, I suggest that "S" cares about the well being of "X" (S and X are persons) means:

1) S considers promoting the well being of X to be desirable for X.
2) S considers promoting the well being of X to be important for S's self-esteem.

Not only do we regard the object of our care as desirable, but it has a relational value to the person who is caring. That is to say, the kind of value that I attribute to my object of care is a value that increases my own sense of self-esteem or worth. My sense of self-worth is a part of the caring relation. Simply put, the things I care about are important to me. It follows from this analysis that caring is not a label for some kind of feeling in the sense of an inner episode. It involves instead a self-involved appraisal. I eventually will suggest that the purpose of remarks of the form "S cares about X" is to make positive or negative appraisals of affective engagement. I will explain this concept in due course.

Caring as Nonethical Appraisal

Given, then, the view that caring as a label for a "natural sentiment," in the sense of a feeling or an inner episode, is false, what does this analysis imply for the concept of nonethical caring? Let us suppose that nonethical caring involves an appraisal, but a nonmoral appraisal. Can this be a basis for deriving ethical caring?

Noddings (1984) wishes to limit natural caring to caring for the well-being of others. For example, she distinguishes natural caring from aesthetical caring. Aesthetical caring refers to our relationship with an object to satisfy the one who is caring. Examples of aesthetical caring, I presume, are "caring about my garden," the "appearance of my house," and "my reputation." However, if an attitude of caring consists, not of a feeling, but of a self-involved appraisal of what we regard as the well being of others, then we require moral standards for deciding what is in the best interests of others. Such a standard implies moral norms. In the absence of any moral norms, what counts as the best interest of others is enveloped into the shifting sands of relativism.

While the concept of "caring about the well-being of others" may suggest a standard for determining what is well-being, no standard is possible by the very definition of the concept of natural caring as nonethical appraisal. I, as a caring person, may have my own conception of what caring about the well-being of others entails; I must recognize, however, that others may have an entirely different conception. Without a shared standard of ethical caring, their notion of caring is as defensible as mine.

The extreme relativity of Noddings' concept of natural caring becomes problematic when the caring person and the person-cared-for have conflicting interpretations of what is in one's best interest. For example, suppose the person I care about has a very different conception of well-being from my own. This person may be engaged in what I clearly perceive as self-destructive behavior. I may express my concern about this to this person. In turn, he or she may become defensive and insist that he or she knows what they are doing and ask me to mind my own business. I may believe that my friend is rationalizing the conduct and decide that I can no longer continue my relationship with this person, because it would be destructive for both of us for me to continue trying to offer my help. Unfortunately, in terms of Noddings' theory of natural caring, there are no grounds for substantiating my decision as the "right one."

Suppose we were to adopt the view that caring about the well-being of others means supporting whatever the person-cared-for considers one's well-being or best interests to be. It follows that if the person-cared-for insists that the pursuit of their interests is in their best interest, the caring person is in no position to differ. I, as a caring person, then, must only act in ways that support others in the pursuit of what they consider their needs and interests to be.

One could point out to someone who appears to be engaged in what one takes to be self-destructive behavior that the pursuit of their self-professed interests contradicts their previously acknowledged ideal of their best interests. For example, I might point out to my friend who has become an alcoholic that she had long ago told me that being a person of moderation was very important to her. However, if the person-cared-for replies that she has changed her conception of her self-ideal, little ground exists for opposition. Thus the caring person who interprets caring for the well being of others in this subjective sense could find oneself supporting others who may be engaged in what one is at best unproductive, or at worst immoral, activities, at least as conventionally understood.

Let us suppose that a friend of mine is passionately engaged in photography. As her friend, I see that her passionate interest, while enabling her to produce very fine photographic art, has certain disastrous consequences for her personal life. She has gone through two marriages, has alienated her children, and is to be unpleasant to be around because of self-centeredness and arrogance. Because we are old friends, she constrains her outrageous ego when we are together. I realize that she is not a happy person. She laments her failed marriages, her alienated children, her lack of friends. As a caring person, I tell her that if she were more interested in others, she can get along better with them. However, she is offended. She tells me that she only cares about her art, and she does not have much time in her life for caring about others. With a heavy heart, I, who care about my friend's welfare, although not giving up on trying to change her, realize that I must accept her as she is.

Ethical Caring

Given the possibility that natural caring does not necessarily include moral appraisal in any standard sense, the derivation of ethical caring from natural caring, in the manner attempted by Noddings (acting in ways that enhance one's ideal of one's self as a caring person), fails to generate ethical caring. Given the relativistic concept of natural caring, at least in terms of the above interpretation, the ethically caring person may at best find herself supporting morally indifferent decisions or even worse, immoral decisions, at least as ordinarily understood.

Consider the following example. Suppose that I am a Nazi commandant of a concentration camp. As it turns out, one of my officers, the lieutenant in care of the gas chambers and crematorium, comes to me with a problem. He is a passionate lover of opera. He has a chance to attend the Vienna opera, but needs to take the day off to do this. I am reluctant to give him permission because we are under considerable pressure to meet our daily quotas of exterminating Jews. I express my reluctance to my lieutenant, but he wants the day off. He promises me that he will work sixteen hours the day before to ensure that he doubles his quota. In wrestling with my decision, I am concerned about doing the best possible job that I can as a commandant. It would be easier to say no to my lieutenant. I worry about whether the gas chambers and the crematorium will hold up to such heavy use for a sixteen-hour period. And yet, I also care very much for music. That along with good books, paintings, and good wine are my passions as well. The lieutenant is not only an officer. He is a dear friend of mine. I realize how important music is to him. Finally, I act in a way that upholds my image of myself as a caring person. I give my lieutenant permission to attend the opera.

By any conventional measure of morality, the Nazi commandant is immoral. Yet, I do not see how that Noddings can show that his conduct is immoral. If one were to reply that the commandant's treatment of the Jews is incompatible with his conception of himself as a caring person, this objection cannot be sustained in terms of Noddings' theory. She emphasizes that one under the guidance of an ethic of caring retreats to a "manageable world." The person acting in terms of an ethic of caring:

is limited by her insistence upon meeting the other as one-caring. So long as this is possible, she may reach outward and enlarge her circles of caring. When this reaching out destroys or drastically reduces her actual caring, she retreats and renews her contact with those who address her. If the retreat becomes a flight, an avoidance of the call to care, her ethical ideal is diminished. Similarly, if the retreat is away from human beings and toward other objects of caring-idea, animals, humanity-at-large, God—her ethical ideal is virtually shattered. (Noddings, 1984, 89-90)

The commandment recognizes that to preserve his own ideal of himself as a caring person, he must not consider the consequence of his decisions for the Jews in the concentration camp. He concerns himself with his family and fellow Nazis.

Suppose Noddings would say that my example of the Nazi commandant is outrageous, and that the Commandant's decision on behalf of the lieutenant is not an example of a caring decision. She might contend that the commandant, given his job of seeing to the imprisonment and murder of Jews, is the very antithesis of a caring person as one who cares for the well-being of others.

The problem a response such as this confronts, as I pointed out above, is that if natural caring does not presuppose any moral norms, there are no grounds for specifying that caring about the well-being of others must satisfy anyone else's criterion concerning what counts as "well-being." However, if one insists on morally normative criteria, then it appears that "natural caring" is ethical caring from the outset.

Given that natural caring implies an appraisal of that object of one's caring as desirable or worthwhile, whether there is an ethical dimension of caring depends on whether or not the object held to be desirable or worthwhile is held to be morally desirable or worthwhile. This presupposes a moral concept of the good. Peters (1981) contends that moral principles serve the purpose of providing criteria of moral relevance. In this interpretation, concern about the well being of others is moral in the sense of respecting the rights of others, or of concern for the dignity of others. If being a Nazi is incompatible with being a caring person, it is so because the Nazi fails to respect the dignity of Jews and other prisoners. He treats his prisoners unfairly or unjustly or denies them their freedom. These moral norms of dignity and freedom are moral principles.

I conclude that for the concept of caring as a self-involved attitude of appraisal to provide any rational grounds for decision making, it must be grounded in moral norms from the outset. Moral norms can be expressed in terms of moral principles. It follows that, instead of dispensing with an ethics of principle, an ethics of care, in effect, presupposes moral norms or principles.

I have discussed at some length Noddings' attempt to derive "ethical" caring from "nonethical caring," because her theory, however commendable, is highly misleading about the concept of caring itself. Moreover, in attempting to derive ethical caring from nonethical caring, Noddings fails to distinguish between two uses of the concept of caring.

THE CONCEPT OF CARING RECONSIDERED

The sense of "care" to which Noddings appeals in her own theory draws on the everyday use, captured by such phrases as "she cares about her family more than her job," or "he cares mainly about his writing." Noddings fails to recognize that her distinction between natural and aesthetical caring is a distinction without a difference, at least in terms of the analysis of the concept of care offered above. I suggested that the various phrases of the form "S cares about X" are appraisals of positive and negative affective engagement. In making such remarks about caring people, we are specifying the object of one's affective engagement in situations, as when we say the person cares about himself or his job or about other people. Additionally, such appraisals often serve to indicate the priority of one's values. Such phrases can be used as terms of moral approval or critique, or simply as statements of evaluation about what one believes is important. In saying that Jones mainly "cares about himself," we are pointing out that Jones is egocentric and not much of a moral person. Sometimes we praise someone for being affectively engaged. If I were to say, "Martha really *cares* about justice or about living a full life," I am emphasizing that she is affectively engaged in some respects. In another circumstance if I were to say "Martha *cares* about justice," I may be emphasizing that she possesses the virtue of justice.

The statement, "he or she is a caring person," captures another use of the concept of caring. The function of this statement is to attribute to a person the moral virtue of compassion, kindness, or benevolence. Such attributes imply that a person is disposed to act in terms of particular virtues such as caring, compassion, kindness, or benevolence. We also may be implying that this virtue is perhaps more prominent in this person's life than other virtues, such as honesty and justice. Although usually intended as a praiseworthy comment, one may be caring to a fault even as one may be just or honest to a fault. There may be an imbalance in one's life such that a person neglects other demands of the moral life. The statement, "she is too honest for her own good" reveals a lack of moral balance. A person who is "overly honest" might be one, when presented with a dilemma between two conflicting values (had an affair and wrestles over whether to make a clean breast of it with his wife), may inflexibly make the honest decision to the exclusion of considering other factors (here compassion, i.e., considering whether telling his wife will hurt her feelings).

We should be compassionate and benevolent, and it is likely that these virtues are lacking in some males in our own society. However, because of the socialization process, females may have developed this virtue to the exclusion of self-regarding virtues such as self-assurance. We understandably may ask if one in a particular context should be such a caring person.

I would be remiss if I did not emphasize that not only is the possessing of the virtues of compassion and kindness part of what it means to be a virtuous person, but these virtues provide a perspective for making the right moral decisions in dealing with relations involving friends and family, and others. In many situations involving relationships, the appropriate moral decision is so concrete that appeals to principles are, if not irrelevant, not what is needed for making a good moral decision. One realizes that one wants to do the caring or compassionate or kind thing, that is, act in terms of the principle of beneficence, and often the difficulty is in deciding what the caring thing is in the concrete situation. For example, a parent's child is rebelling against school and wants to drop out. What is the caring course of action in this circumstance? Appealing to moral principles offers no guidance. The parent must attempt to understand the child's conflict, the possible problems in the school setting, aspects of the family dynamics, and then attempt to make a decision concerning what the parent believes is in the child's best interest. It is with problems such as this, that the literature of the ethics of caring is enormously helpful. I should not be interpreted as criticizing this aspect of this approach to ethics. I have mainly intended to point out the limitations of the concept of caring and especially that it cannot provide us with a general criterion for moral obligation. In conclusion, we want to morally educate people who are affectively engaged with moral issues. We want people to care about justice and integrity, and we want people to be not merely just and honest, but compassionate as well.

FEMINIST ETHICS

Considering the difficulties with Noddings' theory, we might ask what promoted her to attempt to divorce the concept of caring from moral principles. This enterprise, I believe, results from Noddings' feminist's conviction—to borrow Carol Gilligan's (1982) phrase—that a caring focus is essentially a female perspective, while a moral principles focus is essentially a male perspective. Noddings (1984, 8) says: "An ethic built on caring is, I think, characteristically and essentially feminine—which is not to say, of course, that it cannot be shared by men, any more than we should care to say that traditional moral systems cannot be embraced by women."

A considerable body of literature documents that women have a greater tendency to think in terms of a focus on caring, instead of justice or rights. I agree with Gilligan who contends that any adequate theory of moral education must consider this. However, attempting to develop an ethic exclusively in terms of a focus on caring is not only problematic because of the conceptual problems discussed above. It is also problematic because of the inconclusive nature of this research. In the first place, this research suggests that not all women have a care focus. For example, Gilligan, Ward, Taylor and Bardige (1988, xix) acknowledge that a care focus is not characteristic of all women. They say: "Care focus, although not characteristic of all women, was almost exclusively a female phenomenon in three samples of educationally advantaged North Americans. If girls and women were eliminated from the study, care focus in moral reasoning would virtually disappear." Also Belenky et al. (1986) take issue with Gilligan's (1982) claim that as women, who are oriented in terms of care, become more liberated, they began to include their own self as an equal claimant in any moral decision. Belenky and colleagues have formulated an elaborate stage of self-development for women along a continuum of emancipation, ranging from "voiceless" women to those who ultimately develop a strong sense of self and relatedness with others. Belenky and associates point out that women at the stage of breaking away from their previous unemancipated lifestyle are "actively and obsessively" preoccupied with a choice between self and others, and tend to act in terms of their own self as opposed to denying the self and living for and through others. Such women do not attach great value to caring for others.

Second, we must be sure that the research considers not merely gender, but race and class. Cortese (1990, 99-100) finds much of value in Gilligan (1982) and believes that she "has expanded the domain of moral judgment by showing that woman (sic) define themselves through their relationships with others, focusing on care and intimacy, rather than separation and achievement." However, he claims (97) that a "research-based scale of development cannot be applied objectively or universally; it is a product of a certain cultural background at a particular point in time." He states (101) that: "Gilligan acknowledges that the focus on care in moral reasoning is not characteristic of all women. Rather, it is limited to females in advantaged populations. Consequently, ethnicity, race, and social class are more basic than gender in shaping ones conceptions of self and morality."

A related consideration is that evidence suggests that the feminine emphasis on an outlook of caring may be more a result of the sexual division of labor in which women, for the most part, have been relegated to the work of nurture and care of their families. As the feminist historians Amott and Matthaei (1991,14) observe: "Anthropologists have found that most societies across historical periods have tended to assign females to infant care and to the duties associated with raising children because of their biological ability to bear children ." It should not be surprising that women consigned to the work of nurture and care will have developed a caring focus.

On the assumption that a focus on caring is linked to a sexual division of labor, an adequate moral theory must be equipped to address this issue in this way. This brings us back to the problem of Noddings' ethics of caring lacking an adequate theory of justice. Let us assume for a moment that gender differences in ethics are linked to an unjust sexual division of labor in which women have had to be the primary care providers by virtue of their biological ability to bear children. If the sexual division of labor is unjust, we must then conclude that women have been oppressed by men in this regard. In the previous chapter I discussed the tendency of the oppressed to rationalize their situation of oppression through an attitude of compassion or "turning the other cheek." Some of those comments bear repeating here. I think we can benefit from an important insight of Nietzsche's (1969), namely that the oppressed morally rationalize their own situation of oppression. It should not be surprising that oppressed women, forced to be care givers exclusively or primarily, would tend to rationalize their predicament in moral terms that make a virtue out of necessity. Having a caring focus is considered to be virtuous, because one is not allowed to do anything else or conceive of oneself in terms other than that of a caring person. Houston (1989, 92) claims that an ethics of caring will give us prescriptions that contribute to subordination "if there is within the ethics no clear, unambiguous, independent moral worth assigned to the one caring, or some clear directives concerning the importance of the interests of women." Puka (1989), a care ethic advocate, exhibits an awareness of this more radical feminist critique. Puka claims that caring is best understood as an aspect of socialization rather than in terms of cognitive development, as elaborated by Gilligan. Gilligan (1982, 21) acknowledges that when viewed in terms of socialization, caring emerges as "a sexist service orientation in the patriarchal socialization, social conventions, and roles of many cultures." He (19) adds that "care is not primarily a general course of moral development, but a set of coping strategies for dealing with sexist oppression in particular." Oddly enough, Puka retreats from the kind of implications that I suggest above to the view that developing a pedagogy of caring as liberation provides the best approach to dealing with the feminine caring orientation. He even claims to find evidence of this view in Gilligan's writings. No doubt, as a strategy of moral education, emancipatory efforts in relation to one whose outlook is predominately one of caring must involve conceptualizing justice issues in terms of a care orientation. This is no different from the role of liberation theology in working with the oppressed by appealing to their Christian outlook—that can be viewed as an ethics of the oppressed—as a basis for liberation. However, pedagogical relevance does not constitute sufficient evidence for the claim that an ethics of caring is the only way moral concerns can be conceptualized.

To continue, if a caring focus is linked to an unjust sexual division of labor, this may further help us understand why an ethics of caring may not serve justice issues very well at all. Without a conception of justice, women who are victims of gender discrimination are deprived of an empowering concept for understanding their oppression. In terms of a caring focus, becoming emancipated only means that one must care about oneself as well as others. One is not encouraged to interrogate the very roles in which one has been subjected. Perhaps one should be free of having to be such a devotedly caring person. We may do women a great disservice if we deny them the extremely empowering notion of justice as part of their moral outlook.

7

The Ethics of Teaching

The overarching goal of integrating ethics into the classroom is to help students develop their capacity to engage in critical thinking about ethical issues. A secondary goal, which I believe by now clear, is to promote moral growth among students.

For the instructor to be effective accomplishing these goals, he or she needs to bear in mind some of the ethical aspects of teaching. Failing to teach in an ethical way will surely undermine the attempt to promote moral growth through the introduction of ethics into the curriculum. In this chapter, I wish to discuss some important aspects of the ethics of teaching.

The enterprise of teaching in a public school, college, or university, has a moral dimension in a liberal society (Goodlad 1990). A liberal society is one in which persons must strive to promote the good of all. In such a society the good of all is secured by allowing people to pursue their own conception of the good life, subject to the limitations of fairness and respect for the freedom of others to pursue their own sense of good. Some philosophical statements of the liberal view of society emphasize the liberal integrity of the individual to the exclusion of the fundamental concept of the common good. However, this alternative view is derived from the traditional notion of the self as an atomistic individual. In contrast, the view that I endorse, *liberal communitarianism,* assumes that individuals are social beings. As moral beings we come to have a self-understanding of ourselves as social beings who recognize a fundamental obligation to promote the good of all (Lisman 1991). We recognize the importance of promoting a sense of community. Of course, the liberal notion emphasizes that the individual is not to be sacrificed for the sake of the common good. The well-being of all is secured in a society that respects the dignity of individuals and protects the right of individuals to pursue their own good, subject to the limitations of fairness and respect for the autonomy of others. However, upholding the good of all involves more than merely allowing each person to pursue his or her own individual life style. This reconstructed conception of liberalism involves the notion that individuals must be willing to uphold those customs and practices that provide for intersubjective bonds of trust. Upholding the moral practices of promise keeping and truth telling are two examples of bonds of trust. Besides bonds of trust, it is important that the liberal society is committed to principles of justice. There must be a fundamental commitment to fairly distributing social goods. This, then, is the liberal conception of society that provides the framework for the moral imperatives of teaching. A thorough defense of liberal communitarian theory is the subject of a book in itself, and I obviously have only sketched a minimal outline of the essentials of the theory.

The liberal tradition of education is one in which public schools develop capacities that people must acquire to be contributing members of a liberal democratic society. These capacities include self-direction, fairness, and citizenship. Let me comment on each of these capacities in turn.

AUTONOMY

Greene (1988, 118) defines "autonomy" as follows: "To be autonomous is to be self-directed and responsible; it is to be capable of acting in accord with internalized norms and principles; it is to be insightful enough to know and understand one's impulses, one's motives, and the influences of one's past." I want to comment on the critical notions implicit in Greene's statement, self-direction, self-governance, responsibility, and the notion of self-worth.

As Barrow and Woods (1988, 99) point out, a person is self-determining or self-directed "if I do what I choose to do, whether my choice is sensible or not from my own or anybody else's point of view." An individual fails to be self-directed if he or she is subject to the control of other people or externally imposed rules, such as a prisoner whose daily activities are structured by physically enforced rules. People also can fail to be self-directed if they are acting under the influence of drugs or by irrational passions. A good example of the latter is Florentine Ariza in *Love in the Time of Cholera* (Marquez 1988) whose decision about his vocation, about how he spends his life is, at least during his early manhood, completely governed by his unrequited love for Fermina Daza.

We also may not be self-directed when we are indoctrinated, that is, when a person has been influenced to come to hold certain beliefs regardless of the evidence for those beliefs. For example, a young child may be raised to believe that African Americans are inferior to Whites and be influenced to hold this belief despite evidence to the contrary.

Minimally then, as an aspect of autonomy, young people need to be encouraged to be self-directed. This means providing them with opportunities to make choices, to exercise judgment, and to encourage a school community that respects the rights of students to be self-directed. However, being self-directed is not sufficient for autonomy. Being autonomous implies that one is self-governing, that is, that one makes rational or principled decisions.

A rationally self-directed person will base one's decisions on the appropriate evidence. If the decisions are about the everyday world, such a person will base decisions on the appropriate practical evidence, including sense experience and our core of practical knowledge. Moral decisions will be principled decisions.

The autonomous person is also responsible. This is one of the most problematic areas. Being responsible for one's decisions, among other things, means that we are accepting responsibility for one's own choices. As Strike (1990a, 41) claims, morally responsible people "may not delegate responsibility for their moral lives to others." The French existentialist Jean Paul Sartre has emphasized that one of our problems is our tendency not to accept responsibility for our decisions. We are tempted to pretend that we were "forced" into making decisions, which in reality are the product of our own intentional choices. This is an ongoing problem for children and adults alike.

A problem that exists concerning promoting a sense of responsibility among students is the failure to clarify two notions of responsibility. Responsibility in the accountability sense means holding someone accountable. When teachers talk of instilling a sense of responsibility, they sometimes mistakenly have this notion in mind. The other sense of responsibility refers to our ability to acknowledge and accept that we are self-determining agents of our lives. As I have just suggested, children and adults experience difficulty in accepting responsibility for their actions in this second sense. Children may attempt to evade personal responsibility by pretending or denying that they made the choice or decision to do what they did. They may claim that someone "made them do it," or that they were "told to do it." A related evasion of personal responsibility is that of the tendency to deny that one is responsible for the consequences of one's actions. The student may say that he did not do anything but hit another child. They were not responsible for the student who decided not to come to school the next day out of fear of being hit again. There are, no doubt, situations in which it is difficult to decide whether someone is responsible for the consequences of a course of action. Sometimes, a person may not be responsible for something that happens following an action. For example, a student may repeatedly tease another student. Sadly, a week later this student attempts suicide by taking an overdose of his parent's sleeping pills. It would be highly unlikely that merely making fun of another student would drive one to suicide. However, the student who did engage in teasing may feel guilt and remorse. A wise teacher, while not condoning the teasing, would surely want to reassure the student that, although he or she should not tease other students, he or she was not responsible for this drastic course of action.

Critical to one's sense of autonomy is the notion of self-respect. This is also important for developing a sense of fairness. Strike (1990a, 43) observes: "self-respect is an aspect of equal respect. People who believe that human beings are objects of worth and are, thereby, entitled to be treated with dignity and extended equal rights are entitled to believe this of themselves. Second, self-respect is a psychological requirement of an individual's capacity to secure his or her own rights and to respect those of others. People who lack self-respect are, as a consequence, likely to think themselves unworthy of equal treatment."

The teacher or instructor has a responsibility to promote a sense of self-worth among students. It is important to draw a distinction between the notions of self-esteem and self-worth. Although self-esteem is often used interchangeably with the concept of self-worth, self-esteem, as it is currently used in psychology, is advanced as a morally neutral concept. People are encouraged to "feel good about themselves." However, as I have suggested in the chapter on feminist ethics, the emotions are "moral" and attaining emotional growth involves moral growth as well. I shall not discuss this issue further here. The important notion here for the concept of autonomy is the notion of self-worth. Teachers are obligated to promote a sense of self-worth among their students. Students need to come to a recognition of their fundamental sense of dignity. The way that teachers can do this, is as Kant suggests, by treating them not merely as a means, but as an end. Students are quick to catch on to a teacher who exploits his or her own students.

FAIRNESS

As I have already suggested, the very core of the moral point of view involves the recognition that one must regard one's own self-interests impartially; that is, we must accord mutual respect to others and not attempt to advance our own individual self-interests at the expense of others. The teacher needs to promote this sense of fair-mindedness in the students.

Strike (1990a, 44) points out that one of the important factors for contributing to a sense of justice is that "individuals believe that their society affirms their own worth because of its view of justice." The important point here is that people do not acquire a sense of justice primarily on the basis of argument. Rather "they experience its contribution to their lives." Schools, as a major socializing institution, have an important responsibility to help establish this sense of justice.

There are other two important aspects of justice, distributive justice and critical pedagogy. As I explained elsewhere, the core notion of distributive justice is the notion that "equals should be treated equally and unequals unequally." The practices and rules that we implement in society and in schools must be fair practices. Persons should not be treated differently without a justification for doing so. For example, it would be blatantly unfair to allow only the boys to do board work in the classroom to the exclusion of young females. Similarly, people should be treated differently if there is justification for doing this. There might be some justification for putting some students in remedial math and reading classes, provided that the classes do not become permanent groups serving to track students.

As these examples suggest, the manner of the teacher can have an influence on the students' perceived sense of fairness. Students are quick to note favoritism and unfair treatment by teachers. The teacher, then, has many opportunities to promote a sense of justice by his or hear treatment of students.

Teachers also need to engage in critical pedagogy. Giroux (1988) has extended the ideas of Paulo Freire to the public school. Giroux claims that morally committed teachers, or teachers who are committed to being "transformative intellectuals," have a fundamental responsibility to help students attain a better understanding of the cultural hegemonic nature of schooling and society, as well as to develop the basis of a moral critique of the political economy.

The values and outlooks of students are not politically neutral outlooks. They reflect ways those students have of orienting themselves within the culture. Economically disadvantaged children evolve ways of dealing with having less than their middle-class counterparts, such as by rebelling against school. Such activities unfortunately only tend to keep them in the socio-economic condition against which they are rebelling.

Giroux (1988, 103) suggests that there are at least three ways that teachers can help students become more critically aware of cultural hegemony. In the first place teachers need to analyze the "discourse of production." This involves helping students gain a better understanding of the nature of economic inequality, including that they themselves may be victims of inequality. It also involves attempting to understand the ideological frameworks, such as the media, which encourage an outlook according to which people do not attain a structural understanding of the political economy. For example, the media tends to portray the "drug problem" as solely a product of immoral individuals, rather than seeing this problem as rooted in the breakdown of our urban infrastructures.

The second important aspect of critical pedagogy is the "analyses of textual forms." Students need to learn how to read their school texts and curriculum materials critically. They need to be on the lookout for those textual materials that tend to suppress dissident voices or outlooks that reinforce a nonstructural understanding of society.

The final aspect of critical pedagogy is the "discourse of lived cultures." Students must understand that they are engaged in "self-production," that is, that they "give meaning to their lives through the complex historical, cultural, and political forms that they both embody and produce" (Giroux 1988, 105). Such an approach involves being attentive to the subjectivities of the students—the histories, dreams, and experiences that they bring to school. This approach will serve to confirm the "experiences of those students who are often silenced by the dominant culture of schooling"(Giroux 1988, 106). It also will help students to have a better grasp of "how power, dependence, and social inequality structure the ideologies and practices that enable and limit students around issues of class, race, and gender" (106).

CITIZENSHIP

The final capacity that teachers need to instill is a sense of citizenship. There are two central notions here, community and democracy. Let me take up each of these in turn.

As I suggested, a liberal theory of education often emphasizes the importance of the individual's right to pursue his or her own conception of the good to the exclusion of the importance of upholding the good of all. Although we should support the good of all, individuals are not subservient to society.

However, students need to recognize that individuality can only flourish within community. As individuals we require social allegiances as a basis for individual growth, much as a plant requires proper soil conditions for its growth. As many writers have documented, we are witnessing a significant failure of community, accompanied by an emphasis on materialism and narcissism. The individual reigns supreme in our society, aimless, anxious, and distrustful of one's neighbors. I believe that the breakdown of community is linked to the conflict of our market economy with the imperatives of democracy.

In this context, the morally committed teacher has an important responsibility to help create a classroom as a moral learning community. What would such a classroom be like? To provide a brief sketch, it would be a place where students would learn to work cooperatively, rather than in competition with each other. It would be a place where students are encouraged to articulate their own concerns in an atmosphere where unequivocal respect for the rights of others to express their views is encouraged. Teachers would emphasize the importance of working together and of creating intersubjective bonds of trust.

The other important aspect of citizenship is the need for students to acquire a working understanding of the democratic process. Students should be offered the opportunity to engage in democratic decision making in the classroom and in the school in general. Teachers should explain the democratic process as they attempt to carry out that process. Finally, teachers should make the effort to help students gain a better understanding of the democratic process of society.

THE TEACHER AS MORAL EXEMPLAR

Fenstermacher (1990, 134) has argued that the morality of the teacher has a considerable impact on the morality of the student. The teacher can act morally by holding oneself up as a possible model. With this approach "the teacher acts justly while assisting and expecting just conduct from students; the teacher shows compassion and caring, seeking these traits from his or her students; the teacher models tolerance while showing students how to be tolerant."

Fenstermacher (1990) suggests that the moral character of the teacher can be considered "manner." A manner is an aspect of everything the teacher does in the classroom. Just as teachers possess some manner that defines the moral character of their teaching, so learners have a manner that identifies their moral development. Thus despite the subject being taught, the teacher, as a moral exemplar, has a basic moral responsibility to exemplify the virtues of self-direction, fairness, and citizenship.

Teachers or instructors who teach with purpose and think with determination model self-direction. Teachers also must treat the students as self-directed beings. Of course, there is a limitation here. Capacities of self-direction vary among students, given their level of maturity. Teachers, like parents, have a responsibility to guide students along with providing them with opportunities to exercise self-direction, i.e., to make responsible decisions. Young children, no doubt, will flounder if they have too little outside direction, just as older, more mature students, will tether at the bit if they are not given enough rein to set their own direction. Bearing in mind these limitations, the ethical teacher must encourage the development of the capacities of self-direction by treating students as morally autonomous.

Second, the teacher or instructor should model fairness by treating the students fairly in every way possible. The fair teacher is a fair grader, gives each student his or her due, and attempts to provide a balanced discussion of controversial issues, being careful to present both sides of an issue.

Finally, the ethical instructor models the virtue of citizenship by creating a classroom climate in which students are encouraged to respect the rights of all, but also work for the good of all. Such a teacher may adopt teaching strategies that encourage this, such as cooperative learning. Group activities will provide an atmosphere in which students are encouraged to work with each other. The moral teacher will not be reluctant to inject an element of competition into the classroom. But competition will not be pursued for its own sake. It will always be a device to encourage students to gain self-reliance. The ethical teacher will always provide encouragement and support for those who do not excel in competition and find ways that those students can be recognized.

8

The Case Study Approach and
Conducting Ethics Discussions

Beauchamp (1989) claims that the case study approach to presenting ethical issues focuses critical thinking on a specific problem. It stimulates reflection on what ought or ought not be done, and the problems provoke individual and group decision making about personal and social issues. The case study approach to teaching is widely recognized and used in teaching across the curriculum. Consequently, I will not go into a historical discussion and analysis of this pedagogical approach. (I refer the reader interested in this to Beauchamp). Instead, I shall limit my discussion to the application of the case study approach in the classroom.

As applied to ethics, the case method attempts to provide concrete examples of ethical issues or dilemmas in which students can develop ethical insight through analysis of a case study. They gain practice in ethical decision making by choosing a course of action, following an analysis of the case in question. As previously stated, a dilemma is an ethical situation in which two or more values or principles are in conflict or where one is encountering difficulty applying a value or a principle to a situation. Examples of case studies are included in each of the academic discipline chapters. Ethics cases are essentially stories or vignettes in which persons are confronting ethical dilemmas or decisions. Case studies can be as simple as a few sentences in which an ethical conflict is presented. Alternatively, one may say that a medical doctor told his female patients that he was providing donor sperm when he was providing his own. Did he do the wrong thing? Or, one can provide a detailed example of a case study.

Except fiction, which presents a special case discussed in a separate chapter, there are three types of ethics cases that one may consider. First, there are case studies that deal with the application of a moral principle to a situation complicated by factors such as technology. The use of animal organs for human transplants might be such an example. Leaving aside the difficult moral question of the ethics of harvesting such organs, inserting these organs in humans raises a serious ethical question. We believe strongly in the principle underlying such transplants, namely to uphold the Hippocratic Oath and alleviate or prevent suffering. However, are we justified in transplanting animal organs for this purpose? If using animal organs does not present any serious health risk, one might ask if these transplants are compatible with the dignity of persons. This illustrates the first kind of case, applying a principle to a complicated situation.

The second type of case concerns situations in which people are involved in a conflict of self-interest against respecting the interests of others. For example, someone has an opportunity to benefit from insider trading information in a stock deal. Or a student is tempted to cheat on an exam. As we shall see, research ethics involving issues of honesty is an important topic for the natural and social sciences and might be a good way to incorporate ethics discussions into one's courses.

Finally, there are cases that involve conflicts of moral values or principles. The abortion issue illustrates such a dilemma. Everyone agrees on the underlying principles of respect of life and autonomy. However, the issue of abortion features these two principles in conflict. Which principle should get precedence, the right to life or right of choice? Many important dilemmas of the day, and those within academic disciplines, are these sorts of dilemmas. Using the case study approach involves selecting personalized and contextualized examples of these three conflicts and providing an opportunity for students to analyze and discuss them.

THE INSTRUCTOR'S RESPONSIBILITY

The instructor has several responsibilities when using a case method approach. The instructor needs to assign ethics cases for discussion. They are usually included at the end of textbook chapters, especially in business. If not included, the instructor may wish to develop one's own cases. Other possibilities include having groups of students develop cases. Students often respond enthusiastically to this and welcome the opportunity to draw upon their own experiences. It also is very effective in occupational areas for practitioners to come as guest speakers. Guest speakers, drawing from their own work experience, provide convincing cases, which offer insights into actual work situations. The instructor should encourage the guest speaker to highlight ethical dilemmas, or else the speaker may describe a professional experience. Regardless, the instructor needs to focus the class on the underlying ethical issues involved in the case.

The instructor needs to be a good discussion facilitator. Being a good facilitator involves guiding discussions through remarks and questions that provoke critical thinking. Instructors must make sure that important points are considered. Since many ethics cases provoke strong reactions, it is critical for the instructor to establish ground rules of tolerant discussion. The instructor needs to make sure that all points of view are presented and that all students have an opportunity to express their opinions.

In executing the role of impartiality, the instructor, at the outset of discussion, should refrain from exhibiting agreement or disagreement with the various positions presented. When a student expresses a rambling or angry statement, it is helpful to simply rephrase the essence of the statement and ask for input from other students. For example, if during a discussion on poverty, Tom responds angrily that "I'm sick and tired of all those welfare cheaters. I think they should starve in the street!", the instructor might respond by saying, "Well, Tom believes that people in poverty may be taking advantage of their situation. Does anyone disagree with this?" It also is effective to respond to unfounded generalizations, such as this, by asking the student, "Why do you believe this?"

Finally, the instructor may wish to take a final position on the viewpoints at the end of the discussion. I avoid taking a position on extremely controversial issues, because students who disagree with me may feel let down and that they have "lost" the debate. This also may encourage younger students to parrot the instructor's views trying to please the instructor. However, if a student asks me my position on an issue, I defer giving my view until the conclusion of the discussion. But then I will reveal my view, unless the issue is so controversial that the class is extremely divided. I believe it is valuable to disclose one's view from time to time. I comment further on this below.

The student's role in the discussion of case studies is to be actively cooperative throughout the process of discussing the case study. The student must synthesize material on his or her own, learn to separate irrelevant from relevant information, and develop expertise in judgment so as to arrive at a decision concerning how the issues of the case study should be handled. Below is a brief synopsis of a generally accepted method for discussing a case study.

Seven Step Method for Discussing a Case Study

1. Describe the pertinent facts of the case.
2. Describe the ethical issues of the case.
3. Identify the stake holders in the case study, that is, those who have a claim to participate in this decision.
4. Alternate solutions to the problem should be presented.
5. The ethics of the alternatives need to be discussed.
6. The participants in the discussion should identify the practical constraints under which the decision must be made.
7. The students should decide what action they would or should take if they were in the situation.

Let us take a case study and apply these steps to it.

Case Study: The Kevorkian Case

Several years prior to her death in 1990, Janet Adkins noticed slips in her memory, including her ability to play the piano (*NY Times* 1990). About a year before she died, doctors told Mrs. Adkins that she had Alzheimer's disease. All doctors who saw her agreed she had Alzheimer's. Mrs. Adkins arrived at the decision to commit suicide. Derek Humphrey, Director of the Hemlock Society, said, "She was a very balanced woman, a churchgoer. She put the question of suicide to her Unitarian minister, and he was in agreement with her philosophy. She and her family were in counseling for about six months with a most experienced counselor." She tried experimental treatment. She went to three doctors in the Portland area and asked them to help her die. They would not take the risk.

Mrs. Adkins held a bachelor of arts degree in English literature from Portland State University. She lived in a wealthy area of Portland, and her husband was a successful investor. She lived a very active life which included hang gliding, riding in a hot air balloon, hiking in the mountains of Himalaya, and climbing Mount Hood. She was reported to have beaten one of her sons in tennis just a week before her death.

Mrs. Adkins heard about Dr. Jack Kevorkian through a magazine article and an appearance he made on the "Donahue" show. She chose Dr. Kevorkian to assist her suicide because she believed in what he was doing. She flew to Detroit on a weekend in June. Following a weekend of dining and shopping with her husband, she met Dr. Kevorkian at a restaurant near his home in Holly, Michigan. Dr. Kevorkian had spent a couple of days trying to find a place to carry out the procedure. After being turned away by motels, funeral homes, and the landlords of vacant office spaces, he settled on using his Volkswagen van. He installed a cot, new sheets, pillowcases and curtains.

He and Mrs. Adkins drove to a campground in Oakland County. Dr. Kevorkian hooked Mrs. Adkins up to the machine, consisting of an intravenous tube and three bottles, one containing a saline solution, one thiopental sodium to induce unconsciousness, and the third potassium chloride. He attached her to the saline intravenous tube and to an electrocardiograph machine in order to monitor her heart and to be certain it had stopped. Dr. Kevorkian inserted an intravenous tube into Mrs. Adkins' arm and dripped harmless saline solution through it. Mrs. Adkins then pressed a button that stopped the saline and replaced it with thiopental, which causes unconsciousness. After a minute, the machine switched solutions again to potassium chloride, which stops the heart and brings death within minutes. Her husband and a friend waited at a hotel. After determining that her heart had stopped, Dr. Kevorkian called the local police to tell them what he had done.

This case actually could be discussed in a psychology, sociology, or in a health sciences course. Applying the case study approach outlined above (1) the instructor would first make sure all relevant information is provided. Did Mrs. Adkins really have Alzheimer's disease? What was her mental state of mind? Was she making a competent and informed decision to die? What was the law in Michigan regarding such a procedure? What were Dr. Kevorkian's motives? Was he assisting in suicides out of a desire to respect the dignity of persons or was he seeking publicity? (2) What are the pertinent ethical issues? Clearly, there is the issue of a right of a person to take their own life to avoid a loss of dignity from a debilitating disease. There also is the issue of whether it is morally right for a physician to assist someone in committing suicide. (3) The stake holders, or people directly affected by the decision need to be considered. What about Mrs. Adkins' husband and children? What would be the effect upon them of her decision to commit suicide? (4) What about alternative courses of action, such as for Mrs. Adkins to visit other Alzheimer patients at her stage, or even to visit people in a more advanced stage of the disease? (5) What would be the ethics of her deciding to be placed in a nursing home when the disease progressed? (6) Were there any practical constraints in evaluating this decision? Would Mrs. Adkins have been receptive to taking any other course of action? Finally, (7) what do the students who are discussing this issue believe to be the right course of action and why? Of course, some students will have made up their minds about the morality of this case prior to any discussion. But some students, upon learning more about the nature of Alzheimer's disease, may change their mind from opposing Mrs. Adkins' decision to supporting it. It is important to ask the students to support their own beliefs with reasons.

STRATEGIES FOR PRESENTING AND DISCUSSING CASES

There are a variety of ways that case studies can be presented and discussed. The instructor can simply present a case or have students read a case study and then lead the discussion. Or students can work on cases in small groups and then report on their discussion to the class. Ask someone to be the group recorder and perhaps someone else to report to the class. I try to have students take turns with these responsibilities, to constrain aggressive students from monopolizing the discussion. I often ask the group to appoint someone who has not been saying much in class to be the reporter.

Role playing is an excellent way to present ethics cases. I provided a role play example in the appliction section of chapter four. Other role playing activities are given in Part III. This technique can be used in conjunction with a class discussion of case studies. For example, an instructor can ask one or more of the students to role-play the case study by assuming a character in the case, defending that character's position by reference to moral principles. I observed a writing class in which students role-played the Anita Hill/Clarence Thomas Senate hearing. Students assumed the identity of the characters in this scenario. An instructor can use a role playing discussion to introduce the case study itself. The *Ethics in America* video series provides good examples of using role playing to discuss ethical issues. When engaging in this type of role playing, the instructor should select people to represent the positions of the stake holders and ask the participants to defend their positions.

Sometimes students resist taking on a role with which they disagree. On balance, there is great value in encouraging students to play along. Students report after playing such a role that they gain a better understanding and appreciation of their opponent's point of view. A successful role playing activity should serve as a vehicle for expressing the seven steps of a case method. After serving as the facilitator of the role play activity, the instructor should call on class members to explain and defend their own decision involved in the case study. Below is a synopsis of the steps in a role playing activity.

Steps in a Role Playing Activity

1. Briefly describe the case study.
2. Identify the stake holders.
3. Have stake holders (or stake holder groups) prepare their position.
4. The instructor, serving as facilitator, leads the stake holders in a discussion.
5. Debriefing by instructor
   a. Identify the ethical issues.
   b. Have the class discuss what their decision would be regarding the case study.

FORMS OF MORAL DISENGAGEMENT

One of the problems that an instructor encounters in an ethics discussion is the moral disengagement of students. I mean by this the resistance of students to discuss ethical issues seriously. Disengagement takes several forms. It can take the form of skepticism, of deep-seated doubt about moral knowledge. "What is the point of moral inquiry?" Or it can represent subjectivism, a form of skepticism in which moral values are considered to be expressions or statements of feeling. This is expressed by the statement, "If it feels good, do it!" It also can be relativism, the view that everyone's moral beliefs are equally valid. This is expressed by the claim, "It's right for me if I believe it to be right." I have dealt with these counter-ethical perspectives in the Counter-Ethical Theories chapter.

Relativism results from a variety of attitudes. It may only reflect a commitment to good manners and tolerance. As I stated in the previous chapter, a student may be reluctant to criticize the views of others for fear of offending someone else. On the other hand, relativism may be avoidant behavior. The student may be using this perspective as a pretext for avoiding difficult thinking. By saying, "It's all relative," the student may be attempting to avoid having to get involved in a discussion requiring concentration and hard thinking.

Two closely related forms of disengagement are ethical egoism, the view that one should pursue one's self-interest in everything one does, and affective disengagement, not caring about being a moral person. Ethical egoism is expressed by statements such as "What's in it for me?" I have criticized this theory in a previous chapter. However, I have found that criticizing this theory often falls on deaf ears, because this point of view represents one of the most complex forms of moral disengagement. Ethical egoism and affective disengagement share one factor in common. Those who have these attitudes are, in effect, opting out of the moral point of view. These forms of disengagement can be seen as products of our general social malaise in which many people are civically disconnected. I hope that the service learning movement will prove to be an effective way to combat this problem.

At the same time an instructor can get students involved in ethics discussions simply by being tolerant of narcissistic and affectively disengaged students. Ethics discussions evoking fundamental moral principles, such as trust, caring, and justice, remind them of values they do hold. The more they discuss these issues the more convinced they become that they are not ethical egoists after all.

Still another form of disengagement over some issues is due to moral imbalance, that is, having either a well developed sense of justice or compassion but not both. As I discuss in the chapter on the ethics of caring and feminist ethics, research suggests that males on average approach ethical issues with less compassion than females. In this respect, males have much to learn from females.

STRATEGIES FOR COMBATING MORAL DISENGAGEMENT

Other than following the suggestions above, there are other things the instructor can do to cope with these forms of moral disengagement. First, the instructor can ignore subtleties and presume the best among students. Perhaps their disengagement is a result of confusion in the home, church, or in society. You can help them cope with intellectual difficulties simply by providing an opportunity for critical discussion of ethical issues.

Let students be teachers. Many faculty members may fear that they do not have a sufficient knowledge base of an ethical issue to conduct a solid discussion. However, what is more often the case is that the instructor is not aware of how much more sophisticated he or she is than students. Giving students the opportunity to discuss issues among themselves in class or in small groups will ensure that they discuss issues in terms of their own developmental level. Often students can teach themselves better than can the instructor.

The instructor may find it productive to discuss forms of moral disengagement as a social phenomenon. I have suggested that some forms of disengagement may be due to our civic malaise. Bellah et al. (1985) provides an excellent discussion of this problem.

The instructor also can counteract disengagement by practicing advocacy. As previously indicated, instructors must model moral engagement. Modeling moral engagement can have an important counter-effect on some relativistic students. Some students will benefit from an encounter with an intellectually and morally engaging instructor. If an instructor is never willing to express his or her own view, he or she loses an important opportunity to model the essence of critical thinking, namely taking a thoughtful stand on an issue and exhibiting intellectual and moral engagement.

The instructor can promote the classroom as a moral learning community. This can occur when the instructor is willing to be an ethical teacher. I discussed aspects of this responsibility in the preceeding chapter. I also discussed above how ethics cases studies can be effectively presented by means of small group discussion, or by means of what is commonly referred to as cooperative learning. This form of learning is not merely an excellent way to present ethics case studies, but it also can help create a moral learning community.

Bricker (1989, 49) argues that the hidden curriculum of working alone, typical of much classroom work, camouflages the social nature of knowledge by making knowledge look like it is a private, personal phenomenon. Students begin to think of themselves as persons who are constituted by the knowledge they have. Bricker (44) contends: "The hidden curriculum of working alone for knowledge prvents students from seeing the *social nature* of knowledge and thus limits her development of autonomy." According to Bricker (46) academic knowledge is grounded upon inhabiting a community of persons who "use the same rules together." Students share "forms of life" (47). Morally, students are "individuated from each other, but they are also joined together by the rules that provide coherence and their discourse" (48). The basic point here is that autonomy or authentic individuality requires community. At the same time working collaboratively produces gains in social connectedness.

The instructor can further counter moral imbalance and draw students into ethical discussion by honoring the different perspectives that students represent. Young students often parrot their parents' views. As Brookfield (1991) suggests, basic ideologies often represent unexamined basic assumptions and are very threatening for students to confront. Criticizing these views may make students feel that their own sense of selfhood is under attack. The instructor should refrain from being overtly critical of these students' beliefs and allow them the opportunity to think through issues in their own terms. At best the instructor may only plant seeds of critical thought; it will take time, sometimes years, for students to change their outlook.

Also, as I indicate in the chapters on multiculturalist and feminist ethics, there are ethnic and gender differences in approaches to ethics. While I am critical of the attempt to develop moral theories based on these differences, the instructor needs to perceive how people frame and approach ethical issues in terms of gender and ethnicity. The wise instructor will work at seeking the common grounds of understanding that are often presented in very different ways. The chapters on multiculturalist and feminist ethics provide some indication of ethnic and feminist differences in approaching ethical matters, and a large bibliography exists especially pertaining to feminist ethics. The most important works in this area are mentioned in the chapter on feminist ethics.

Finally, the instructor needs to respect ideological differences underlying ethical views. In my experience of dealing with controversial issues such as abortion and poverty, students are divided on these issues in terms of deep ideological differences. Some oppose abortion due to religious convictions. Others tend to blame people for their poverty out of an ideology of individualism, the belief that individuals are the primary reality and are solely responsible for whatever befalls them. As with students who have never questioned their fundamental, home-taught values, the instructor usually can be more effective by encouraging students to consider alternatives without pummeling them with criticisms.

In conclusion, I encourage the instructor to promote an atmosphere of impartial, critical thinking about discipline-appropriate ethical issues. The instructor needs to be tolerant of extreme opinions and encourage students to examine the grounds for their beliefs. Finally, through opportunities of cooperative learning and by modeling engaged, critical thinking, the instructor can create a classroom environment that will draw many resistant students into serious moral discussion.

Part III

Integrating Ethics into the Curriculum

9

Ethics in the Social Science Curriculum

Despite the sustained academic effort to construe the social sciences as value-free, a case can be made for the notion that the social sciences are not free of ethical considerations. Bellah (1976) examines a number of classical social thinkers, including de Tocqueville, Durkheim, and Weber, and maintains that the views of these, and other social thinkers as well, imply certain fundamental ideas about the relation of the individual to society, including a conception of what the good life is. Contrary to the notion that the purpose of social science is to provide the most effective means to predetermined societal ends, Bellah contends that social science must make both ends and means the objects of rational reflection.

It does not take too much reflection to understand why social science must come to this recognition. Social science studies the same kinds of beings that we are, namely, moral beings. Any thorough and useful study of human beings must consider this. Of course, a social scientist might reply that these disciplines, except for psychology, do not study individual beings, whether moral or not. Instead, social sciences are disciplines that mainly study social institutions. However, social institutions are normative institutions. A primary social institution, such as the family, is not merely a biological unit. It is a unit organized in terms of moral norms. As Berger and Luckmann (1967) point out, these and other secondary institutions, such as the church and schools, play an important role in socializing the young into the prevailing ethical norms of society.

The advocate of a value-free social science may agree that it is appropriate to study the values perpetuated within a social institution, such as the schools. But they may contend that it is not the duty of the social scientists to take sides, despite those values. If the schools, for example, are serving to reproduce a class-divided society, as conflict theorists claim, it might be argued that it is not within the purview of the social scientists to take sides on the question of whether schools should be in the business of cultural reproduction.

At the very least, the social scientist needs an understanding of fundamental moral notions, such as freedom and justice, to be able to understand in what way a given system under analysis is serving the interests of justice. For example, the functionalist sociologist may even fail to see that certain aspects of institutions may be disfunctional because they are perpetuating injustice.

Social scientists, like natural scientists, also are often in the best position to make recommendations about how our society might go about solving our social problems. To shy away from this on the grounds that it is not one's duty as a social scientist to do this, is to relinquish what well may be one's moral responsibility as an informed intellectual.

Finally, the social scientist need not be in complete agreement with the notion that social inquiry implicitly has ethical aims to recognize that it is appropriate to confront students with ethical implications of social science. Social problems, such as poverty and the plight of women, are useful topics for dealing with ethical implications. For example, in relation to the issue of poverty, the instructor can point out that whether or not one has a structural view of poverty will affect one's moral judgment about the justice or injustice of poverty. For example, if one believes that poor people are the main cause of poverty, i.e., that poverty is an expression of irresponsibility, then one may not believe that we have an obligation, as a society, to try to do something to reduce poverty. On the other hand, if one regards poverty as structural, one may argue that there must be a fundamental change in the political economy to provide more jobs for people in poverty. Discussions such as these will help students not only recognize ethical implications of the social sciences, but attain a better understanding of the value of the academic subject itself as a contributor to better understanding of the ethical needs of society. Discussing ethical issues of the social sciences can reinforce the recognition that social science research is relevant for clarifying ethical issues and that clarifying certain ethical issues helps students gain a better understanding of the social science discipline.

In the remaining part of this chapter and the next, brief discussions are provided of several topics that are appropriate for integrating ethics into a sociology or psychology course—gender equity, race and social equality, and research ethics. These merely are suggestive topics. Many other topics would serve equally well, including population, drugs, street crime, AIDS, energy, and the environment. Finally, I offer a section of classroom applications.

GENDER AND EQUALITY

Amy Walker, a seventeen-year-old student at Santa Teresa High School, wrote a paper on battered women for her English class (Goldston & Hendrix 1994). She wrote about case histories of women who had been sexually, physically, and mentally abused. In her paper she said that she had suffered repeated mental and sexual abuse by her boyfriend. Amy wrote that her boyfriend raped her after they had been together about a year and a half in August, 1990, when he was showing her his father's new home. Amy said she tried to block out the incident and did not tell anyone. She continued seeing the boy and having intercourse with him. Shortly after the alleged rape incident she became despondent and was placed on twenty-four hour suicide watch indefinitely. The couple's parents agreed that they should not see each other anymore, but they kept meeting secretly until March of 1991 when Amy wrote her paper. Her teacher, Mary Navarro, believed that she was required by law to tell the authorities about Amy's situation. She reported the allegations to Children's Protective Services of Santa Clara County and advised Amy to file a report with police. After the allegations were made public, Amy and her mother complained to the school principal, Mike Welch, and two associate principals that she was being harassed by her ex-boyfriend. However, the principal sided with the boy. They did not see any reason to get involved. Welch said: "We can't go on a witch hunt. There are two sides to every story." Amy was removed from the American government class that she and her ex-boyfriend attended. The boy remained in the class. The boy yelled in a hallway as Amy and a friend were walking by: "Yes, I raped you, but where's the proof? You're the neighborhood slut." When Amy and her friend reported this incident to the principal, he said that he had trouble believing them because no adults had heard the comments. After news stories came out about the incident the associate superintendent requested that the principal provide a written report. As a result, the principal acknowledged that "his own awareness of the issue had grown and that services offered by the Rape Crisis Center would be advertised in the school newspaper." In reporting the rape incident to the police officer, Amy showed the officer a threatening note her former boyfriend had written. The officer read the note but did not make a copy of it, and the note disappeared from her purse the next day at school. The officer did not refer Amy to a rape crisis counselor. Amy did not graduate that year because she failed two classes, the American government class from which she was removed and her English class.

As an ethics case study, we must ask if Mike Welch, the school principal, handled Amy Walker's situation ethically. This is a complicated case because it concerns the rights of both Amy and her ex-boyfriend. At one level this could be construed as a "she said, he said" case, where there is insufficient evidence to determine who was telling the truth. But based on the evidence before us, it appears that Amy at least had friends who were backing up her side of the story, and apparently she had shown a police officer a threatening note from her boyfriend. Of course, one cannot be sure that the threatening note was not provoked by the boyfriend's response to "true" or "false" allegations. Nevertheless, Amy's friends were backing up her story.

The other aspect of the case concerns whether Amy was treated fairly in being removed from the American government class. Typical of many such dilemmas, it is not that two principles are in conflict, as with issues such as abortion (right to life against freedom of choice), but whether all parties in question are treated fairly. As mentioned earlier, the formal principle of justice states that no one should be treated differently unless there is justification for doing so. Was Amy treated fairly in being removed from the American government class while her ex-boyfriend was allowed to stay in the class? At the very least, one could argue that Mike Welch treated Amy unfairly by removing her, instead of the boyfriend, or by not removing both of them from the American government class, and by not allowing Amy an opportunity to pass the course.

This is a good example of the kind of ethical dilemma or ethics case study one could use in a sociology class, especially concerning the topic of the social condition of females in contemporary American society. The way she was treated illustrates the biases that prevail against women in many situations in our society. There is a broad sociological question that needs to be dealt with on this topic, namely in what ways and to what extent are women subordinate to men? There are also a couple of pertinent ethical questions. Are men and women in all relevant respects equal, and assuming they are equal, what are morally acceptable relatations between males and females? A sociology instructor may wish to spend most of one's time on the sociological issue, but it is appropriate to deal with the other two questions as well.

Are Women Subordinate to Men?

While it is beyond the scope of this chapter to provide any definitive answer to this question, I wish to highlight some of the sociological concepts and material appropriate for framing a discussion of this issue. It is important at the outset to clarify the difference between the terms, "female" and "male" and the terms "feminine" and "masculine." The first pair of terms refers to ascribed traits, that is, biological sexual differences. The second pair of terms refers to achieved characteristics, i.e., culturally learned differences between men and women. Gender, then, is socially constructed; the concept refers to social characteristics, such as differences in hair styles, clothing patterns, occupational roles, and other culturally learned activities and traits (Robertson 1987).

In most societies, men and women are expected to play specific gender roles, the behavior patterns, obligations, and privileges considered appropriate for each sex. Historically, in American society men have been assigned the role of breadwinner and women the role of homemaker. The "man's world" outside the home was viewed as a harsh and heartless jungle in which men needed strength, ambition, and aggression. The "woman's world" was the home and her job was to comfort and care for husband and children, maintain harmony, and teach her children to conform to society's norms (Thio, 1992, 272). This basic division of labor has produced many popular stereotypes, serving to rationalize the respective masculine and feminine roles. These stereotypes include seeing men as ambitious, aggressive, strong, and athletic, while women are regarded as shy, easily intimidated, passive, weak, and dainty. It is appropriate for women to be concerned about their appearance and aging, but not men. Men should restrain their emotions and not cry, but women may be emotional and cry easily. Women continue to experience the legacy of this patriarchial treatment of women in the form of sexism.

Sexism

In Western society the traditional roles of females and males are not only substantially different but also unequal (Coleman & Cressey, 1992). While women have been treated unfairly in a number of areas—family, education, jobs—it can be said that the underlying cause of unfair treatment is sexism. Simply put, sexism is the belief that women are inferior to men. Sexism is revealed in the many ways that males and females are compared. For example, different definitions of mental health are applied to men and women. Mature women are characterized as submissive, dependent, unadventurous, excitable, and concerned with their appearance. A man with these characteristics is considered immature. Mature men are considered independent and courageous. These sexist stereotypes cause women generally to be perceived as incapable of pursuing traditional "masculine" careers. It also influences interaction between men and women. Women typically give low-status signals such as smiling, nodding, holding their arms to their bodies, or keeping their legs together. Men use high-status gestures by smiling infrequently, holding their heads still, and assuming relaxed body postures (Thio 1992). In more specific terms, sexism is manifested in the institutional life of families, education, and employment. Let us briefly survey some of these examples.

Family. Weis (1988, 184) contends that women are in a "double bind." Women historically have defined themselves primarily in terms of home and family but, in fact, work outside the home. Rather than alter social interactions and labor processes within the home, a "double day" or second shift occurs in which labor in the home is added to hours spent in wage labor. "Employed women continue to do 4.8 hours a day of housework compared to the 1.6 hours their husbands do." One reason for this phenomenon is that the sexual division of labor is the primary mechanism that maintains the superiority of men over women; because of lower wages for women in the labor market, women are encouraged to marry and ultimately live out the double bind.

Hoschild (1989) points out that even when men share more equitably in the house work, striking differences exist between men's and women's roles. For example, women do more of the daily jobs; women juggle several things at once while men do one thing—go to the park with the children or prepare the dinner—and women spend proportionally more time doing housework than with children, while men spend proportionally more time with the children than doing housework.

Education. In many aspects of our educational system, females are treated differently than males. In the elementary school classroom many activities are gender-linked. Teachers ask girls to water the plants and boys to clean the blackboards. Boys are more harshly disciplined but also receive more teacher time and praise. Although girls achieve higher grades throughout their public school education, as measured by standardized tests of achievement, boys tend to do better in math and science and girls do better in reading, writing, and literature (Ballantine 1989). One of the interesting problems concerns gender differences in achievement motivation. Studies of female college students reveal that bright females are caught in a double bind in which they worry about failure and success. Either the bright woman fails to live up to her own standards of success, or she academically succeeds and by that defies societal expectations of the "feminine" role. Females frequently surpass males in elementary school in performance and achievement, but as they enter adolescence began to think in terms of their future, often in favor of the "ideology of romance" (Weis 1988). This tendency has been observed particularly among working-class females who distance themselves from educational achievement through reading romance novels and focusing on romance and marriage as their plan for adulthood. These females create a specifically female anti-school culture that consists of interjecting sexuality into the classroom, talking loudly about boyfriends, and wearing makeup. Marriage, family life, fashion and beauty contribute massively to this feminine anti-school culture, serving to illustrate the contradictions inherent in so called oppositional activities. "Are the girls in the end not doing exactly what is required of them—and if this is the case, then could it not be convincingly argued that it is their own culture that itself is the most effective agent of social control of the girls" (193-194).

Jobs. Although the gap between men's and women's pay has narrowed in recent years, it continues to be significant. In 1975 a woman working full time earned about 59.5 percent as much as a man working full-time, and in 1991 that figure was 72 percent (Coleman & Cressey 1992, 262). A woman with a college degree earns slightly more than a male high school dropout, while a male college graduate earns half again as much. Also, most women in the work force work in low-paying clerical or service positions.

Table 9.1
Women's Work: Less Prestigious, Lower-Paying Jobs

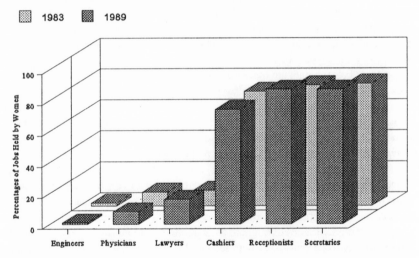

Adapted from Coleman & Cressey, *Social Problems* (New York: Harper Collins College Publishers, 1992), 265.

It could be argued that gender roles, as they presently exist in most societies, are morally indefensible because they reinforce a sexual division of labor that functions to subordinate women to men. One-third of the world's formal labor force do four-fifths of all "informal" work, but receive only ten percent of the world's income and own less than one percent of the world's property. Gender roles are structured such that females are expected to perform job functions different from those of males. Another part of our gender roles is that women are expected to earn less money than, and be shorter and younger than, their sexual partners.

Although slowly diminishing, the prevailing view of female roles affecting employment opportunities is that the primary responsibility for a woman is either to be a successful wife and mother, or to be attractive to men in general. This feature of a woman's role does not directly subordinate women to men, although it does assume that a woman's nature and value are given mainly in terms of her relationships with and acceptability to men. This characteristic is supported by current advertising and suggests that women can be whatever they want, nuclear physicists, professional athletes, or workers on the Alaskan pipeline, as long as their jobs do not interfere with their roles as wives and mothers or with their attractiveness.

The other aspect of the current version of female roles bearing on work and employment is that sexual attractiveness is determined by the approval or disapproval of men. This may not seem different from many other roles whose success is dependent on approval of others. Many men are supervised in their work, and the success of their work is partly dependent upon the evaluation of their supervisor. The problem for gender roles is that this particular role relegates women as a group to a position subject to the approval of men, and hence to a lower status.

From a sociological perspective, we can see that it is quite likely that Mike Welch, the principal, may have held sexist attitudes toward Amy Walker and may have minimized or disregarded her allegations that she was abused and raped by her boyfriend. When confronted with examples of sexism, some defenders of casting females in a subordinate role to males may attempt to defend their practice on the grounds that females really are not equal to males. This brings us to the second question, are males and females in all relevant respects equal?

Fair Treatment

The Biological Argument for Gender Differences

The central issue for many concerning gender equity is the biological argument. Those who advocate this argument contend that gender differences are based on biological considerations in which females are "weaker" and more "caring" and have a "natural" inclination for playing a nurturing role. For example, Goldberg (1982) claims that natural differences exist between the sexes that makes a male-dominated society inevitable. Goldberg claims that there is a difference—a hormonal one. It is argued that female and male brains differ in structure because of the prenatal influence of a testicular hormone and that this structural brain difference causes later differences in behavior. Because of hormonal differences, males are inherently more aggressive than females. This greater aggressiveness assures male domination of the high-status roles in society.

According to Goldberg (1982), it is efficient to socialize women into less competitive roles. Most women would lose in competitive struggles with men, because men have the aggressive advantage, and thus women would be forced to live adult lives as failures in areas in which the society wanted them to succeed. It is women, as a matter of fact, who would not allow girls to be socialized in ways so that the vast majority of them would be doomed to adult lifetimes of failure. Even if there is no biological propensity to adopt maternal and nurturing roles, Goldberg believes that a society should socialize women away from roles that men will attain as a result of their more aggressive natures.

Trebilcot (1982) counters that whether there are natural or innate physiological differences between females and males, this has little bearing on the issue of whether society should reserve certain roles for females and others for males. Trebilcot suggests that females are on the average shorter than males, but some females are taller than some males. The shortest members of the population are females, and the tallest are males, but there is an area of overlap, with some men being very short and some women being very tall. It also is usually assumed that for psychological traits some degree of overlap exists and that the degree of overlap varies for different characteristics. For example, let us suppose that men generally are more aggressive than women. Even if the least aggressive members are females and the most aggressive are males, there is an area of overlap with some very aggressive women and some unaggressive men.

Trebilcot (1982, 152) accepts for the purposes of argument the claim that natural psychological, behavioral, and role differences are inevitable. But she denies that it follows that there must be gender roles, that is, "that the institutions and practices of society must enforce correlations between roles and sex." In the first place, why should a society bother to direct women into some roles and men into others, if the pattern occurs despite the nature of society? In the second place, while one might argue that if correlations between sex and roles are inevitable, institutional enforcement of these correlations must occur. Trebilcot contends that this is not necessary. She says (152) "there could be a society in which it is held that there are inevitable correlations between roles and sex but institutionalization of these correlations is deliberately avoided." The only thing that would be inevitable is that most women would perform a certain role and most men will not. A particular role may not be inevitable for any individual. Trebilcot concludes that if it is a value in society that people should be free to choose roles according to their individual needs and interests, then there should not be sanctions enforcing correlations between roles and sex, because such sanctions would tend to force some individuals into roles for which they have no natural inclination and which they might otherwise not choose.

Finally, one might argue that Goldberg's concept of aggression is somewhat unclear. If aggression means that use of force and violence to master or to subdue, then being aggressive in our kind of society may not be so desirable. Take, for example, the business world. Many companies are moving toward self-directed management models in which people are being asked to work as a team in making important decisions. Team-work requires cooperation, not aggressiveness. So even if aggression were a characteristic of many males, it may not be desirable in the emerging work ethos. Assuming then that morality requires that males and females be treated equally, we might ask about the nature of morally acceptable relationships between males and females.

Morally Acceptable Relations Between Males and Females

There are several areas in which women deserve more equal treatment. In the first place, some feminists and other advocates of women's rights argue that women should not be treated as sex objects. Advertisements focus on women's bodies to sell a variety of products. Films and records cast women in demeaning relationships. The Amy Walker case study highlights that not only are there countless cases of violent attacks on women, including date rapes, but that women who report these violent attacks are frequently considered more at fault than the provocateurs.

Second, women need to be treated more fairly in education and work. Teachers must avoid playing favorites to males and expecting less of the females. And clearly, women deserve to be hired on the basis of their abilities to perform the duties expected of them in the workplace. Of course, if a woman, or a male for that matter, is physically unable to perform the demands of a given job, it is not discrimination or unfair treatment not to hire such a person.

Finally, women need to be treated fairly by their spouses in their homes and families. This is probably the area where there continues to be the greatest amount of unfair treatment. Okin argues that the family is the first school of justice. Okin (17) says that "unless the first and most formative example of adult interaction usually experienced by children is one of justice and reciprocity, rather than one of domination and manipulation or of unequal altruism and one-sided self-sacrifice, and unless they themselves are treated with concern and respect, they are likely to be considerably hindered in becoming people who are guided by principles of justice."

RACE AND SOCIAL INEQUALITY

George Johnson, a white male, graduated from Yale University with a B.A. in economics, a minor in business administration, and a 3.6 GPA (Barclow 1994). He applied to the management training program at Northeastern Bell. He was not hired. He learned that Northeast Bell has an affirmative action plan that includes a program of preferential treatment to offset the lack of African Americans in management. Instead of hiring George, the company hired Frank Walters, an African American applicant from Webster College, a Black institution, for the the management training program. Frank has a B.A. in government and a 2.9 GPA. George believes that he was discriminated against because he is White and that Northeastern's preferential treatment program in morally unacceptable. Do you agree with George?

George's plight certainly typifies a widely held perception of the White population in our society that affirmative action in hiring is practiced in the private and public sector, and that White employees are losing jobs to Hispanics and African Americans. As to whether or not this perception conforms to reality is a good question for a sociology class. But the deeper question is whether any instance of affirmative action is morally justified. Dealing with this dilemma will lead us into two other questions:

To what extent does racism exist in our society? What steps should be taken to reduce racism? Turning to the first question, most sociologists agree that a high degree of institutional inequality for ethnic minorities exists in the United States. This is reflected in education, work, and in law and justice.

Racism in Our Society

When we consider various aspects of our society, there is overwhelming sociological evidence that racism exists. According to the dictionary, racism is defined as "a belief that race is the primary determinant of human traits and capacities and that racial differences produce an inherent superiority of a particular race" (*Webster's Ninth New Collegiate Dictionary*, 969). In this section, I focus on the plight of African Americans. A complete sociological treatment of this issue would examine the situation of Hispanics, Native Americans and Asian-Pacific Americans as well. Bearing in mind the history of slavery and segregation of African Americans, it is generally understood that African Americans have been treated unfairly in a variety of ways. But what is not so widely agreed upon is to what extent unfair treatment continues to exist and what remedies should be taken to ameliorate the situation. In terms of contemporary unfair treatment, much of the debate centers around whether the plight of many African Americans is traceable to their history of slavery and segregation, or whether their plight is due to their failure to take advantage of opportunities that have been presented starting with the civil rights movement of the 1960s. Both sides of this issue are taken into consideration in the following discussion. There are several areas sociologically that must be examined to obtain a reasonable appraisal of the extent to which African Americans continue to be treated unfairly, particularly in education and jobs.

Education

Blacks, as well as Hispanics and Native Americans, receive significantly less education than Whites. For example, in 1989, 78 percent of whites had graduated from high school, whereas only 65 percent of blacks and 51 percent of Hispanics had so graduated. For African Americans, the source of educational inequality is rooted in domination. Most African Americans received little schooling during the period of slavery, and after emancipation they were educated in segregated schools (Coleman & Cressey 1992). In 1954 the Supreme Court ended legal segregation, but school segregation has continued mainly as a result of segregated housing patterns in cities. Courts have ordered that school children must be bused from one school to another to achieve racial balance. But protests and conflict have made the courts shy away from this remedy.

In addition, internal discrimination has existed within the schools. Teachers frequently have lowered expectations of African American students and put them into non-college tracks and in lower-ability groups (Spring, 1991). At the same time,

African American students in large urban ghettos form their own street culture partly as a reaction to circumstances of poverty, as a way of coping with unstable family life, and as a response to a sense of economic hopelessness. Ogbu sees several related factors contributing to school failure (Weis, 1988). Because African Americans have

Table 9.2
Decline in College Enrollments Among Minorities

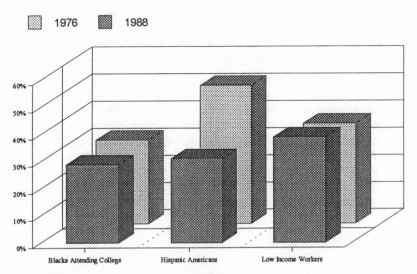

Adapted from Spring, *American Education: An Introduction to Social and Political Aspects* (New York: Longman, 1991).

faced a job ceiling or techno-economic barriers, they have developed alternate survival strategies, that is, ways of making it outside of mainstream education and jobs. This diverts them into non-academic pursuits. Further, they may promote personal attributes or competencies that are not necessarily congruent with standard school practices for academic success. From observing their parents' situation and that of other adults in their communities, African American youths suspect that their chances of making it through education and mainstream jobs are not very good. As they get older, they become increasingly disillusioned and begin not to take their school work seriously. Their distrust arises out of a history of conflict between Blacks and the public schools and between Blacks and White authorities. Because of this history many African Americans distrust the schools When children distrust the schools and the people who control them, as their parents do, it is difficult for them to accept, internalize, and follow school rules of behavior for academic achievement. Minorities usually react to their subordination and exploitation by forming ambivalent or oppositional identities and oppositional cultural frames of reference. That is, minorities develop an identity system or sense of peoplehood that they perceive and experience not merely as different but as in opposition to the social identity system of their dominators, or in the case of Blacks, "White oppressors." Racial minorities define attitudes and ways of acting as not appropriate for themselves because these attitudes and ways of members of the dominant group are the "White ways." Minorities define opposing attitudes and behaviors as more appropriate for themselves.

This oppositional social identity and the oppositional cultural frame of reference affects school achievement for Blacks because African Americans equate school learning with the learning of the culture of the dominant group, or White culture. It is believed that this learning requires the giving up of Black culture. Many African Americans believe that to succeed academically, they must learn to think and act White with the inevitable outcome of losing one's African American identity, abandoning Black people and Black causes, and joining the enemy, namely, White people. Unfortunately, many of the attitudes designated as "White" include attitudes that are essential for school success, such as speaking standard English, working hard in school to get good grades, being on time, etc. Students who elect to "act White" frequently face opposition from their peers. Ogbu concludes that the lag in academic performance of Black students is not adequately explained in terms of class struggle and class oppositional process, if social classes are defined solely in economic terms. If we take racial stratification seriously as a distinct type of stratification, it generates its own oppositional process that cuts across class boundaries because it is tied to the minority-group members' sense of peoplehood or collective social identity.

Employment

African Americans and Hispanics often have low-status and low-paying jobs. Whites are more than twice as likely as Blacks or Hispanics to have a professional

Table 9.3
Lower Income and Higher Unemployment for Minorities

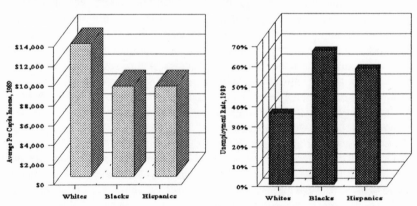

Adapted from Coleman & Cressey, *Social Problems* (New York: Harper Collins College Publishers, 1992), 174.

position. Moreover, in 1989, the average African American family earned only 57 percent as much as the average White family, which is down from a high of 61 percent in 1970. Also in 1989, only 4.5 percent of White workers were unemployed, while 8 percent of Hispanics and 11.8 percent of African Americans were without work. Although educational inequitities can explain much of this inequality, minority members receive, on the average, less pay than whites with the same level of education. For example, an African American family headed by someone who has completed four years of high school has about the same income as a White family headed by someone with only eight years of education.

Remedies

The most controversial "remedy" for the plight of African Americans has been "affirmative action," giving preferential treatment to African Americans in hiring. Those in favor of some degree of preferential treatment usually present either a backward looking argument or a forward looking argument. The backward looking argument contends that African Americans are owed some degree of compensation for the past history of slavery and segregation. It is argued that affirmative action provides one attempted remedy for this situation. The forward looking argument maintains that African Americans are economically behind Anglo Americans because of the history of slavery and segregation. This population has had to attempt to economically catch up under conditions stacked against them. So long as Anglos dominate business, educational, and political leadership, African Americans have limited opportunities to catch up. It is concluded that the best remedy for the future situation of African Americans is to have affirmative action policies that will enable African Americans to begin to attain needed positions of leadership in business and education.

There have been three major criticisms of affirmative action. The plight of George in the above example illustrates the basis for contending that in trying to remedy the plight of African Americans, Anglos often are victims of "reverse discrimination." In the Supreme Court Decision, *Regents of the University of California v. Allan Bakke*, in 1977, a mixed verdict upheld the right of an educational institution to consider race as a factor in university admissions but held that in this particular case, Allan Bakke was discriminated against. Bakke, a thirty-three-year-old engineer, had applied to medical school at the University of California Davis. He was turned down because he held a grade point average lower than the cutoff point for Anglo American applicants but an average higher than African Americans who were admitted under an affirmative action policy. Despite the outcome of this decision, the debate over whether affirmative action programs are morally justified continues.

One criticism of affirmative action is a utilitarian argument. It has been argued that affirmative action, rather than providing a remedy for the economic plight of African Americans, actually has made their situation worse. It is alleged that affirmative action only results in a backlash against affirmative action policies. Affirmative action policies have contributed to a widely held perception that many Whites have lost jobs to African Americans. Second, it could be argued that continued and increased racism is aggravated by affirmative action policies. Hence, there may be increased hostility toward African Americans because of affirmative action.

Finally, the largest issue over finding economic remedies to the plight of African Americans is the welfare dependency debate. In the 1960s liberal scholars contended that the ingrained cultural characteristics of ghetto-specific behavior ultimately do not determine behavior or success. Instead cultural values result from specific social circumstances and life opportunities and reflect one's class and racial position. Underclass Black's limited aspirations or failure to plan for the future is not a result of different cultural norms but the consequence of restricted opportunities, a bleak future, and a sense of resignation resulting from unhappy personal experiences (Wilson 1987).

This line of analysis was called into question in the 1980s with the growing problems of inner-cities, including black male joblessness, single household families, and drugs. The extreme rise in inner-city social dislocations, following the passage of the most sweeping anti-discrimination and anti-poverty legislation in the nation's history could not be explained by the 1960s concept of ghetto-specific behavior (Wilson 1987). As a result a neo-conservative critique emerged, finding expression in books such as *Thinking About Crime*, *Wealth and Poverty*, *Civil Rights: Rhetoric or Reality*, and *Losing Ground*. The most influential of all these books was written by Murray (1984), who advanced the welfare dependency theory. Murray argues that poverty is a result of federal programs that have effectively changed the rewards and penalties that govern human behavior. This book provoked a variety of liberal criticisms, including Wilson's (1987). Murray contends that the availability of food stamps and increases in Aid to Families with Dependent Children (AFDC) payments have had a negative effect on poor Black family formation and work incentives. On the other hand, liberal critics have pointed out that the real value of these two combined programs increased only from 1960 to 1972. After that time, their value declined sharply because states neglected to adjust AFDC benefit levels to inflation. During this time, there were no reversals in trends of either family composition or work effort.

Moreover, the increased joblessness among Black males in urban ghettos cannot be explained by the welfare dependency theory because single adults do not qualify for AFDC. Of course, conservatives will contend that jobless Black males are a product of welfare mothers who have not taught their children a sense of personal responsibility. This view overlooks the fact that many welfare mothers do teach personal responsibility and that in many cases Black males cannot get a job because of discrimination.

Murray also neglects the fact that the unemployment rate in 1980 was twice that of 1968. "When unemployment increases, poverty also rises" (Wilson 1987, 17). Murray maintains that the slowing of the economy had nothing at all to do with the failure of the poverty rate to decline in the 1970s, but liberals maintain that the economy was the major cause of the failure of poverty to decline in the 1970s. Without the benefit programs that Murray attacks, the poverty rate would have risen further. In an excellent documentary about the Shaw district of Washington, D.C., *Throw Away People*, Roger Wilkins contends that the Black underclass of the 70s and the 80s was a result of the history of slavery and segregation in which Blacks migrated to Eastern and Northern cities to find industrial work. Blacks were forced to live in segregated neighborhoods. Until the 1960s, Blacks could support families on wages earned with industrial based jobs. During the civil rights movement, the college-educated and professional Blacks took advantage of new opportunities and moved out of the black neighborhoods into more affluent suburbs. They left behind the elderly, the poor, and the unskilled. When the more affluent and educated Black population moved out of the ghettos, a strong stabilizing influence left the ghetto. The recession of the 70s saw the loss of industrial jobs, leaving the Black ghettos even more enmired in poverty. Then the drug scene emerged, providing as Wilkins said, one version of the American dream.

CASE STUDIES AND CLASS ACTIVITIES

Paul Sloan - Psychology 101, Community College of Aurora
(Lisman 1992a, Project Reports, 138-40)

One full class session was spent on small group discussion around the ethics of a "violence as entertainment" movie that would appeal to adolescent youth gang culture. This occurred at the time we covered the part of the course in psychology that focused on perception. The power of visual perception as an influence on persons, both subliminal and dramatic, was discussed, a handout was given and another instructor and I played the parts of the movie producer-director and a psychologist having a meet-the-press type debate on the effects of violence on the screen.

This was followed by a written homework assignment, answering an essay question about community responsibility for the freedom of expression that we value in this country. The advantage of writing after the classroom discussion was to give them more time to think about it. This was taking special time to dwell on ethics as it relates to exploitation of the senses and perception of people who are healthy and people who are emotionally and psychologically damaged by neglect or abuse in their upbringing. I felt it was a good timely topic that had some application from our knowledge of growth and development, the changes that adolescents experienced, and the extension of gender roles of aggressiveness into adulthood.

Case Study

Sam Peckenpaw is a movie producer and director who believes in portraying violence realistically on the screen so that people will see how futile and destructive it really is.

Doctor Joyce Brothers believes that violence is destructive and causes people to act violently by predisposing them to use it as a solution to conflict. She believes that violence can and does affect behavior in people who are impressionable, especially those vulnerable to emotional damage.

If you were on a committee in metro Denver which has the responsibility and the power to decide whether to allow this movie (which shows an exciting gang drive-by shooting scene) to be rented at video stores and shown on cable television, what questions would you have of the two above people?

If the committee chose to allow for the movie to be readily available and rated the movie "R", then how could the community take responsibility for those who were emotionally damaged and who might act out their tendency toward violence on others?

Kathleen Cramm - General Psychology 101, Community College of Aurora
(Lisman 1992a, Project Reports, 151-52)

To help students in my General Psychology 101 class develop skills in ethical decision making and to incorporate ethics into the general curriculum, I chose the following activities:

1. Included a course objective to explore ethical issues in psychology.
2. Helped the class identify and discuss the ethical issues identified by in the psychology text.
3. Presented Kohlberg's and Gilligan's models of ethical decision making when teaching the chapter on gender issues in psychology.
4. Had the class identify and discuss an ethical issue using the two models.
5. Presented a case study that focused on specific text material for class discussion.
6. Included ethics-related topics for papers.
7. Included an essay question in which the class was to consider ethical issues as well as content issues.

One of my objectives in teaching is to help the student develop thinking skills and move from "black and white" understanding of issues to appreciating the complexities that affect contemporary life. In the discussion of using animals in research and the potentially harmful uses of psychological knowledge, the class engaged in lively debate.

I believe one of the most important issues in Carol Gilligan's findings is that too often research on male subjects has been generalized to females without the consideration of possible gender differences. In presenting Gilligan's model, I asked the class to decide which model seemed to fit them best. Both males and females chose Gilligan's model, although I believe there was some gender typing—including women who chose Gilligan's model because they thought they "should" fit a model based on women's experience.

The class worked in groups and chose from three issues: abortion, the Hill/Thomas hearings, and the Heinz case, which was in the text. Both in this class period and in the case study later in the semester, students tended to rate their decision making at one of the highest stages. Also, they seemed to oversimplify the issues, perhaps because they were not personally involved. At a future time, I would focus more on helping students explore the "self-interest" issues and on seeing how their moral decisions might be affected when the dilemma actually involves loss to themselves.

The final case study was loosely based on the experiences of a woman who had been a speaker in the class and involved the ethics of using operant conditioning on human subjects. The class easily agreed that the experiment was unethical. However, they disagreed in their reasoning. It was clear that many students used Gilligan's ethics of personal relationships rather than Kohlberg's general moral principles to justify their decision. In an effort to help the class explore the real world application, we discussed other ways in which people may be socialized to violence—including military training and football—and whether this socialization is ethical. In the future, I would expand this discussion.

Case Study in Ethics

Professor Higgins, a well respected professor at MIT, has obtained a government grant to study the effects of operant and classical conditioning on behavior. He wants to answer the question as to the limits of conditioning—can people, for example, be conditioned to lie, steal, kill, and if so, under what conditions. The government is interested in the results because it is believed that such knowledge will help to understand and counteract terrorism. Because of the nature of the study, the grant award is classified information and the subjects cannot be told what the experiments involve. The subjects are young adult volunteers who are told they are performing an important service for their country. They have agreed to make a two-year commitment in exchange for college tuition when they complete the study. You are an associate of Professor Higgins and are aware of the secret study.

As a group decide:

1. What are the ethical issues?
2. Whose interests are involved? Who is affected by the decision and what stake do they have in the outcome?
3. What do you believe is the ethical answer?
4. Using Gilligan or Kohlberg, what stage of moral development does your ethical decision fit into?

Cases for Sociology

1. A Homeless Person (Reported in the *St. Cloud Times*, Oct. 6, 1989)

Sharon Lenger, forty-eight, has a bachelor's degree in psychology and an associate of arts degree in drug counseling. She worked as a residential counselor in a home for abused and molested adolescents in California until she was severely assaulted by one of the residents. Because of the injuries sustained in the attack, she was unable to work in the home and moved out. She received workers' compensation, but this was not enough to sustain her in California because it was based on her low salary and did not take into account the free room and board provided at her place of work. She moved to Minnesota to live near her sick and elderly parents. Then the state of California stopped her worker's compensation payments. She needed further surgery because of the assault injuries, so she applied for medical assistance and general assistance. Now she receives $203 a month in general assistance payments, not enough to pay for food and a place to live. Currently she is staying at an emergency shelter run by Catholic Charities and describes herself as one step away from the street. In other words, she is a homeless person.

Does Sharon Lenger have right to adequate shelter? If so, how should this be provided? (White 1994, 299).

2. Protective Exclusion in the Work Place

The Supreme Court recently ruled on a case involving Johnson Controls, in which this company's "protective exclusion" policy, which prevents women during child bearing years from working in areas carrying a risk of lead poisoning, is being challenged. Many companies that deal with developmental toxins, or products toxic to the fetus, have such policies of "protective exclusion." The only way a woman who is of childbearing potential can work in such toxic areas is to be sterilized.

The grounds for the exclusion is to protect the fetus. Thus, it would not be sufficient for such women to sign a waiver for any harmful effects from a teratogen (substances that deform a developing fetus). Du Pont, which has a similar policy, states "the waiver of subsequent claims by the female worker would be of no legal significance because the deformed fetus, if born, may have its own rights as a person which could not be waived by the mother." An Illinois State Supreme court upheld this position. The courts have ruled that a child injured at birth has the right to sue the hospital for damages resulting from the mother's transfusion with the wrong blood type (Beauchamp 1989, 36).

Women's groups argue that "protective exclusion" is sex discrimination, especially because there is growing evidence that the reproductive systems of men are also adversely affected by various industrial chemicals. Defenders of the exclusion policy consider the sex of the excluded party as irrelevant on the grounds that the only issue is that of protecting the susceptible fetus. Women are excluded because they are capable of becoming pregnant and bringing the fetus into the workplace.

As an issue of fairness, one needs to consider whether female employees of childbearing potential are being treated differently without justification. It would certainly not be fair not to allow women to do a given job just because they are female. But does the position of being pregnant and working in a job near a developmental toxin justify excluding such females from these jobs?

3. Senator Bob Packwood (This story has been widely reported in the newspapers.)

Bob Packwood is a Republican senator from Oregon. His supporters claim that he has been a friend of women's causes; he hired a majority of women for his staff long before others became sensitive to the issue of sex discrimination, and he has been a longtime and unwavering advocate of abortion rights. Yet he seems to have a problem with women. He is charged with grabbing and kissing several women against their will. The most prominent example is a female reporter he kissed after a routine interview in his office. The reporter was shocked and offended. Packwood has publicly apologized, blaming his behavior on alcoholism. Furthermore, Packwood was not in a position of power or authority over the reporter; she was not hired, promoted, or fired because of her reaction to Packwood's kiss. Nevertheless, the Senate Ethics Committee charged him with sexual harassment. (Packwood has since resigned under the threat of being removed from the Senate.)

Packwood admits that his behavior was rude and offensive. But does it constitute real sexual harassment? (White 1994, 330-331).

4. Selling a House

Suppose that Bob and Mary Smith have been trying to sell their three-bedroom house for two years. The house is only five years old, and it is located in a pleasant middle-class neighborhood of Denver. The house has been appraised at $200,000, and the Smiths started out asking that much money for the house. But they have come down in price several times, and now they are asking for only $150,000. They feel that they cannot really go any lower in price because they have a $100,000 mortgage on the house, and they have spent at least $50,000 on various improvements. One day their real estate agent calls and says he has qualified buyers who are willing to pay $150,000 for the house. The only problem is that the buyers, Ralph and Sara Jones, are Black. The real estate agent advises the Smiths to turn the offer down. He points out that the house is in an all-White neighborhood, and that if they sell to Blacks, the property values in the area will go down dramatically. He has seen this happen in east Denver where houses that once sold for $500,000 are now selling for $50,000. Also, the real estate agent claims that the neighbors will be very angry if the Smiths sell their house to Black people. On the other hand, the Smiths have a legal right to sell their house to qualified buyers, and the Joneses are definitely qualified. Ralph Jones is a successful lawyer, and his wife Sara is a grade school teacher. They have three children, and they would be delighted to have the house.

Should the Smiths sell their house to the Joneses or not (White 1991, 288)?

10

Research Ethics

The primary dilemma of social science research ethics involves the conflict between two rights: the right to research and to find knowledge, and the right of individual research participants to self-determination, privacy, and dignity (Frankfort-Nachmias & Nachmias 1992). Most social scientists believe that research involving human participants requires the informed consent of the participants. The U.S. Department of Health and Human Services guidelines governing research under its grants requires that a signed consent form be completed if research participants are placed at risk of pain, physical or emotional injury, the invasion of privacy, or physical or psychological stress. In addition, participants should know that their involvement is voluntary.

THE MEANING OF INFORMED CONSENT

The recent controversy over radiation experiments that were performed on mentally handicapped people and on soldiers near nuclear test sites in the 1950s illustrates the importance of providing subjects an opportunity to give their informed consent to any proposed research. Informed consent can be defined as the procedure in which individuals choose whether to participate in an investigation after being informed of facts that would be likely to influence their decision. This definition (Frankfort-Nachmias & Nachmias 1992) involves three elements: competence, voluntarism, and full information.

Competence

The underlying assumption of the principle of informed consent is that participants can understand their participation in the research. Such understanding assumes that the participant is responsible and mature. Persons considered incompetent include young children, comatose patients, and mental patients.

Voluntarism

Informed consent also assumes that the participant freely gave consent. Ensuring voluntary consent is critical in contexts where positions of authority are involved, such as in prisons, mental institutions, hospitals, and public schools.

Full Information

The federal guidelines for social science research recommend that clients give reasonably informed consent. Researchers should provide the participant with the information that a reasonable and prudent person would need to make a competent decision. Reasonably informed consent requires a fair explanation of the procedures and its purpose. Researchers should explain to the subject that he or she is free to withdraw from the procedure at any time. It is widely agreed that informed consent is the most general solution to the problem of how to promote social science research without encroaching on individual rights and welfare. However, not all ethicists would grant that informed consent is an absolute requirement.

THE ETHICS OF DECEPTION IN SOCIAL SCIENCE RESEARCH

One of the classic cases taken up in the ethics of deception on social science research is Stanley Milgram's (1974) obedience to authority research. Below is a synopsis of this research from Milgram's perspective. Following is a presentation of two perspectives on this kind of deceptive research from a consequentialist and a non-consequentialist perspective.

Obedience to Authority

Between 1933 and 1945 millions of innocent people were systematically slaughtered on command in Nazi Germany. Milgram (1974, 1) observes that "Obedience is the psychological mechanism that links individual action to political purpose. It is the dispositional cement that binds men to systems of authority." The Nazi extermination of European Jews was the most extreme instance of abhorrent immoral acts carried out by thousands of people in the name of obedience. Although obedience to authority has been praised as a virtue, it takes on a new aspect when it serves a malevolent purpose—it is transformed into a heinous sin.

Milgram claims that the moral question is whether one should obey when commands conflict with conscience. Conservative philosophers argue that society is threatened by disobedience. They believe that even when the act prescribed by an authority is an evil one, it is better to carry out the act than to question authority. Milgram wished to observe people in situations of obedience.

He set up an experiment at Yale University, which eventually involved hundreds of subjects and was carried out in other laboratories. While there were variations, the basic experiment involved having two people come to a psychology laboratory to take part in a study of memory and learning. One of them is designated as a "teacher" and the other a "learner." The experimenter explains that his study is concerned with the effects of punishment on learning. The "learner" is led into a room and seated in a chair. His arms are strapped to prevent excessive movement and an electrode is attached to his wrist. The experimenter tells him that he is to learn a list of word pairs; whenever he makes an error, he will receive electric shocks of increasing intensity. Milgram observes that the real focus of the experiment is the "teacher." After watching the "learner" being strapped into place, the "teacher" is taken into the main experimental room and seated before an impressive shock generator. Its main feature is a horizontal line of thirty switches, ranging from 15-450 volts, in 15-volt increments. There are also verbal designations that range from SLIGHT SHOCK to DANGER—SEVERE SHOCK. The "teacher" is told that he or she is to administer the learning test to the person in the other room. When the "learner" responds correctly, the "teacher" moves to the next item; when the "learner" gives an incorrect answer, the "teacher" is to shock the "learner." The "learner" is to start at the lowest shock level (15 volts) and to increase the level each time the man makes an error, going 30 volts, 45 volts, and so on. The "teacher" is a genuinely naive subject who has come to the laboratory to participate in an experiment. The "learner," or "victim," is an actor who receives no shock at all. The point of the experiment is to see how far a person will proceed in a concrete and measurable situation in which the subject is ordered to inflict increasing pain on a protesting victim. At what point will the subject refuse to obey the experimenter?

When the learner-actor supposedly begins to experience discomfort he or she groans or grunts at 75 volts. At 120 volts the victim complains verbally; at 150 the "learner" demands to be released from the experiment. The victim continues to protest as the shocks escalate, growing increasingly vehement and emotional. At 285 volts "his response can only be described as an agonized scream" (Milgram 1974, 4). The "teacher" encounters a difficult dilemma. On the one hand, the suffering of the "learner" presses the "teacher" to quit. On the other, the experimenter, or the person conducting the experiment, is perceived as a legitimate authority to whom the subject feels some responsibility. "Each time the subject hesitates to administer shock, the experimenter orders him to continue" (4). To extricate himself or herself from the situation, the subject must make a clear break with authority. The purpose of the investigation of the experiment was to "find when and how people would defy authority in the face of a clear moral imperative" (4).

Milgram observes that one might have expected that the subject would refuse to obey the experimenter at the first sign of the "learner's" discomfort. However, Milgram found to his surprise that ordinary individuals would comply with the experimental instructions. Many subjects experience stress and protest somewhat to the experimenter. But a substantial number continued to the last shock on the generator.

To the suggestion that those who shocked their victims were sadists, Milgram replies that almost two-thirds of the participants fell into the category of "obedient" subjects, and they represented ordinary people drawn from working, managerial, and professional classes. Thus, this explanation is highly questionable.

Milgram contends that the most fundamental lesson of his study was that ordinary people can become agents in a terribly destructive process and that when asked to carry out actions contradictory to basic standards of morality few people can resist authority. If people are asked to render a moral judgement on what constitutes morally appropriate behavior in this situation, they unfailingly regard disobedience as proper. However, many of the subjects in the experiment were unable to realize their values in action and continued the experiment although they disagreed with what they were doing.

Milgram claims that the force exerted by the moral sense of the individual is less effective than social myth would have us believe. Though such prescriptions as "Thou shalt not kill" occupy a pre-eminent place in the moral order, they do not occupy a correspondingly intractable position in human psychic structure. Milgram (1974, 7) says, "A few changes in newspaper headlines, a call from the draft board, orders from a man with epaulets, and men are led to kill with little difficulty." Even the forces involved in the psychology experiment will go a long way toward removing the individual from moral controls.

Milgram asks what keeps the person obeying the experimenter. First, there are a set of "binding factors" that lock the subject into the situation. These factors are politeness, a desire to stick with his initial promise of aid to the experimenter, and the awkwardness of withdrawal. Second, adjustments in the subject's thinking occur that undermine one's resolve to break with authority. One such adjustment is the tendency of the individual to become so absorbed in the narrow technical aspect of the task that the individual loses sight of its broader consequences. Another adjustment in the obedient subject is for the individual to see him or herself as not responsible for his or her own actions. "He divests himself of responsibility by attributing all initiative to the experimenter, a legitimate authority " (Milgram 1974, 8).

Another adjustment is that the person acting under authority does not really lose his morals; he gets a radically different focus. His moral concerns shift from the morality of what he is doing to the learner. He focuses on a concern for how well he is living up to the expectations that the experimenter has for him. Similarly, in war time a soldier does not ask whether it is good or bad to bomb a hamlet, because he does not experience shame or guilt in the destruction of a village. Instead, he feels pride or shame, depending on how well he has carried out the mission assigned to him.

Another adjustment at work is what Milgram terms "counteranthropomorphism." Psychologists have observed the primitive tendency among people to attribute to inanimate objects and forces the qualities of the human species. A countervailing tendency is that of attributing an impersonal quality to forces that are essentially human in origin. For example, when the experimenter says, "The experiment requires that you continue," the subject considers this to be an imperative and goes beyond any merely human command. He does not ask the obvious question, "Whose experiment? Why should the designer be served while the victim suffers?" (Milgram 1974, 9) The "teacher" failed to realize that human agent had faded from the picture, and "The Experiment" has acquired an impersonal momentum of its own.

Milgram observes that many subjects devalue the victim because of acting against him. Comments such as "He was so stupid and stubborn that he deserved to get shocked," were common. Once acting against the victim, these subjects considered it necessary to view him as an unnecessary individual, whose punishment was rendered inevitable by his own deficiencies of intellect and character.

Some people studied in the experiment were in some sense against what they did to the learner and may protest even while they obeyed. "Some subjects were totally convinced of the wrongness of what they were doing but could not bring themselves to make an open break with authority" (Milgram 1974, 10). Milgram claims that they failed to realize that subjective feelings are largely irrelevant to the moral issue at hand as long as they are not changed into action. Milgram believes that nature has designed us with a fatal flaw. The individual virtues of loyalty, discipline, and self-sacrifice are the very qualities that bind men to malevolent systems of authority and engines of war.

A Consequentialist Defense of Deception in Research

Elms (1982, 234) defends the Milgram form of deception in social science research on consequentialist grounds. He maintains that deception is justified under the following conditions: "When (1) there is no other feasible way to obtain the desired information, (2) the likely benefits substantially outweigh the likely harms, (3) subjects are given the option to withdraw from participation at any time without penalty, (4) any physical or psychological harm to subjects is temporary, and (5) subjects are debriefed as to all substantial deceptions and the research procedures are made available for public review."

Elms maintains that deceiving the participants in social science research is often the only way to conduct the research. This is so when it is important to create a realistic experiment. Moreover, several alternate strategies will not accomplish the objective of the research. For example, asking people to tell about themselves is ineffective because their self-disclosure will be selective. People also may not know how they would behave if they are presented with hypothetical situations by the researcher. People also are reluctant to admit to destructive patterns of behavior, such as child abuse or racial and sexual prejudice.

Elms, in taking a consequentialist position, considers certain criticisms of such a calculus. Many think that deceptive experiments should not be used because the subjects may be psychologically harmed. Elms replies that the psychological harm experienced is presumably only short lived and is certainly much less than the "harm" that subjects encounter from many other decisions they make, such as getting married, having a baby, or going to college.

Elms cites the Milgram obedience study as an example of experimental deception that inflicted psychological harm on the subjects. The subjects shocked the "victim" unmercifully with little persuasion from the experimenter and in the face of much resistance from the "victim." They had the option throughout the experiment of quitting any time and many did so. Elms acknowledges that during the debriefing, when the participants were confronted with their willingness to inflict pain on innocent "victims," some may have been distressed by this realization. However, Elms insists that the researcher has no more responsibility to help the subject cope with this kind of self-discovery than preachers, teachers, or novelists, who "induce such knowledge in anyone whose attention they could momentarily catch." According to Elms (1982, 237), what was remarkable was not that the subjects suffered persisting harm, "but that they suffered so little, given the intensity of their emotional reactions during the experiment itself."

Elms also considers "indirect harms" that might result from a deceptive study. To the claim that deceptive research will generate a greater distrust of social scientists and of other people in general, Elms (1982, 237) replies that these concerns are exaggerated. The public does not see social scientists as the "sacred protectors of the truth." Moreover, "abuses of public trust by politicians, physicians, lawyers, ministers, business leaders, and other supposedly trustworthy individuals touch much more directly on people's lives than the encapsulated deceptions of social scientists."

Elms asks, given the minor harms of properly conducted social science research, what then are the benefits? He acknowledges that few social scientific research studies produce any immediate benefits to participants or to society. At best, we can expect that this type of research will contribute to the general body of social scientific knowledge. Elms (1982, 238) observes, "Any insistence that social science research always meet criteria of immediate utility would make it a mere adjunct of business, government, and military interests and would frustrate forever its development as a source of basic scientific discoveries useful in a broad range of applications."

Elms acknowledges that research projects differ in their degree of potential benefits, and that we must take this into consideration when trying to determine, as a consequentialist, whether the estimated benefits outweigh the estimated harm. He says that we must be satisfied with making only rough estimates of benefits. He cites the Milgram experiments as an example of an experiment that generated a greater balance of benefits over harms. Elms claimed that Milgram's experiments helped us obtain a better understanding of how ordinary citizens could be drawn into a Holocaust-like phenomena of inflicting pain and torturing innocent people. Second, we have benefitted in the years since the publication of the experiments. We now have a generation of college students who have a better understanding of how they could under certain circumstances be as obedient as the sternest Nazis. Elms (1982, 240) speculates that Milgram's studies have "generated enough introspection and discussion to diminish significantly the likelihood of another Holocaust-like phenomenon, at least in this country."

Elms recognizes that some research procedures may have the potential to psychologically harm the subjects in significant enough ways. Examples of this are studies in which a subject fills out a personality questionnaire and then is told falsely that the questionnaire reveals hidden homosexual tendencies or other characteristics that derive from the subject's own self-image. While some people may handle this without any difficulty during debriefing, Elms (1982, 241) claims that "a false imputation of homosexuality or neurosis, made by a psychologist, may continue to raise self-doubts well after the psychologist has changed stories." Elms maintains that this kind of research should be constrained in the same way as medical research.

The debriefing period is the time for limiting or eliminating several potential harms of deceptive research practices. First, anxiety and other unpleasant emotional reactions can be diminished by giving the subject a sense of the value of his or her participation as a research subject. Second, the debriefing process can restore a sense of honesty to the researcher and bring him or her back toward the human level of the subjects. Third, debriefing can provide a model to researchers of how deception can be used without destroying the integrity of human social contacts or the autonomy and self-esteem of the subjects involved. Finally, debriefing serves to increase the level of publicity connected with the research.

A Non-Consequentialist View of Deception in Research

Macklin (1982) defends a non-consequentialist view regarding the use of deception in social science research. She opposes Miligram's research, because of concern for the potential harm to subjects involved in deceptive research. She cites several examples. The Milgram experiments themselves resulted in some patients experiencing extreme emotional distress. There is also the danger of lowered self-esteem. In another harmful experiment, subjects, without being warned in advance of the effects of the use of a drug, were given a drug that induced in their subjects a temporary interruption of respiration. Subjects reported "horrific" experiences. In one example, Army recruits were "passengers aboard an apparently stricken plane which was being forced to 'ditch' or 'crash land.'" They were terribly frightened. There also have been experiments in which "an isolated subject in a desolate area learned that a sudden emergency had arisen (accidental nuclear radiation in the area, or a sudden forest fire, or misdirected artillery shells, depending on the experimental condition) and that he would be rescued only if he reported his position over the radio transmitter which has quite suddenly failed." This creates great anxiety and fear in the subjects. In another experiment, a subject was distressed when he was told that he was "responsible" for an explosion that seriously injured another soldier. Finally, there are examples of "emergency bystander studies," staged events with the behavior of bystanders observed—fake collapse on subways, with blood trickling from the mouths of "injured" victims. She asks, "what if a bystander had a heart attack in these circumstances?" Macklin (1982, 211) concludes that "the risk of significant harm to subjects in social scientific experiments is greater than some would have us believe."

Macklin claims that it would be a mistake to think that the informed consent doctrine as it is understood and adhered to in the biomedical domain rests solely on the ethical principle demanding that people be protected from undue harm. A Kantian strain underlies the doctrine of informed consent—a strain expressed in language such as "the dignity of human beings," "the need to respect personal autonomy," and an individual's "right to decide" what shall be done to his or her person. The individual's right to decide has little to do with the probability or degree of harm that may befall a person because of participating in an experiment. Macklin (1982, 211) maintains the principle that should govern social scientific investigations is "contributions to knowledge, however great, do not justify treating human subjects in a manner that fails to respect them as persons."

Macklin is critical of appeals to the "significance" of social science research as justification for overriding the rights of individuals to be informed. In the first place, researchers, who are biased toward the assumed value of their field, may provide an exaggerated assessment of the significance of an experiment. In the second place, social science lacks a systematic theory into which new research findings can be integrated.

Macklin considers Elms' defense of Milgram's obedience studies. Elms claims that the effect of Milgram's study is that it may help society alter conditions that promote destructive obedience in society. Macklin replies that it is far from certain that Milgram's model can be systematically applied to society.

PRIVACY

An important right in social science research that needs to be respected is the "right of privacy," the right of the participant to control information about oneself. There are three aspects of privacy that merit comment: sensitivity of information, settings being observed, and dissemination of information (Frankfort-Nachmias & Nachmias, 1992).

Sensitivity of Information

Some personal information, if revealed or made public, is threatening. This could include religious preferences, sexual practices, income, racial prejudices, and attributes such as intelligence and honesty. The greater the sensitivity of the personal information, the more safeguards need to be in place to protect the privacy of research participants.

Settings Being Observed

It is assumed that the extent to which the setting is private, that consent must be secured. For example, it would be considered unethical to intrude into people's homes without their consent. However, as the Laud Humphrey's research demonstrates in the case study below, it is not always clear when the setting of the research is public and when it is private.

Dissemination of Information

This aspect of privacy concerns the ability to match personal information with the identity of research participants. In *Small Town in Mass Society*, the researchers described the inhabitants of a small town in upstate New York in such detail that the residents were easily recognizable. The townspeople staged a protest against the publication of this research, wearing masks, bearing the fictitious name they were given (Frankfort-Nachmias & Nachmias, 1992).

Two standard methods of protecting the privacy of research participants are anonymity and privacy (Frankfort-Nachmias & Nachmias, 1992). Anonymity requires that the identity of individuals be kept separate from the information they give. One method for ensuring anonymity is not to acquire names or other means of identifying participants in a research project. The related method of securing privacy is confidentiality, that is, not revealing names or other identifiers about participants, such as social security numbers, street addresses, and phone numbers. Also confidentiality can be further protected by using crude report categories, year instead of date of birth, and profession but not specialty within profession.

Macklin claims that in attempting to determine appropriate ethical standards for disclosure, we need to distinguish among three types of observation research:

1. *Scrutiny of public records.* This does not constitute treating people as a means solely. The researcher is using written information, not human beings, as a means to researchers' ends.

2. *Observation of public behavior.* Observation of public for purposes of research is no more an invasion of privacy than watching people in those same settings out of

mere curiosity, though it may be rude. However, those being scrutinized may feel intruded upon, that is, that one's every movement is being watched. Macklin (1982, 204) observes, "It is reasonable to expect that whatever one does in public, curious onlookers will be present. It is, however, not a legitimate expectation that social scientists are likely to be lurking about at any moment observing one's actions and taking notes." Engaging in such observation, then, seems to clash with the Kantian prescription against treating people solely as a means. Macklin claims that, while it is true that to observe people in public places without their knowledge or consent is to treat them as means to the researchers' ends (and not as ends in themselves), it is not clear that such observation is unethical. The rude onlooker who stares is violating a precept of etiquette, not a moral norm. The important obligation is to preserve anonymity. "Like the scrutiny of public records, the observation of public behavior need not require that informed consent be obtained, so long as the subjects' anonymity is strictly maintained and so long as the setting is truly public."

3. *Participant observation research.* Urban anthropologists studying their own cultures can easily use this technique of disguised participant observation. Macklin (1982) claims that they justify their use of this technique by appealing to the absence of risk to subjects, principally achieved through preserving anonymity in published results. This was the case for Humphreys' (1975) research on homosexual activity. Below is a synopsis from Humphreys' view of his research. I then return to Macklin's critique of this research.

Tearoom Trade

Tearoom Trade is a book about the experiences of Laud Humphreys (1975) who provided a sociological enthnographic study of male homosexual behavior in public restrooms, which in the homosexual argot were called "tearooms." Humphreys carried out his task by going to public toilets in parks and positioning himself in the restrooms as a "Watch Queen," a voyeur, ostensibly serving as a lookout for the police or for anyone who might be engaged in homosexual conduct in the restroom.

In explaining his approach as an ethnographer, Humphreys (1975, 25) was convinced that there was only one way to watch highly discreditable behavior and that was to pretend to be in the same boat with those engaging in it. "To wear a button that says 'I Am a Watchbird, Watching You' into a tearoom, would instantly eliminate all action except the flushing of toilets and the exiting of all present." Being deceptive was especially important because his "research required observation of criminal acts." A second reason for deception was to prevent distortion. Even if he could find a few men willing to continue their sexual activity while under observation, how "normal" could that activity be? The researcher could not be sure that he was observing a "performance," rather than a more "natural activity," in the sense of men engaging in sex as they would when not being observed by a non-homosexual.

Thus Humphreys (1975) opted to pass as "deviant." He played the role of a "Watch Queen." Typically Humphreys was situated at the door or windows inside a public restroom from which he was able to observe the means of access to the restroom, as well as much of the homosexual activity itself. When someone approached the restroom, as a lookout he would cough, then nod when the coast was clear or when he recognized an entering party as a regular. Humphreys noted that there were several kinds of lookouts: those waiting to get in on the action, voyeurs who masturbated while observing sexual acts, and voyeurs who appeared to derive sexual stimulation and pleasure just from watching the others. Humphreys said that he adopted the latter role.

Humphreys conducted his observations at park tearooms. He sat in his car and with a concealed tape recorder, noted the license plate numbers of the cars of the men who went into the restrooms, including, whenever possible, brief descriptions of the car and its driver. Then Humphreys went into the restroom to observe the homosexual activity. He verified that the recorded license numbers belonged to men he actually observed engaging in homosexual activity inside the restrooms. This procedure enabled him to get some idea of those who tended to frequent various restrooms.

Humphreys became an accepted person with some of the homosexuals. He would walk out of the tearooms and talk with them. When he became sufficiently familiar with about a dozen of the men, he disclosed his actual purpose for being in the tearooms and was able to get them to agree to subsequent interview sessions. However, he was not completely satisfied with this form of sociological investigation. He felt that the men who consented to the interview were not representative of the tearoom population. Humphreys (1975, 37) said, "I could engage them in conversation only because they are more overt, less defensive, and better educated than the average participant."

He sought another way to interview these men where he could continue to conceal his actual purpose. With the assistance of "friendly policemen," Humphreys was able to gain access to the license registers, pretending that he was engaging in market research. These registers provided him with the names and addresses of those in the sample, as well as the make of the automobile. He correlated this information with his descriptions of the automobiles he had observed. He determined that a large majority of the participants were locals, with a smaller percentage representing traveling salesmen and members of the military. He then looked at the homes and the neighborhoods of the participants. He realized that the majority of his participant sample were married, and nearly all of them were quite secretive about their deviant activity. Faced with the problem of how to interview more than his initial willing respondents, he sought further means for conducting deceptive interviews.

At about this same time, Humphreys was asked to develop a questionnaire for a social health survey of men in the community, which was being conducted by a research center. He realized that the research instrument would provide him with nearly all the information he wanted on the men in his sample: family background, socioeconomic factors, personal health and social histories, religious and employment data, a few questions on social and political attitudes, a survey of friendship networks, and information on marital relationships and sex (Humphreys 1975, 41).

Humphreys obtained permission of the director of the research project to conduct interviews. He inserted his deviant sample of 100 men on a random basis into the list of those to be interviewed. He (1975, 42) said that "only one trusted, mature graduate student and I made all the interviews of my respondents."

Humphreys stressed that he took great care to protect the privacy of his respondents.

None of the respondents were threatened by the interviews. His master list was kept in a safe-deposit box. Each interview card, kept under lock and key, was destroyed after the interview. No names or other identifying tags appeared on the questionnaires. And although he recognized each of the men interviewed from the tearooms, there was no indication that they recognized him. He was careful to change his appearance, dress, and automobile from when he had passed as deviant. He also allowed at least a year's time to lapse between the time he had observed the respondents in the tearooms and the interviews.

He interviewed about 50 of his initial list of 100 "deviants." As a result of the interview process, he gained a better understanding of these married men, including their motivation to seek sex with other men in public restrooms. Many of these men claimed that one of the reasons they sought sex outside the home was because of diminishing intercourse with their wives. When asked how often he had intercourse with his wife, a lower-middle class male, replied, "Not very much the last few years. It's up to when she feels like giving it to me—which ain't very often. I never suggest it" (Humphreys, 1975, 114).

One of the contributing factors to their diminishing sex life was religious teaching, especially Roman Catholic, which discouraged women from using birth control measures. Consequently, the wife was afraid to have sex, for fear of becoming pregnant. Humphreys observed that these men turn from the unsatisfied marriage bed to the alternative outlet, which was quick, inexpensive, and impersonal sex. Any personal, on-going affair, requiring money or hours away from home, would threaten an already shaky marriage and jeopardize the most important thing these men possess, their standing as father of their children (115). An additional reason for seeking a sexual outlet with men was because sex with women has romantic connotations, associated with the need for commitment and courtship rituals. Seeking sex with men, then, enables men to be free from all the usual romantic attachments of sex associated with women.

Humphreys suggested that in the past, before the vice squads narrowed the options, these kind of men would probably have made regular visits to cheap houses of prostitution. Humphreys found no indication that these men sought homosexual contact as such. Rather that they wanted a form of sexual release less lonely than masturbation and less involving than a love relationship. Unfortunately, the newer form of sexual release was more stigmatizing (Humphreys 1975, 115).

While the majority of the men were married, and primarily heterosexual, Humphreys claims that some were drawn into becoming homosexual by the tearoom trade. This viewpoint, of course, contradicts the view that homosexuality appears to be fixed at an early age. A lesser number of his sample, both married and unmarried were bisexual; others were closet gays. A few were overtly gay.

Humphreys made some interesting observations about the "morality" of these men. They obviously were engaged in their own kind of deceptive activity. Since their sexual activity was socially frowned upon, these men adopted a defensive shield to ward off social disapproval. These men, observed Humphreys (1975, 135), "are not only concerned with avoiding trouble but are involved, as well, in the creation of a social image, in presenting themselves as respectable members of society," assuming what Humphreys calls the "breastplate of righteousness."

Humphreys also noted that the men's fear of exposure and stigmatization served as an intervening lens through which the effects of other social characteristics were filtered and distorted. Humphreys (1975, 139) states, "Social conservatism is revealed as a product of the illegal roles these men playing the hidden moments of their lives." These men adopted right-wing social and political attitudes. They also reflected a similar "uprightness" in their home life. Their performance of duties as a husband, father, neighbor, and friend served to give credence to their life of respectability. By all appearances, the men's marriages were "smoother" than those of Humphreys' control sample (145).

Humphreys found that the majority of the political liberals in his sample were in fact avowed gays. He found that these men seemed more accepting of their own sexual natures and more intent upon establishing love relationships with others.

Macklin on Participant Observer Research

Macklin (1982) contends that deceptive methods of the participant observer are not justifiable for the following reasons:

1. Indeterminacy about what will be truly significant research.
2. Ignorance of the possibility that such information would come to light by other means.
3. To sanction the use of deceptive research methods on "bad" groups is to open the door to likely abuse.

According to Macklin, incomplete disclosure is justified in at least two contexts. The investigator should not have to fully reveal his hypotheses to his subjects, because that would invalidate the research. Second, the investigator need not disclose the reasons for selecting the subjects when disclosing this may be psychologically harmful to the subjects. For example, telling someone that they were selected for an experiment because they are latent homosexuals or greedy may be upsetting to these subjects. Participants should not suffer lowered self-esteem by being told that their personal characteristics are undesirable or socially unacceptable.

CASE STUDIES

A Lady in Distress

In this study (Catalyst 1991, 4-5) the male subjects were asked to participate in a questionnaire survey, purportedly being conducted by "the Consumer Testing Bureau," a market research organization "interested in testing the market appeal of a number of adult games and puzzles" in exchange for a modest sum of money. As they filled out the questionnaires, they were exposed to an emergency. They were tested alone, with a friend, or with a stranger (co-subjects), and their responses were observed.

Upon arrival for his appointment, the subject was met by an attractive and vivacious young woman (secretary) who showed him to the testing room and gave him the questionnaire to fill out. While he answered the questionnaire, the secretary said that she had a few things to do next door in her office, but would return in 10 or 15 minutes to give further instructions. The office door was open and easily accessible from the testing room. While the subject (and co-subjects) worked on their questionnaire(s), they heard the secretary moving around in the next office, and opening and closing drawers. After a couple of minutes, they heard a loud crash and a scream as the chair fell over. "Oh, my God, my foot...." "I...I...can't move...it. Oh, my ankle. I...can't...can't...get...this thing off...me." The secretary moaned for about a minute longer, getting gradually more subdued and controlled. This whole sequence was pre-recorded on high fidelity tape, but the subject (and co-subjects), next door, had no way of knowing that. The main dependent variable of the study was the type of response made to the emergency and the length of time before that response was made.

Questions for Discussion

1. Are there any ethical problems with this experiment? If so, what are they? If the experimenters had merely observed situations of bystanders' response to situations involving the distress of others, would your answer be the same?
2. Should the experimenter obtain informed consent from the subjects concerning the deception? If so, is there any way of obtaining consent?
3. Should the subjects be debriefed? If so, how? What should be said to subjects? Should there be different debriefings for those who did and those who did not come to the woman's aid?
4. Are the subjects' rights being violated? If so, how?
5. Could the subjects be harmed because of their inclusion in the study? If so, how?

The Hand in the Till

In this experiment (Catalyst 1991, 6-7), male undergraduates witnessed a (staged) theft while waiting for an interview. In one condition, each subject was the sole witness; in another, two subjects were present.

Male college freshmen were asked to volunteer to participate in an interview for a modest sum of money. After arriving for their interviews, the subjects were greeted by an attractive female receptionist and directed toward a waiting room. Among the subjects was a short, clean-cut, conservatively dressed student. This participant (C) was a confederate of the experimenter.

All of the subjects were told that they would be individually interviewed by a team of experts from the Institute for the Study of Consumer Practices on the reactions of college students to the urban environment of New York City. They were also told that since the interviews were running behind schedule, they would be paid in advance.

When paying the subjects, the receptionist pulled several large and small bills out of an envelope in full view of all subjects. To emphasize the presence of the large amount of money in the envelope, she asked the subjects if anyone had change for a twenty. After paying the subjects, she put the remainder of the money (between thirty and fifty dollars) back in the envelope, and placed the envelope on top of the desk. Shortly afterward, she left the room to speak to an interviewer.

Just after the receptionist left the room, C walked over to the desk, and pretended to fumble with a magazine lying on top of the desk. Seemingly trying to hide his actions but in full view of the other, real, subjects, C then took the cash from the envelope, picked up the magazine, and returned to his seat. He did not say anything. If a subject questioned him about taking the money, he either ignored the comment, continuing to leaf through his magazine, or innocently answered, "I don't know what you are talking about."

A couple of minutes later, the receptionist returned. Now, the subjects could report the crime and confront C directly. After about half a minute, the receptionist sent C to his "interview." The subjects now had an opportunity to report the theft without directly confronting C.

Finally, each subject was called into his interview. If the subject did not tell the interviewer then, the deceptions and purposes of the experiment were explained. The dependent variable of interest was the proportion of subjects reporting the theft spontaneously to the receptionist or the interviewer.

Questions for Discussion

1. Are there any ethical problems with this experiment? If so, what are they? If the experimenters had somehow managed to record an actual theft, would your answer be the same?
2. Should the experimenter obtain informed consent from the subjects concerning the deception? If so, is there any way to obtain consent?
3. Should the subjects be debriefed? If so, how? What should be said to a subject who did not reveal the theft to the experimenters at any point when he had the opportunity to do so?
4. Are the subjects' rights being violated? If so, how?
5. Could participating in this project as an actual subject pose any harm to the individual? If so, what would that harm be?
6. Is the social importance of the experiment relevant to your answer? If so, how?

11

Ethics in the Science Curriculum

Some who have written about the relationship between science and ethics have contended that the traditional view of science as an unproblematic body of knowledge about the natural world should be replaced with a view of science as a social activity in which socio-ethical goals are incorporated into the conception of science itself (Gosling & Musschenga 1985). However, one need not agree with the notion that values are an implicit aspect of the scientific enterprise to realize that scientific application involves ethical questions. Dubos (1971, 270) contended that as modern technological innovations are the direct result of scientific research, "scientists can no longer afford to stand aloof from social problem." In the past the social effects of science manifested themselves slowly. However, today effects are immediate and extend into every aspect of society, for good and for evil. Dubos (270) says: "The scientist has convinced society that his efforts deserve to be generously supported because he has become one of its most effective servants. As a penalty for his dependence on public support and for the influence that he has gained he cannot escape being made responsible for his activities, even if their results are different from what he had hoped."

Examples of some ominous areas of scientific research are not hard to find. Genetic research may provide scientists and our society with the resources to eradicate diseases and alter intelligence. New birth technologies are providing an array of options regarding childbirth. The production of military weapons carries with it not only the dangers of nuclear, chemical, and biological weapons, but also involves the waste of material and intellectual resources. To alleviate the problem of worldwide starvation, pesticides, fertilizers, and genetically altered planting seeds are used. These issues concern the balance between providing sufficient food and protecting the environment. With medical advances it is now possible to prolong life, but this possibility brings with it a whole range of problems for an aging population: Should medical resources be used to provide vital organs for the aged at the expense of resources for younger people? Should voluntary euthanasia be legalized? We have a host of concerns about the environment, especially pollution of land, water, air, and the upper atmosphere. Scientists must wrestle with these concerns. In the area of information technology, computerization has produced an efficient storage, search, and retrieval of information and the production of new information, but this technology threatens "increased central control over the population, the misuse of information, lack of privacy, and opportunities of criminal acts" (Frazer & Kornhauser, 1986).

Dubos argues that the scientist can no longer be satisfied with merely describing, classifying, and inventing. "This happy phase of social irresponsibility is now over, and the scientist will be called to account for the long-term consequences of his acts" (Dubos 1971, 271). The scientist must recognize that he or she cannot predict many long-range consequences of his or her research, because they depend on factors outside the scientist's control. In this regard the scientist has the responsibility to be alert to the unexpected consequences of research. While the scientist cannot predict the remote consequences of activities, he or she can typically provide techniques for recognizing them early. As an example of what can be done, extensive studies on the potential danger of radiation exposure were launched when it became apparent that nuclear research would lead to applications for both war and peace.

Dealing with the ethical issues concerning the uses of science is not only important for the training of scientists, but it is also important for the non-scientist taking course work in science. Frazer & Kornhauser (1986) point out that if the public has a better knowledge and understanding of the social and ethical issues of science and technology, it can be better involved in policy making. These authors also warn against the danger of a society "becoming divided into a minority having some knowledge and understanding of science and its social issues, and the majority who feels that science is too difficult to understand, not of its concern, and that it is being manipulated" (32). This could lead to hostility toward science.

Infusing ethics into the science curriculum also can help instructors provide students with tools that will enable them to evaluate the consequences of science. According to McInerney (1986, 178), they need tools such as "probabilistic thinking; an appreciation for the often value-laden nature of the scientific enterprise; the tentativeness of science; the need continuously to suspend final judgment and to make decisions based on the best information available; and the inherent shortcomings of models that forecast the outcomes of technology applied in this or that way." Students need to be able to distinguish between scientific expertise and charlatans, as well as that which "masquerades as science," such as the appeals of creationists, or those who challenge genetic technology, relying on exaggeration and half truths (178). The issue over "fusion in a bottle" in 1989 is illustrative of the problem. In Utah, scientists declared that they could generate nuclear fusion by a chemical process. However, no one could replicate their experiment. These scientists had evidently rigged their results to gain publicity and financial backing.

An additional benefit of raising ethical concerns in science instruction is that this can help the non-scientist better appreciate the need for mastery of the appropriate scientific facts and concepts. A student who can come to see that not only does scientific research have ethical implications, but that a knowledge of the research is necessary to evaluate ethical implications, has an additional motive for understating science as well. Infusing ethics into science can help the student understand the relevance of ethics for science but also appreciate the relevance of science for ethics.

Following are discussions of environmental ethics and genetic research as examples of topics for various science classes.

THE ENVIRONMENT AND ETHICAL THEORY

A Case Study

The Plight of the Dolphins

Andrew Davis (1992) describes a typical tuna fishing episode involving dolphins:

For a moment, only a pod of leaping dolphins creases the rippled stillness of the ocean. A score of the sociable mammals are swimming and diving together in a random migration that has endured for millennia. Then, the chatter of a helicopter breaks the quiet, joined by the high-pitched whine of racing speedboats. Overtaking the dolphins, the boats pull in front and begin herding the now-terrified pod into a circle. Just behind, a 200-foot fishing boat, the bizarre fleet's mother ship, turns to one side and begins laying a mile-long curtain of nylon net around the cauldron of churning water.

But it is not dolphins that the fishermen are after. Underneath is a school of the dolphins' perennial ocean-going companions, yellow-fin tuna. The dolphin serves as an expendable lure. Although wet-suited rescuers try to help the dolphins over the edge of the tightening net, many are left behind. As the net is cinched tight, the dolphins become entangled, gasping for air, and slowly drowing. Any of the dolphins alive when the net is winched aboard are crushed by the cascading tons of tuna on the ship's deck. Over the last 30 years, more than six million dolphins have died this way.

This fishing technique is known as the "purse seine." This was developed in the late 1950s. This technique has boosted tuna catches in the Eastern Tropical Pacific (ETP) from 115,000 tons in 1961 to approximately 217,411 tons in 1985, according to the Inter-American Tropical Tuna Commission (Davis 1992).

During this period, the number of dead dolphins has risen dramatically. For example, in 1959, 71,000 northern spotted dolphins were killed. By 1965 an average of 1,000 dolphins a day were dying in the nets of 100 fishing boats. Since 1960, approximately six million dolphins have been killed by purse seiners (Davis 1992).

The most threatened species of dolphins are the northern offshore spotted dolphins, the variety used by the fishing industry to spot the yellow-finned tuna. The dolphins gather in bands of a few hundred (Brower 1989, 36). Schools of spotted dolphins, spinner, and common dolphins have a symbiotic relationship with schools of yellow-finned tuna, and dolphins and tuna travel together. "The association is most common in the Eastern Tropical Pacific (ETP) the warm waters west of Mexico, Central America, Colombia, Ecuador, Peru, and Northern Chile" (Brower 1989, 37).

Tuna fishermen have taken advantage of the symbiotic relationship, searching for dolphins to find the fish. Dolphins are fairly easy to spot. For example, spotted dolphins "are the greatest broad jumpers of all cetaceans, raise white fountains in the ocean on coming down" (Brower 1989, 37). "Spinner dolphins, whirling like dervishes as they exit the water, make centrifugal re-entries that scoop holes in the ocean" (Brower 1989, 37).

Until recently the fish underneath the dolphins were caught by rod, line, and baitless hook. All this changed in the early 1960s, with the application of purse-seining techniques to tuna fishing. Typically the dolphins sighted in the ETP are rounded up with "seal bombs" (underwater explosives) thrown from speedboats, as the tuna are encircled by a mile-long fence of net, its upper edge buoyed by a line of floats—the "corkline"—its lower edge hanging several hundred feet deep. Brower (1989, 37) describes the techniques as follows:

Cables draw the bottom of the seine tight, trapping the dolphins and any tuna swimming underneath. Toward the end of each "set" on dolphins the crew is supposed to follow a procedure called back-down, which is intended to allow the dolphins to escape over the corkline of the net, but often—in darkness or on high seas, from equipment failure, human error, or some unexpected panic by the dolphins—something goes wrong and dolphins will die.

Sam LaBudde, an environmental activist, surreptitiously boarded a tuna fishing boat as a deck hand and videotaped the dolphin sets, involving the purse seining of tuna. He concocted a story in Mexico and got a job aboard the *Maria Luisa*. Using a camcorder in 1987, he documented dolphins sets in which dolphins were killed in tuna fishing. In one episode he recorded, "One to two hundred eastern spinner dolphins died, trapped under the canopy, in that first set. When the carcasses had been disentangled from the net and dumped, shark bait, the crew had their catch—a single yellow-fin tuna" (Brower 1989, 44).

In another episode of the *Maria Luisa*, LaBudde was in Costa Rican territorial waters. They got permission to fish in these waters. LaBudde says, "To celebrate we went and wiped out probably five percent of the world's population of these Costa Rican spinners in a single afternoon" (Brower 1989, 46).

Brower (1989, 47) describes the use of seal bombs to round up dolphins: "A fisherman in a yellow hard hat runs forward and hurls a seal bomb into the water off the stern. He is trying to drive the dolphins toward the escape panel at the rear of the net. The dolphin bombing produces no noticeable effect. (It will fail, indeed, and in this set at least two hundred dolphins will die.)"

One concern is the effect of the seal bombs on the dolphins. The dolphins have no ears as such in the sense that terrestrial mammals do. Primarily dolphins hear through their jaw bones that are hollow and filled with a sound-conducting oil, and through an oil-filled sac inside the mellon. Dolphins have an extreme sensitivity to sound. The seal bomb, landing on the point of a dolphin's "hearing" jaw, succeeds in scrambling its faculties for a time in the dolphin set. How long afterwards will the jaw go on ringing? Brower (1989 , 48) says "Blind dolphins have been known to survive in the wild, guided by exquisite acoustic images of their prey and warned by echoes of the dangers around them. A deaf dolphin, however, is a dead dolphin."

The environmental legislation, the 1972 Marine Mammal Protection Act (MMPA), was created to prevent this slaughter of the dolphins. This legislation gave jurisdiction over marine mammals to the federal government rather than to the state. Its objective was to decrease the allowable dolphin kill each year. This act made it illegal to "harass, hunt, capture or kill" any marine mammal. It also banned the importation of marine mammals and marine mammal products such as seal-fur coats and spermaceti-based cosmetics. A research program was funded for the development of dolphin-saving gear and techniques, and an observer program was set up (Brower 1989, 38).

The MMPA also established stringent protection for marine mammals determined to be threatened species or those determined to be below the Optimum Sustainable Population (OSP). The OSP is defined as "the range of populations sizes between the highest number that an ecosystem will support and what is generally maintained to be 60 percent of the species' historic pre-exploitation level." The government also had tried to restore populations that had fallen below that level. As a result of the MMPA, whales, walruses, polar bears, sea lions, sea otters, and dolphins have been protected. Due to this legislation, some species have been on the increase. For example, the harbor seal population of the Pacific Northwest is increasing at a rate of seven percent a year, and the California sea lions at five percent (Davis 1992).

Other species, however, especially the dolphins, have not faired as well. Part of this has to do with the lack of enforcement of the MMPA. Over the past twenty years, the aims of the the the Reagan administration did little to hide its disdain for environmental concerns.

Before the act took effect, the tuna industry was granted a grace period to try and solve the problem of "incidental take," resulting in the death of dolphins in purse seines. Despite the fact that the MMPA states that dolphins' mortality should be "reduced to insignificant levels approaching zero," the U.S. tuna fleet is allowed to slaughter 20,500 dolphins each year. The MMPA did bring about a steady decline in the number of dolphins killed. For example, in 1975, 166,645 died in U.S. nets by the conservative official estimate. In 1977 the official underestimate was only 25,452 (Brower 1989, 38). Over the next four years, the National Marine Fisheries Service (NMFS), the government agency charged with enforcing the MMPA, clamped down on the number of dolphins allowed to die until it stopped, in 1981, at 20,500 (Davis 1992). This quota was extended indefinitely in 1984. Under Reagan, funds for research on dolphin-stabling gear were greatly reduced, regulations were relaxed, and enforcement was softened. Since the MMPA's passage at least 800,000 dolphins have died in U.S. nets. "The dolphin kill by tuna fishermen in the ETP continues to be the greatest slaughter of marine mammals on earth" (Brower 1989, 38).

One way that fisherman skirt the law is by underreporting instances of injured or dead dolphin. NMFS observers tell stories of threats, bribes, and how records disappear and data sheets and lab work-ups are thrown overboard.

Fishermen are resistent to switching to alternative means of fishing for tuna, because this is the most effective way to catch mature tuna. One fisherman, August Felando, told Brower that he believed that the dolphin were there for the taking. Brower was unsure over the distinction drawn between banning the killing of dolphin and permitting the killing of tuna. He (1989, 56) says that tuna are "miraculous creatures, hydrodynamic marvels wrought in silver and gold, the finest things in their line, just as dolphins are the finest in theirs. Making this moral distinction between killing dolphins and killing tuna is a little peculiar." One of the differences between the two is that the dolphin is so much more intelligent. But is intelligence sufficient criterion for valuing dolphins more than tuna?

The argument that Brower gives against dolphins sets in the tuna fishing is that it is not expedient in the long run. If it continues it will simply eliminate the use of dolphin as a tool to find tuna. Brower (1989, 56) observes, "the tuna seiner locks himself into a system that compels him to destroy the dolphins that his predecessors have used for a millennia to find fish."

The MMPA enforcement of the U.S. tuna industry has resulted in a reduction of the number of tuna boats flying under the U.S. flag. However, the tuna fisherman have not abandoned dolphin sets. Fishermen have simply reflagged and are fishing under the auspices of other countries thereby escaping the MMPA.

A Scientist's Perspective: Who Should Pay?[1]

In the words of Thomas Jefferson, "We have a moral obligation to pay our own debts rather than pass them on to the next generation." In these times, his words speak clearly to the deficit spending and accumulating debt of our Federal Government, but they also speak to the travesty of environmental degradation. Although the warning signs of impending environmental collapse are becoming increasingly obvious, what we should do about it is not entirely clear.

Regulations designed to protect the environment must achieve a delicate balance between the rights of a complex array of effected parties. Environmental protection often displaces workers, and sometimes even requires people to change their way of life. Because of the dramatic effects that environmental decisions have on people, they must always be made with care and compassion.

The most basic consideration here is our relationship to our environment. The way people think about our relationship to our environment typically falls into one of two schools of thought; environmentalist or cornucopian. Cornucopians are anthropocentrics who believe that our environment is a resource that exists for our use. In this view, people come first, and the environment's role is supportive. This has been the common viewpoint for much of the history of civilization, as humanity has broadened its boundaries to cover essentially all of the inhabitable land on earth. We have been fruitful and have multiplied, and we have harnessed the earth to provide us with the essential resources to sustain our civilization.

Environmentalists do not look at the environment as something that is apart from us and there only for our exploitation. In this view, the protection of our environment is a key to our continued success, environmentalists see us as being responsible for the well-being of the environment and of all of the species that make up earth's living community.

At the heart of the difference between environmentalists and cornucopians is the idea of sustainability. The two schools of thought both agree that it is a vital goal, but they

---

[1] This section contributed by Douglas Petcoff.

differ about what role we should play in attaining it. Environmentalists call for an active role in preserving the environment and guarding against environmental decay. They feel that the moral thing to do is to preserve the environment for the future. Cornucopians argue that the environment is highly resilient and will absorb our impact. If this is true, then denying resources to people who need them seems wrong.

The arguments between environmentalists and cornucopians usually become extremely complicated in terms of defining the fine line between use and overuse of resources. While the best and highest use of a given resource isn't usually clear, it is clear that most of our resources are finite. Ecologically, the earth is a closed system. Simply put, nutrients cycle and energy flows. Except sunlight, everything that we depend on for our survival is found here on earth in limited quantities.

Since quantities of resources are limited, all living things must compete for them. Competition for resources can occur at most levels. Two different species may compete for a given resource; this type of competition is known as interspecific competition. An example would be competition between snakes and skunks for the eggs of some unwitting ground bird. Humans are aggressive competitors with other species. When ground is cleared for a new housing development, the native species are displaced, often into uninhabitable territory. Many prairie dog holes have been bulldozed so that a new home could be built.

We have been so successful that our ever-expanding population has overwhelmed most species. Over the last 50 years, most species have become extinct as a direct result of human activity. It has become apparent that if a species is to survive, it must adapt to a coexistence with humans. Such urban species as pigeons, fox squirrels, and cockroaches are doing fine. Grey wolves, grizzly bears, and many species that are limited to small patches of tropical rainforest are on the way out.

The result of these extinctions is an irreversible decrease in biodiversity. The dangerous thing about this loss in biodiversity is that diversity is correlated with stability. As we cause a reduction in the number of species, we cause a reduction in nature's ability to adapt to us.

Another type of competition for a limited resource occurs between members of the same species and is called intraspecific competition. While different species are adapted to different niches (ways of life)—which tends to reduce competition between them—become members of the same species are adapted to the same niche, and therefore compete head to head. This type of competition is far more fierce than interspecific competition and is generally limited by mechanisms that limit the number of individuals within a population. Humans have not acted to limit population size, and people must compete, in increasing numbers, for the same limited resources.

The maximum number of individuals that can be sustained for an unlimited time is referred to as carrying capacity. Given unchecked population growth, a time will come when we will overshoot the earth's carrying capacity. It is possible that we have already surpassed carrying capacity. It is also possible that we can look to technology to allow us to increase carrying capacity.

We have, in fact, greatly increased carrying capacity already. The agricultural revolution that started ten thousand years ago provided us with reliable food resources that allowed a huge increase in the human population. Advances in agriculture in this century, highlighted by the "green revolution" of the 1970s, have provided us with hybrid crop plants that provide remarkable yields compared to what was available before. These triumphs of human ingenuity and technology, coupled with the development of medicine, have allowed us to dramatically expand our population.

But agriculture, as we now practice it, is a resource and energy-intensive enterprise. We are committed to the use of fossil fuel burning machinery, synthetic fertilizers, irrigation, pesticides, herbicides, fungicides to kill just about anything except the crop of interest. This agricultural practice is called monoculture. We rely almost exclusively on large expanses of single crops and are limited worldwide to a few different crops. Monoculture is the antithesis of biodiversity and is extremely susceptible to damage from drought or disease. In short, monoculture is a house of cards; upon which depends the future of our species.

Are we living on borrowed time? We have been externalizing the cost of our lifestyle on the environment, and the environment is showing signs of stress. Eventually, someone is going to have to pay for the environmental degradation that we have allowed to occur. As consumers and as members of a democracy, we must all bear some responsibility. We must decide who should pay to ensure a healthy environment. Should we increase fees to businesses? Should costs be passed on to consumers? Should we move manufacturing out of the country and make other countries pay? If we cannot decide, then future generations must pay for our limited vision.

Environmental Ethical Theory

Environmental ethical theory attempts to provide a systematic framework for addressing the concerns of the environmentally concerned, including those within the scientific community dealing with ethical dilemmas, such as the case of the dolphins. However, in turning to environmental ethics, we are confronted with an initial problem of moral theory. Traditional utilitarian and deontological theories do not readily lend themselves to providing a moral framework for understanding environmental issues. Instead, there are alternative approaches currently touted among environmental ethicists. There are basically three approaches, anthropocentric, sentientist, and ecocentric. Utilitarian and Kantian concepts are interwoven within these theories, as we shall see.

The anthropocentrics adopt the position that human benefit is the fundamental criterion for making environmental decisions. It is essentially a utilitarian view. Baxter (1983) epitomizes this view. He takes a cost-benefit approach. The fisherman, Felando, in the dolphin case study, in advocating that the tuna are there for taking, and that we are within our rights to do what we need to do to get them, represents the most calculating version of utilitarian thinking as applied to the environment. But even Brower could be interpreted as being something of a utilitarian when he argues that the sole basis for protecting the dolphin is that it is not expedient to be killing them in the long run. The anthropocentric view fails to explain our sense that maintaining a sustainable environment seems to be inherently or intrinsically worthwhile.

Sentientist approaches appeal to the interests of sentient beings as the basis for determining our obligations to the environment. An important advocate of this view is Singer (1993). He maintains that sentient beings are regarded as having inherent value. LeBudde seems to adopt this view as he finds himself repulsed by the captain of the fishing boat eating dolphin flesh. Sentientists are utilitarian in maintaining that we ought to maximize pleasure and reduce pain. The basic difficulty with sentientism is that it does not provide us with any criterion concerning ethical decisions confronting non-sentient aspects of the environment.

The ecocentric approach represents the most comprehensive view toward the environment. The core of this view is that moral consideration must be extended to all of nature. (Mapes & Zembaty 1992). Taylor (1991) represents this view from a Kantian perspective. As previously stated, Kant grounded the individual in a set of universal moral principles, rules, and judgments supportive of the notion of human dignity and respect for persons as ends in themselves. His main purpose was to establish the a priori principles of morality that apply, not merely in the abstract to all rational beings qua rational beings, but to all human beings qua human beings. Taylor maintains that we should adopt a "biocentric outlook" on nature, defined as a respect for "the interdependence of all living things in an organically unified order whose balance and stability are necessary conditions for the realization of the good of its constituent biotic communities" (448). In relation to the dolphins, Taylor would claim that to eliminate dolphins is to violate the respect for the interdependence of all living things. Taylor insists that to adopt this kind of attitude of respect for nature is to take the Kantian stance that "one wills it to be a universal law for all rational beings" (447).

More comprehensive ecocentric views are those of Leopold (1983) and Callicott (1989), a current exponent of Leopold's view. Callicott claims that "ethics are peculiarly (if perhaps not uniquely) the human means of achieving social organization" (65). He suggests that we can distinguish between morality as a description of social organization from morality as perceived subjectively by the members of society. For example, the commandment, "Honor thy father and thy mother" can be regarded, objectively, as a socio-biological description of a human society organized in such a way that pair bonding in a nuclear family is central. In contrast, from a subjective viewpoint, this is perceived as an imperative. Callicott goes on to maintain that, by taking the concept of the community as the core value, a case can be made for extending our moral concern for having a fundamental respect for our environment and the integrity of ecosystems. Callicott claims that we should respect the broader environment as contributing to the stability of the whole ecological environment. The intricate network of ecological relationships is important for all levels of communal stability, human beings included.

This view suggests the need for a broader ethical framework than is provided by either utilitarianism or Kantian ethics. A communitarian ethical framework seems to fit better with this line of analysis. Although, I only briefly mentioned it in the beginning, an attractive communitarian view is liberal communitarianism, the view that maintains that we ought to strive to promote the good of all alike in ways that promote respect for autonomy and fairness. We recognize that we ought to promote the good of all, because of the nature of our understanding of ourselves as socially constituted beings. As social beings, we come to understand that we are a part of community and that we, as individuals, can only flourish in meaningful community, a community founded on the moral notions of promoting the good of all in terms of fairness and autonomy. We are obligated to promote the good of all, including our neighbors, as a matter of social necessity. Following Callicott, the concept of community is extended to include all of nature, and we are therefore obligated to work for a sustainable environment. This view could be criticized for extending the concept of "community" to include the natural environment. The natural environment is not ordinarily what we refer to by means of the term community. Second, even if a case can be made for this inclusive use of the concept, how does this ethical framework provide us with a way to make hard choices among competing priorities and resources within the community. Granted that a sustainable environment includes clean air and water, for example, but so does a vigorous economy. When we look at the heated debates over "jobs" versus the "environment," simply appealing to a sustainable environment does not provide us with an adequate guideline for resolving these dilemmas. I am not saying that this theory cannot provide these guidelines; only that they are not clearly manifest.

With respect to the strained use of the concept of community, it would be better to regard a sustainable environment, not as identical to the community but, as essential to the sustainment of community. Thus as we confront environmental dilemmas, we look at what must be protected for the sake of sustaining community. This interpretation may invite the criticism that this theory lapses into a version of an anthropocentric theory, where now we are valuing nature only in terms of its contribution to the good of all as community. A possible gambit around this difficulty may be found in distinguishing between the intrinsic value of the environment versus its extrinsic value. Taking the latter concept first, something is considered extrinsically valuable if it is good as a means to the attainment of some other valued purpose or end. For example, we may value an automobile for transportation. In contrast, something is considered intrinsically valuable if it is considered valuable for its own sake. Aristotle argued that happiness or a life well-lived is the only thing intrinsically valuable. Without engaging in a debate with this Aristotelian claim, one could argue that we regard a sustainable community as intrinsically valuable. And a sustainable community includes a sustainable environment. Some environmental philosophers, such as Rolston (1988) may contend that as long as we talk about nature as intrinsically valuable in this sense, we are operating from an anthropocentric view. For on this line of analysis, it has been alleged that only that which is "inherently valuable," i.e., valuable in itself, apart from satisfying any human interest, can be truly regarded as non-anthropocentric. I just do not think that it makes any sense to talk about nature as "inherently valuable." If there were no human beings (or valuing creatures) in the universe, it seems to make no sense to talk about the inherent value of nature. In a billion or so years, the planet earth will be nothing but a cosmic piece of mineral left over from the effect of the death of the sun. The Aristotelian sense of intrinsic value, again, that which is valued for its own sake, admittedly presupposes that humans are the ones who are doing the valuing. But again there is a large distinction between valuing something for its own sake and valuing something as a means to some purpose. If nature or the environment were valued only extrinsically, I would concede that this form of valuing is an anthropocentric view.

Turning to the second difficulty of the Leopold/Callicott view, perhaps one could argue that when we confront dilemmas over how to protect the environment and jobs, we have to operate from a basis of what is absolutely necessary for a sustainable community, and thus prioritize our decisions regarding what resources to protect, regardless of jobs, on the grounds of what resources are essential for the sustainment of community. In some cases, as with clean air and water, we could make the case that these resources must be provided, even if it means that certain companies are forced to go out of business. Much more work needs to be done to further elaborate and defend this version of liberal communitarianism, but that would be the subject of another book.

ETHICAL CONSIDERATIONS IN MODERN GENETICS

A Case Study: A Cloned Embryo

Last year a scientific controversy resulted over the experiment of Jerry Hall and his associates which took place at the In Vitro Fertilization and Andrology Laboratory at George Washington University in Washington, D.C., on October 22, 1993 (Elmer-Dewitt 1994). Hall had successfully cloned 48 microscopic embryos from 48. This achievement set off one of the fiercest medical ethics controversies since the birth of the first test tube baby 15 years ago. Many believed that a line had been crossed, a taboo broken (Elmer-Dewitt 1994). It is important to emphasize that there is a vast difference between the achievement in this respect and the Jurassic Park type. This latter type of cloning, which has not been achieved, is the cloning of a complete sentient being from an adult cell. All cells contain within their DNA the information required to reproduce the entire organism. However, in adult cells, access to parts of that information has been switched off, and scientists do not yet know how to switch it back on (Elmer-Dewitt, 1994).

The type of cloning achieved by Hall and Stillmann was no different from that which has been done with livestock. A reason for their interest in determining if this type of cloning could be done with human embryos is related to the difficulties of in vitro fertilization. Couples who have trouble conceiving can have their sperm and eggs mixed in a Petri dish, and the resulting embryos transferred to the mother's womb. Most of these attempts are unsuccessful. Some couples can only produce a few embryos, because either the male's semen is scarce or the woman's ovaries are running out of eggs. Hall and Stillman wanted to see if it was feasible to increase the supply of embryos through cloning. They worked with abnormal embryos that would not live for very long anyway. In all, 48 embryos were cloned and none lived for more than six days.

Hall and Stillman were amazed by the negative reaction to their experiment. They were motivated by a desire to relieve the suffering of infertile couples. However, critics complained that if such cloning were widely practiced, it could lead to abuses. Arthur Capalan, director of the Center for Bioethics at the University of Minnesota, pointed out that couples who faced the probability of having children with cystic fibrosis or hemophilia may wish to clone several embryos for the DNA procedure that can be performed on embryonic cells, snipping off the DNA defective cells. However, some embryos die in the process. Having extra embryos might enhance the success. Or a hopeful mother who faces chemotherapy and possible sterility might wish to bank a few embryos for future use. Or consider the possibility that a couple could set aside clones of their children; so that if one died, a duplicate could replace it. Suffice it to say, the medical possibilities raise a storm of ethical questions.

A utilitarian might argue that whether such cloning should be legally sanctioned has to do with whether we as a society will be better off in the long run by allowing such procedures. On the other hand, a Kantian might argue that such medical experiments and possible uses of embryos are against the concept of respect for persons. But as with the case of abortion, one could counter that embryos are really not persons. Thus from a Kantian perspective, the focus might be on the long-term effect of our basic respect for persons in a society that condones such practices. Would, for example, having the ability to "order" a clone from a photograph of possible babies decrease our level of respect for human beings? Or would being able to set aside a clone for a replacement of a dead child be compatible with the respect for personhood? These questions require much greater analysis and thought than I can provide here. In what follows, additional information about DNA is provided.

A Scientist's Perspective: Human Somatic Gene Therapy[2]

A physician-researcher as been studying the possibility of gene therapy for a congenital immune deficiency syndrome caused by a single gene defect—adenosine deaminase deficiency (ADA). He has had occasional success with genetic treatment in a strain of monkeys who have a similar condition, but the response has been erratic. Other researchers do not feel that he has sufficient scientific understanding of the mechanism of treatment to begin human trials. However, he feels that children who are dying of this condition and who have failed to respond to other therapies should be offered the opportunity to participate in a trial of his technique. Regulatory agencies have reviewed the physician-researcher's protocol but have withheld approval pending further animal studies. The parents of one of his young patients has come to him in tears, requesting that he "do something" to try to save their child. Given that the appropriate regulatory agencies have denied approval, what should this researcher do?

In September of 1992, a party was held at the National Institutes of Health (NIH) to celebrate the success of the world's first foray into human gene therapy. The guests of honor were two girls, aged six and eleven. Both of these girls had been born without the ability to make an enzyme called adenosine deaminase (ADA)—they had been unlucky in the genetic lottery of which we are all products.

The exact function of ADA isn't important here, but the medical consequences of not being able to produce it are severe. Without it you have no immune system—you

---

[2] This section contributed by Douglas Petcoff.

have no ability whatsoever to fight off infection. The name given to this disorder is severe combined immunodeficiency syndrome (SCIDS), which is also known as the "bubble boy disease." The fate given to children born with this condition is life within a sterile environment. A life without being touched, without ever having direct contact with another living thing, lest the child get infected and die.

But the technology of gene therapy, which essentially gives us the ability to replace missing or defective genetic information, is an option, the potential for a different fate. Exactly two years before the NIH celebration, two brave little girls accepted the option, and opened a door that will change the world. Not that they were interested in changing the world; they were more interested in the possibility of going to school, of playing with other children, of being able to be touched without fear of it costing them their lives. Because of their therapy, they have been able to do these things—to be normal kids.

Who could deny these girls the option that allowed them to be normal? The technological advances in genetics that made this possible have to be seen as good, as worthwhile. But the development of this technology has led to ethical dilemmas that could not have been envisioned just a few years ago. Somewhere between the desire to be "normal" and the desire to be "improved" we enter into an ethical quagmire.

The same techniques that allowed two little girls to be well give us the potential to drastically alter any species we want to, including our own. We have the technology to create a "master race" far superior to what we are today. Our ability to manipulate and purify our species at this time is beyond Hitler's wildest dreams.

There are two different approaches to gene therapy, somatic cell therapy and germ-line therapy. Somatic cell therapy involves treatment of body cells that do not belong to the lineage that yields sperm or eggs. Germ-line therapy treats sperm, eggs, or any cells that may give rise to these gametes, such as any embryonic cells prior to determination of germ-line cells. The consequences of the two approaches are different, as are the ethical implications.

Somatic cell gene therapy effects a change within an individual in such a way that the change cannot be passed on to that individual's children. This allows problems to be corrected in a manner that is similar (although far more powerful) to more traditional forms of medicine. The NIH SCIDS therapy was a somatic treatment. Blood was drawn from each of the two girls, from which white blood cells were isolated. Functional copies of the gene that encodes the missing ADA enzyme were introduced into these cells. The girls' "genetically engineered" white blood cells were then returned to them.

At this point, with their genetically engineered white blood cells making the enzyme that is needed for normal immune function, the girls went about living fairly normal lives. The primary limitation to this technique is that the cells live only for a few months, so the procedure has to be repeated several times a year.

In addition to SCIDS, human somatic cell gene therapy is in various stages of testing for various cancers, AIDS, cystic fibrosis, and several important disorders. This list is growing at an ever increasing pace.

Germ-line gene therapy allows us to change not only an individual, but also the genetic traits of that individual's offspring. Of the early experiments in germ-line gene therapy, the "mighty mouse" experiment is perhaps the most famous. In this experiment, multiple copies of the human growth hormone gene were injected into fertilized mouse eggs, and the engineered eggs were implanted into the uterus of a surrogate mother mouse. She gave birth to engineered mice that grew much larger than their normal siblings. This type of genetic engineering has tremendous potential for enhancing yield from crops and domestic livestock, but has not been developed as a viable treatment for humans because of ethical considerations.

The technology that has given us gene therapy has also been used to develop sensitive and highly accurate tests that can be used to screen for a number of genetic conditions. For example, a test is available that will tell someone if they carry the gene for Huntington's Disease, which causes the nervous system to degenerate. Since this gene has a dominant effect, but is expressed late in life, testing positive means you will get this disease—and there is no cure. Because of the way that the technology works, genetic tests are far easier to develop than are treatments. As such, this situation exists for a number of genes, including cystic fibrosis and Tay-Sachs disease. Since most of these diseases are recessive, testing positive merely means that you have a chance of passing the bad gene on to a child. In cases where there is no cure for a genetic condition that is tested for, the test is useful for reproductive decisions, such as who to marry (Hasidic Jews do not allow two people who carry the Tay-Sachs gene to marry, since every child they conceive has a 25% chance of being born with this deadly disease), whether or not to conceive a child in cases where both parents are carriers of the same bad gene, or whether or not abort a pregnancy when a genetic test of embryonic or fetal cells indicates that the child will be born with the disease.

The moral questions that are raised by modern genetics fall into three different categories: 1) How much does it cost and who should pay? 2) Is there a limit to how much we should change an individual or a species? 3) What should sensitive information about an individual's genetic status be used for and who should have access to it?

With respect to the costs of gene therapy and genetic testing, these considerations are similar to those posed for any other aspect of health care. The cost of gene therapy for a single individual can be a huge burden on society. Should insurance companies be required to pick up the tab, without limitation?

This technology also has the potential to lower health care costs. If individuals who would otherwise be chronically ill, with extended stays in hospitals, can be made relatively healthy, their cost to the health care system may go down dramatically, at the same time their lives become more productive. But there is also an eventual down side to this. For example, consider the girls in the SCIDS gene therapy trial. Their eggs still have the faulty gene, so if they have children some day, those children will receive a bad copy of the gene from their mothers. Since SCIDS is a very rare disease, it is unlikely that they would also receive the bad gene from their fathers. Since SCIDS is a recessive disease, one good copy of the gene is enough for normal immune function. However, the long term effect is that by keeping people with severe genetic defects alive long enough to bear children, we are increasing the number of bad genes in our gene pool, and in time we will increase the number of people born with severe diseases. Should we restrict their reproductive rights as a price of the therapy?

In drawing the line between fixing a problem and enhancing the human phenotype, who decides how far we should go? This issue is also not unique to genetic engineering, as anabolic steroids and growth hormone are already used to increase size and strength beyond what is natural. However, the potential for enhancement is far greater with genetic engineering. While correcting the genetic defect that destroys the immune system in SCIDS seems to be clearly desirable, should we develop "therapies" that can be used to enhance athletic prowess or intelligence? Should we search for genes involved in eliciting ethical behavior (although "ethics genes" seem far-fetched, genes have been found that have been implicated in schizophrenia, and various other behavioral phenomena)?

The issue of enhancing what it is to be human is especially apparent with germ-line therapy. We have the technology to do whatever we want to our species. List the things that you wish you were—taller? better looking? smarter? The sky is the limit. Would you want these things for your children? Who wouldn't?

Couples who can't have children because of male infertility often go to sperm banks to acquire sperm for artificial insemination. These couples typically display a new car shopping attitude towards their choice of a sperm donor. The necessary qualifications to be a sperm donor read like a spec sheet for a master race—over six feet tall, athletic, high IQ, handsome, perfect eyesight, etc. Would you expect a woman to purposefully seek out the least genetically endowed father for her child? The new genetic technology will bring about lots of these decisions, along with the consequences for deciding wrongly.

What constitutes a wrong decision? At what point does correcting a defect become enhancing a characteristic toward some idealized state? These questions take us to the heart of our feelings about diversity and our feelings about discrimination. In choosing what traits to correct or enhance, we are choosing what traits we will discriminate against. We must proceed very cautiously. With all the potential for abuse, should we proceed at all? There are at least two healthy girls who would say we should.

CASE STUDIES

Genetics and Ethics

Release of Genetically Engineered Organisms
(Jennings, Nolan, Camp, and Donnelley 1990, 1-13)

Gary Stroble, a researcher at Montana State University, apparently frustrated with the regulatory bureaucracy that oversees the release of genetically engineered organisms into the environment, decided in June of 1987 to inject 14 American elm trees on the university's campus with a genetically modified strain of *Pseudomonas syringae* without waiting for approval of the university's bio-safety committee or for federal approval from the United States Environmental Protection Agency and the National Institutes of Health. Stroble's work was designed to show that the originally pathogenic *P. syringae* could be genetically altered in ways that would cause it to protect non-diseased trees from Dutch elm disease.

Many critics labeled Stroble's actions arrogant and irresponsible, but other researchers admitted that they had been tempted to act similarly because of the overly restrictive nature of current regulations on environmental release of genetically engineered organisms. Stroble could face loss of his job, loss of grant funds, public censure, and possibly criminal charges if the release of the *P. syringae* were held to violate the Federal Fungicide, Insecticide, and Rodenticide Act.

You are asked as a member of Stroble's department to testify to a university review committee convened to consider possible disciplinary action. What would you say about the morality of Stroble's actions and what course of action would you recommend that the committee take?

Environmental Ethics

The School Board Confronts Environmental and Fiscal Responsibility
(Jennings et al. 1990, 4-12)

A district school board is considering whether to eliminate plastic styrofoam trays, plates, and cups in favor of either washable cafeteria products or paper and cardboard products. To insure good insulation, CFCs (chlorofluorocarbons) are used in making the styrofoam products; however, CFCs ascend into the atmosphere, where they are broken down by ultraviolet radiation from the sun. A single atom of chlorine will then destroy about 1,000,000 molecules of ozone. For this reason, scientists estimate that 3-5% of the global ozone layer has been destroyed by CFC, and that these gases are also responsible for 15-20% of the world's global warming trend or "greenhouse" effect.

At one high school, an environmental issues group, Advocates for the Earth, has repeatedly lobbied the school board to change cafeteria products, on the grounds that continued use of the plastic of foam products is environmentally irresponsible. Frustrated after one unsuccessful attempt, some students participated in a cafeteria sit-in, and several were subsequently suspended for refusing to return to class.

As the meeting convenes, the school board maintains that the committee must assess not only the environmental effects but also the fiscal effects of the choice. A case of 500 foam trays, the chairperson notes, costs $13.95, while a case of 500 paper trays cost $49.81, an increase of nearly 400%. 250 foam slide-dish trays cost $11.10, while the same number of paper trays costs $21.15. The annual cost of cafeteria operations at the district's schools exceeds $100,000. The chair observes that the board will consider several alternatives: (1) the purchase of permanent dishes, silverware, and dishwashers to clean them; (2) a switch to paper products, which are easily recycled; (3) the continued use of the foam products, while seeking ways to have them recycled. Options 1 and 2 would so significantly increase the cost of cafeteria operations that money will have to be taken from some other item in the school budget. The school board makes it clear that they will not reduce instructional programs for this purpose, so it is likely that some extracurricular student activities would be reduced or eliminated.

The board has allowed student representatives to make presentations before it makes its decision. What option will you recommend?

Not In My Backyard
(Jennings, et al. 1990, 4-16)

Some 240-260 million tires are discarded annually in the U.S. and landfill space is rapidly shrinking. Officials for the town of West Valley have developed a law they believe will solve their community's financial difficulties and provide at least a regional solution to this aspect of the nation's growing garbage crisis. West Valley residents have been asked to give approval to the town commission's plan for construction of a power plant that would burn some 10 million discarded tires a year.

West Valley would benefit from the plant in many ways. Approval of the plant would likely attract new companies to the town's fledgling industrial park. Some 200-250 local workers would be hired for construction of the plant, and 50 permanent staff positions would be created by the OxKen Energy Company upon its completion. The town would also receive $1 million in property taxes annually from OxKen, which the commission wants to use to reduce local property taxes, buy computers for town offices, build new community ball fields and recreation facilities, and buy new fire-fighting equipment. Other communities may also benefit. The plant will generate 267.5 megawatts of electricity, enough power for 25,000 homes, which will be sold to the regional utility company. And OxKen's incinerator technology will not only help with the tire disposal problem within a radius of some 200 miles, but its pollution control system can be used to trap three pollutants—scrap metal, fly ash, and sulphur—that can be recycled.

However, several neighboring towns believe that West Valley is being given an economic "free ride" at their expense; they feel that the overall regional impact of the plant will have adverse consequences for their communities. Officials of Pleasant Field, for example, are upset that their town will be on the main traffic route to the plant; some 25-30 tractor trailers a day are expected to pass through the town, creating traffic safety problems and necessitating the hiring of additional police and traffic officers. Other local officials have noted that emissions from the OxKen plant will likely be carried by prevailing winds to nearby reservoirs that are the major source of drinking water for many communities. Even though state environmental officials have reported that the plant will pose no environmental hazard, some residents of nearby communities are selling their homes because of fears of air pollution, and an adjacent state downwind from the plant recently enacted a law prohibiting shipping tires across state lines for purposes of burning.

Should the voters of West Valley approve construction of the plant? Are there alternatives to the West Valley plan that are economically feasible and environmentally acceptable?

Science Teaching Activity

Mel Briscoe - Physical Geology, Community College of Aurora
(Lisman 1992a, Project Reports)

The issue under consideration is the construction of a dam. The specific factors affecting the dilemma are as follows:

1. Farmers below the dam had owned and occupied their land since the 1600's when their Indian and Spanish ancestors intermarried and settled on the land which provides their sole source of livelihood. They needed the dam to provide a supplemental water supply to support their increased population and to meet needs for irrigation water which varied seasonally.
2. One hundred miles away, the city had experienced a rapid population growth. The city had increased needs for environmentally clean energy sources. The City Council encouraged development of a dam in the Safford Valley to provide the needed energy.
3. One half-mile below the dam site is the town of Graham which averaged a population of 400 people. The village was built in 1860 by Mormon pioneers.
4. The proposed dam site was surveyed by a team of geologists and engineers from the U.S. Geologic Survey and the Army Corps of Engineers. The chief geologist recommended that the dam NOT be built in the Safford Valley just above the village. The rationale was that the dam site was crossed in one direction by a dozen faults. The dam site was crossed in another direction by one major fault. The rock in the valley is "friable" which means that it could crumble under certain conditions.
5. The dam was built by the government, despite the geologic report. The chief geologist published a statement of his disapproval that the dam was built on this site and disclaimed responsibility for any loss of life or property resulting from the dam breaking.

The class was assigned to role play the following scenario.

It is now 30 years later. The descendants of the original stakeholders in the dam are reconsidering the ethics of building the dam.

- Group One: descendants of the farmers.
- Group Two: descendants of the citizens of the city.
- Group Three: descendants of the residents of the town of Graham.
- Group Four: descendants of the original team of geologists and engineers including a geologist daughter or son of the chief geologist.

The group in the role play must consider the following questions in their discussion.

1. What assumptions does your group make about the present state of affairs?
2. What were the pros and cons of building the dam?
3. What were the ethical issues?
4. What conclusion does the group reach about the ethics of building the dam?

Linda Bisbee - Biology: Nutrition, Community College of Aurora
(Lisman 1992b, A Participant's Handbook, 85-6)

Auroral Laboratories, Inc., announces a new food additive, bimethylcyclopentamidine (BMCP). BMCP has the following properties:

1. It is relatively inexpensive, soluble in both fat and water and easily made.
2. It extends the life of fresh food by roughly three (3) times, maintaining 95% of original nutritional value.
3. In canned or frozen food, BMCP maintains original flavor and color of the product.

It is estimated the BMCP will result in a total food savings in the world of 25.6 billion U.S. dollars yearly and increase the nutritional value and amount of food available, particularly in the Soviet Union and Third World countries. (In the Soviet Union, it is estimated that 25% of all food harvested rots prior to reaching the markets.) In the U.S., it is estimated that BMCP is a $250 million per year industry, of which Auroral Laboratories, Inc., could realize a minimum of 10%. It is also expected to reduce farmers' losses due to spoilage and increase the food supply in the U.S., as well as reduce consumer food prices by an estimated 6.5%.

In animal testing, however, BMCP causes melanoma (a particularly fatal skin cancer in humans) in 25% of all animals whose skin was sprayed with the substance. No animals developed any tumors when BMCP was ingested.

Your group needs to discuss the answers to the following questions:

a) What are the advantages or values of BMCP?
b) What are the disadvantages of BMCP?
c) Should the product be used?
d) What is the mission/purpose of your group?
e) What ethical dilemmas do you see arising from your group's position?

12

Ethics in the Humanities Curriculum

I focus in this chapter on the morally educative value of literature, especially fiction. I am discussing this topic because literature provides a unique way to introduce ethics discussion in the classroom. The curricular integration of ethics works well in many courses in a humanities program besides the study of literature. In the applications section, I provide a number of examples of how one may usefully present discipline-appropriate case studies in English, speech, and history classes. Some novels, short stories, and plays can be used similarly as "cases" when the story presents a typical ethical dilemma, such as Ibsen's *An Enemy of the People*. But using literature as a tool of ethics opens other avenues of moral teaching as well. Literature has the capacity to contribute to the development of moral self-understanding. It also can help us gain moral insight into the experiences of others. Coles (1989) has written persuasively about how literature has influenced and humanized him in his work as a psychiatrist and afforded him understanding throughout the years as he has worked to understand the moral life of children.

THE MORAL VALUE OF LITERATURE

I recognize that the moral role of literature is a contested topic. Many different views currently prevail. This includes the subjectivism of reader response theory (Fish 1980), the ethical skepticism of the post-modern approach of Derrida (1976, 1981), formalistic approaches that disavow moral structure as inherently part of literature, and the moralism of neo-Marxist views. I (Lisman 1984, 1988) critique these theories elsewhere. Booth (1988) has recommended that we not limit ourselves to one interpretation of the moral function of literature, but instead remain open to differences of authorial intent and readers' varying responses. This open-minded attitude is supremely important in making sure that we do not prejudge literature as we approach it. Nevertheless, the history of literature and particularly fiction, exhibits that serious fiction, on the whole, has a moral structure. I have this tradition in mind as I attempt to explicate this structure and then suggest ways that fiction can contribute to moral growth.

An important value of literature is that it has the capacity to deepen our moral understanding. Fiction can accomplish this moral effect because the moral world of fictional characters is in many respects similar to our moral world. We experience ourselves and others as moral beings and recognize situations as morally significant. Similarly, fictional characters are "moral beings" in the same sense. The characters of fiction "live" in a moral community with its implicit moral norms and expectations. Sometimes characters abide by these norms. Often they are at odds with them.

The moral understanding we gain from fiction is not theoretical but concrete. This concrete moral understanding is primarily self-understanding. Moral self-understanding does not refer primarily to our sense of right and wrong or of our obligations, though this is included within this notion. Instead, it refers to the awareness of those distinctively human characteristics by virtue of which we are moral agents, including particularly our sense of moral limitations and possibilities. One of our moral limitations is the fact that we often cannot be sure we are doing the right thing. We often must act being unsure of the outcome or recognizing that there may be unanticipated complexities. In terms of possibility, we are aware of ourselves as autonomous. There are occasions when we experience our autonomy as a burden. We are thrust in painful situations in which what we are convinced is the morally right thing to do may harm others. Ibsen's play *An Enemy of the People* illustrates this well. The Doctor turned the entire town against him because he made public the unsanitary conditions of the town's baths.

Since the characters in fiction also are "moral beings," we are able to increase our comprehension of ourselves as morally contingent and autonomous persons as we enter their moral world. Through reading about these characters we can gain insight into how other moral beings react to moral situations not completely unlike those we encounter.

One might ask, why should we turn to fiction for moral understanding since we are moral beings? To begin with, the best novels are those that through characterization provide us with simulated experiences. Through the contemplative experience of reading we can gain deeper insights into ourselves than we may obtain in real life, where we either may not encounter just the kind of situation being fictionalized, or we do not have the luxury to reflect on the situation before we must act. Dostoevsky provides a good example of a novelist who presents extremely dense stories that focus on the moral concerns of the main characters. Dostoevsky sets the scene with a minimal amount of description and plunges right into the character's urgent concerns.

Second, we also can gain insight into the inner experience of other "moral beings" through fiction. We may come to know what it is like to be a Raskolnikov who murders the old money lender as a crazed Nietzschean test of whether he is capable of devising and living by his own individual moral code. Or we may come to understand something of what it is like to be in the grip of the theistic anomie, or religious alienation, of Kafka's Joseph K.

Third, we turn to fiction precisely because the "moral beings" are not actual people who live down the street. We are fascinated by what happens to people endowed with the "twofold reality" of literary characters. On the one hand, they reflect the historical and psychological reality of members of society, and on the other, they possess all the magical power of an imaginary creation.

Fourth, we can gain by means of fiction an appreciation for concrete, complex moral conflicts. The novel aids us in the imaginative recreation of moral perplexities. For example, Doris Lessing in the *Golden Notebooks* presents us with moral perplexities connected with being a woman and a person of social conscience in the present century. Ralph Ellison in *The Invisible Man* dramatizes the dangers for individuals and society when people define themselves in terms of externally imposed values. Toni Morrison's *Sula* portrays the conflicts resulting from the individual's quest for independence and self-realization in a society that values conformity and offers limited opportunities for personal fulfillment. In *The Yellow Wallpaper,* Charlotte Perkins Gilman presents the ways in which social and sexual expectations can limit an individual's opportunities for fulfillment. Finally, while we may learn a great deal about ourselves through our involvement in moral situations, our biases often make it very difficult to be objective. In contrast, reading a novel often affords us insights into our own experiences or situations that otherwise might be difficult for us to acknowledge. Ken Kesey's *One Flew Over the Cuckoo's Nest* may enable us to learn something about the painful absurdities of our own world as we see it from the perspective of the Chief and McMurphy. Malcolm Lowry's *Under the Volcano* depicts the life of a hopeless alcoholic, affording insights into the depth of despair and pointlessness that it may be very difficult to acknowledge. F. Scott Fitzgerald's *The Great Gatsby* depicts how the values and myths associated with the American Dream shape individual choice. In his short story, "Dry September," William Faulkner writes about a man caught between what he knows is right and the power of those forces that demand a terrible price for his being true to a higher sense of morality. Finally, Hemingway's *The Sun Also Rises* deals with the struggle of trying to find a moral purpose in a society for which he has no hope.

LITERATURE AND MORAL EDUCATION

The surge of interest in the role of narration in moral development (Tappan & Packer 1991) has produced significant insights into the nature and effect of narration in relation to moral growth. It has been argued that narration, or telling stories, is the means by which one gains an understanding of how one is morally situated and a sense of personal sovereignty or empowerment (Tappan & Packer 1991). Story-telling is one of the means by which one makes sense of oneself as a self. Of particular interest here is Tappan's view, based on the work of two Russian semioticians, Lev Vygotsky and Mikhail Bakhtin, in which the "social nature of *language* is the key to understanding how and why psychological functioning has its origins in social processes and social relations" (Tappan 1991, 247). Language, Tappan contends, "mediates the functioning of the psyche in the form of different internalized voices engaged in *inner dialogue*" (248). When children make moral judgments, such as "That's not fair!" or "You don't care!" they are not expressing moral beliefs whose ontogenesis lies within their own individual psyche. They are "expressing culturally specific words, languages and forms of discourse they have heard from others (parents, teachers, friends, etc.) that they now use to mediate their own moral functioning" (249) Tappan believes, and I concur, that moral development proceeds through internalization of social discourse. The moral voices of justice and care, the relational experiences of inequality and of attachment "do *not* acquire their *moral meaning* until *after* the moral voices/languages of justice and care have been internalized." (Tappan 1991, 249). Tappan concludes that a young person's narrative representation of one's lived moral experience provides access to "the semiotic reality of her process of moral functioning in response to that experience" (251).

Good novels exercise their moral effect through theme and character. Of course, it is necessary that the work be stylistically successful, but it is not stylistic success alone that enables a work to achieve its effect. The work must treat characters so we gain insight into motive and purpose. It is not a work's "message" that makes it morally efficacious.

The Morally Educative Function of Literature

In a previous chapter on moral virtue, I claimed that a morally literate person is one who has certain self-directed virtues, such as self-respect, self-responsibility, and a strong sense of autonomy. A moral person also has other-regarding virtues, such as compasssion, a sense of justice, and a sense of civic responsibility. I turn next to how literature can greatly affect the moral virtues.

It is not the purpose of fiction to present moral messages or to advocate a specific moral point of view, although a character in a novel may certainly do this. We should not expect literature to advocate any specific view of what the good life consists of, whether it involves being a person of religious faith or being a humanist or being an "absurd man." Moreover, since whatever deepening of experience we gain through fiction is primarily by means of the literary characters, we expect those characters to embody values in the way people do. Some people are primarily selfish, and others are altruistic. Still others are gripped by a sense of meanness or malaise. Fiction contains characters who exemplify these, and many other norms of life.

The first contribution of literature to moral education is that of intensifying our understanding of moral agency. This includes enlarging our understanding of human possibilities and limits. How does it achieve this effect? Human beings are tempted to deny their ontological limits and possibilities, such as the reality of death, the fact of aging, and the fact that we live in a contingent world. We also at times find it difficult dealing with our freedom of choice and certain moral responsibilities. Many themes in literature deal with these dimensions of the human condition.

One theme is the problem of human autonomy itself. Coping with the reality of human freedom is often extremely painful for individuals. Some people attempt to escape from their essential freedom into an idealistic world of supernatural faith. Others adopt the opposite extreme of deceiving themselves by denying their freedom and attempting to live out their lives in terms of the stereotypes of the masses. A good literary presentation of this latter type of problem is Walker Percy's *The Moviegoer*. Binx Bolling wavers between an unthinking life of earning money and seeking materialistic pleasures and a life of searching for deeper values. Other novels dealing with this theme are Jean Paul Sartre's *Nausea*, Graham Greene's *The Power and The*

Glory, and Ernest Hemingway's *The Sun Also Rises*.

Another important theme is the conflict of the individual and society. This theme, of course, ranges over many different kinds of conflicts, from those of the nineteenth century novels of Emily Bronte and Jane Austen concerning the behavior of individuals in a society with very circumscribed social roles, to more contemporary novels, in which part of the problem confronting individuals is that they do not know or care about what is conventionally expected of them by society. This latter theme is treated in Albert Camus' *The Stranger*, Fyodor Dostoevsky's *Crime and Punishment*, and Joseph Heller's *Something Happened*.

Mark Twain's *Huckleberry Finn* deals with the conflict of individual conscience with social norms. Huck, in his dealings with Jim, struggles with the social norm of regarding Blacks as inferior to Whites and his own judgment that Jim is also a human being. Other novels emphasizing the conflict between the individual and society are William Faulkner's *Light in August*, Ken Kesey's *One Flew Over the Cuckoo's Nest*, and George Orwell's *1984*.

Another theme in literature is the search for self-understanding. This has become a major theme in contemporary literature because of the pervasive sense that there are no longer any "Moral Absolutes." Holden Caulfield in *The Catcher in the Rye* by J.D. Salinger struggles to understand himself at a difficult time of his adolescence when he feels hemmed in by an essentially "phoney" society (Lisman 1989). Many other works deal with the theme of the individual's search for meaning or sense of loss of meaning, including F. Scott Fitzgerald's *The Great Gatsby*, Malcolm Lowry's *Under the Volcano*, and John Updike's *Rabbit Run*.

A final theme is that of moral responsibility. In John Steinbeck's *The Winter of Our Discontent*, Ethan Hawley finds that his desire for financial independence brings him in conflict with what he believes his moral responsibility to be toward his family and his best friend, Danny Taylor. Other works dealing with aspects of this theme are Steinbeck's *Of Mice and Men*, John Knowles's *A Separate Peace*, and William Faulkner's "Dry September."

Literature also can promote the growth of moral sensibility. This can be accomplished in at least two ways. One is by helping us see through morally shallow or inhibiting ways of feeling, particularly stereotyped perceptions (Greene 1978). A work of art, when attended to for its qualities, can release a reader into his or her own inner world. It may jolt the reader into self-confrontation and enable the reader to depart, if only briefly, from comfortable, habitual ways of seeing and thinking.

The other is the more positive contribution of actually enriching our emotional life, including our emotional capacity to respond to others. Great works of literaure possess the power to move and delight a great diversity of persons in imagination.

Literature can play a contra-hegemonic role. I assume that we live in a hegemonic society. Following Antonio Gramsci, hegemony can be described as an organizing principle or world view, ideology, or system of beliefs that is diffused by agencies of ideological control and socialization into every area of daily life (Weiler 1988). Simply put, hegemony is the diffusion of ideals and values that serve to perpetuate the dominant class. Literature serves hegemonic purposes. This is true of popular literary genres, such as mysteries and romance fiction. The detective appeared as a popular hero when business corporations emerged as the focal institutions of American life. "The fantasy of a lonely, but morally impeccable, hero corresponds to doubts about the integrity of the self in the context of modern bureaucratic organization" (Bellah et al. 1985). Some contemporary mysteries, including those by P.D. James and Colin Dexter reflect a change in the value perspective of people immersed in our highly bureaucratized life. These authors create detectives who live psychologically disconnected from their role of detective, while cultivating their interiority. This condition mirrors the current trend of the professional class. Rather than acknowledge this aspect of bureaucratic organization and strive to change organizations, readers seek escape from their plight in mysteries and related genres. Another popular counter-hegemonic novel form is the romance novel. These works serve the purpose of elaborating what has been called the "domestic code" that reinforces the sexual division of labor (Christian-Smith 1990).

Hegemonic works of fiction that reinforce the values of domination must be distinguished from those that reinforce the acceptance of domination.

Literature of Domination

The literature of domination reinforces the values of the dominator in ways that prevent the dominator from understanding one's role as a dominator. A good example of this kind of novel is John Updike's *Rabbit* series. Although Updike's technical virtuosity and his ability to portray the consciousness of a thoroughly upper-middle class man is admirable, his work is mainly social realism. It gives little insight into the life of this man as both dominator and dominated, which I consider to be the distinctive predicament of the upper-middle class in our society. In *Rabbit is Rich* and *Rabbit at Rest*, Harry Angstrom is preoccupied with his sexual relations with his wife and other females. In the latter novel Harry's wife, Janice, has inherited her father's Toyota dealership, which Harry oversees. Harry has gone into semi-retirement in his mid-fifties and delegated the duties of the daily supervision of the dealership to his son, Nelson. Unfortunately, Nelson is addicted to cocaine and almost bankrupts the dealership by stealing from the company. After being confronted with his behavior, the son agrees to undergo drug rehabilitation. While his son is recovering, Harry has sex with his son's wife, Pru. She eventually confides in Harry's wife, who is understandably outraged. When Janice confronts Harry, he responds to this crisis as he has in the past. He runs. He goes to their condo in Florida. After being there for a few days, he wonders why Janice has not tried to reach him. Updike (1990, 468-69) writes: "Then he begins to accept her silence as a definite statement. *I'll never forgive you*. O.K., he'll be damned if he'll call her. Dumb mutt. Rich bitch. Working girl yet. [She has become a real estate agent] Think's she so fucking hot ruining everybody's lives with those accountants and lawyers Charlie put her on to, he's known her so drunk she couldn't get herself to the bathroom to pee."

Here Harry typically refuses to acknowledge his responsibility for what has happened. Because of the way Updike presents Harry, the middle-class readership will tend to identify with Harry's condition, believing that Harry's problem is solely due to his own values and choices and not to his class condition. In this respect this work is hegemonic.

Literature of the Dominated

Hegemonic fiction of the dominated presents the classes in ways that deny readers of this class an empowering understanding of their oppression. Such works also reinforce acceptance of false consciousness, that is, they encourage readers to seek a vicarious identity with the values of the upper classes. Although not a literary example, in the movie *Driving Miss Daisy*, the Black chauffeur is portrayed only in a position of servitude to Miss Daisy. His individual life has little or no significance. When in the end of the movie, Miss Daisy declares that the chauffeur has been her best friend, a very distorted view of friendship has been presented.

Turning to another example, bell hooks contends that Spike Lee's movie *Do the Right Thing* denies the value of Black liberation and upholds the values of racial separatism. Hooks says, "*Do the Right Thing* reassures White views that the 'lunatic' violence erupting in 'segregated' black communities finally hurts black people more than anyone else" (hooks 1990, 175). Hooks also observes that when a crowd of Black people watch as policemen brutally murder a young Black man, this conveys the message that "the White supremacist system of policy and control is intact and black people are powerless to assert any meaningful resistance" (176).

Often, well-meaning people of affluence, perhaps unwittingly, reinforce moral hegemony by "acts of charity," demonstrating that it is better to give than receive and that the solution to the problem is through individual effort. What is masked in such "acts of charity" is not only how the political economy (the structure of affluence) enables the affluent to perform acts of charity at no great personal sacrifice (because they are affluent), but also that such "acts" reinforce the ideology of individuality and the virtue of charity, further disempowering the dominated. Perhaps this is why some people in poverty do not want "handouts." This may simply reflect that they have assimilated the ethics of the oppressor in that they want to "stand on their own feet." However, such a response may stem from an intuitive sense that by accepting handouts they are being drawn into the outlook of the dominator that preserves the gap between the affluent and the poor or between the dominator and the dominated.

A good example of a member of the class defiantly resisting an attempt by the dominator to reinforce the ethics of domination is found in Flannery O'Connor's "Everything That Rises Must Converge" (1989b). The story is told from the point of view of Julian, a recent college graduate, who is a fledgling writer selling typewriters. He accompanies his mother on the city bus where she is enroute to a weight reducing class at the Y. The story is set in the South in the early sixties when the city buses have been integrated. Julian is disturbed by his mother's racism.

During the bus trip before any Blacks get on the bus, Julian's mother makes derisive remarks about having to ride on the bus with Blacks sitting in front. Then a Black woman with a little boy gets on the bus and sits beside Julian and his mother. Julian and his mother and the Black woman and her child get off at the same stop. Julian's mother calls out to the Black child, "Oh, little boy!" She says, "Here's a bright new penny for you." O'Connor writes: "The huge woman turned and for a moment stood, her shoulders lifted and her face frozen with frustrated rage, and stared at Julian's mother. Then all at once she seemed to explode. 'He don't take nobody's pennies!'" (O'Connor 1989, 965).

Such "morally virtuous acts," as that of Julian's mother, conceal the "real" ethics of the oppressor, namely the adulation of power. The Black woman in this story is not cozened by Julian's mother's deceitful act of charity.

Toni Cade Bambara's fiction is a good example of counter-hegemonic fiction of the dominated. Her short story, "The Lesson," is a good example of a counter-hegemonic work. In this story a Black woman, Miss Moore, a friend of the family, takes Sylvia, the resistant street-wise narrator, and some of her Black friends from the ghetto downtown to visit F.A.O. Schwartz, an expensive department store. Miss Moore shows them expensive toys. Sylvia says: "I'm thinking about this tricky toy I saw in the store. A clown that somersaults on a bar then does chin-ups just cause you yank lightly at his leg. Cost $35. Who are these people that spend that much for performing clowns and $1000 for toy sailboats? What kinda work they do and how they live and how come we ain't in on it? Where we are is who we are, Miss Moore always pointin out. But it don't necessarily have to be that way" (Bambara 1989, 74-5).

Having examined the morally educative function of literature, I believe that we can see how the teaching of literature can be an essential part of a pedagogy of moral education. Moreover, the use of literature for the purposes of promoting moral growth can be accomplished in a way that satisfies what would seem to be at least two important criteria of any adequate moral pedagogy—respect for the autonomy of the students and the provision of moral guidance without authoritarianism. By focusing on the implicit moral norms of literature, which in the literary experience can deepen the reader's moral self-understanding, the student's autonomy is respected without encouraging relativism. By allowing the student to be guided by the moral structure of literature, literature can be morally directive without being morally authoritarian.

APPLICATION

Fiction

The Situation of Blacks in the South

"Revelation," by Flannery O'Connor (1989)

After the Civil War, the Constitution was amended to prohibit slavery and guarantee Blacks the right to vote. While some progress initially was made toward extending equal rights to Blacks, toward the end of the nineteenth century, racism gripped the South. A pattern of complete racial segregation gradually emerged (Lockwood & Harris 1985, 93). Beginning in the twentieth century, a wave of *Jim Crow* laws flourished in the South, where 90 percent of the nation's Blacks lived (93).

Jim Crow Laws drew the color line almost everywhere, including disenfranchisement, or denial of the vote to Blacks. This typically was carried out by having a literacy test and poll tax. Poor, illiterate Blacks were consequently excluded from the polls. Other Jim Crow laws included segregated restrooms, theaters or theater seating sections, public water fountains, etc.

In 1896 the U.S. Supreme Court, in *Plessy v. Ferguson,* held that "separate but equal" facilities for White and Black people was constitutional. This decision pertained to a petition by Homer Plessy, who was not allowed to ride in the White section of a train in Louisiana. The Plessy decision placed racial segregation under the protection of the federal government. Jim Crow laws continued to thrive until the 1950s, when the *Brown v. Board of Education* decision declared that segregation of public schools was inherently unequal.

During the era of the Jim Crow laws, the only employment available for most Blacks was poorly paid domestic work. Females served as maids in White households. Black males and women hired themselves out as teams of cotton pickers going from farm to farm. Or they worked as farm hands on a single White-owned farm. Some Blacks, along with some poor Whites, worked as sharecroppers, where they rented farm land from White landowners and in turn had to pay their rent by giving the landowner a certain percentage of the earnings from their crops. The landowners usually extracted an exorbitant fee for the land rental. In addition the sharecroppers had to pay dearly for the seed, fertilizer, clothing, and food staples they purchased from the general store, not infrequently owned by their landlord. They were consequently permanently in debt to the landowners and the general store. As James Agee documented in *Let Us Now Praise Famous Men*, sharecroppers lived in abysmal poverty.

Racism appeared in forms other than segregation laws. Blacks were generally considered by most Whites to be "inferior" to Whites. Instead of acknowledging that Blacks were ill-clothed and underfed, having to eat the cheapest food possible, these factors of their environment were taken to be personal attributes of the Blacks themselves. They were considered naturally "smelly," "dirty," and "lazy," and folks who liked "cheap foods" such as turnip greens, watermelon, and pig's knuckles. Following World War I, 70 Blacks in the South were lynched, several of them veterans still in uniform. During this period, the Ku Klux Klan flourished. This White organization inflamed race prejudice and encouraged racial violence (Lockwood & Harris 1985, 95). The television series *Eyes on the Prize* documents many such abuses of Blacks. One episode of the broadcast deals with the murder of a young Black child by several White men. The men were convicted, but the White judge refused to set any punishment for the offenders.

It is against the background of racism that we need to understand Flannery O'Connor's "Revelation." Mrs. Turpin, has brought her husband, Claud, suffering from an ulcer on his leg to the doctor's office. She engages in conversation primarily with two women, one whom she considers her equal, a middle-class, pleasant sort of person, accompanied by a surly college girl, Mary Grace, and a poorer woman with a sickly boy, whom Mrs. Turpin considers "White trash."

As Mrs. Turpin awaits her husband's turn to see the Doctor, she becomes engaged in conversation with these people in which she shows herself to be considerably prejudiced against Blacks and White trash. At one point she acknowledges to herself that a good upstanding Black is even better than White trash. Throughout the discussion, she identifies with the middle-class woman whom she considers pleasant, and by casting knowing glances, is assured that the two of them see eye to eye about their evident superiority to the White-trash people.

Mrs. Turpin, however, does not allow Blacks to escape her scorn of the unworthy. She observes about her Black work hands that she has to be friendly to them: "I sure am tired of buttering up niggers, but you got to love em if you want them to work for you" (O'Connor 1989a, 945). Mrs. Turpin seizes every moment to show that she and the pleasant woman share the same value. When the pleasant woman states that what makes people bad are "dispositions," Mrs. Turpin seizes the moment to extol her own virtues as being "blessed" with a good disposition. She says, "The day has never dawned that I couldn't find something to laugh at" (948).

Throughout the discussion Mrs. Turpin has been disconcerted by the pleasant woman's daughter, who has been glaring at her all along. The girl has been reading a book from which she occasionally looks up to stare threateningly at Mrs. Turpin. We learn that the girl is attending Wellesley College in Massachusetts.

Suddenly, the girl throws her book at Mrs. Turpin. She jumps up and chokes the woman with her bare hands. The girl's mother wrestles the girl to the floor and gets help from the doctor who sedates her and asks the mother to take her daughter to the hospital.

Mrs. Turpin, dazed by these proceeds, at one point asked the girl, "What have you got to say to me?" The girl replies, "Go back to hell where you came from, you old wart hog" (O'Connor 1989a, 950).

When Mrs. Turpin and her husband return to the farm, Mrs. Turpin is very disconcerted about being so severely abused and by being called a "wart hog." She felt that she had been singled out by God for criticism. She could not understand why she, who was a respectable, hard-working, church-going woman, had been singled out for such a disrespectable criticism.

She tells her Black farm workers about this episode. They express disbelief and dismay that she would have been so severely criticized. However, Mrs. Turpin, having no respect for these people, and suspecting them of flattery, dismisses their sympathy. She "knew just exactly how much Negro flattery was worth and it added to her rage" (952).

Finally, that evening at sunset, Mrs. Turpin has a vision in which she is able to reconcile her self—doubts and dismiss this unsettling criticism that has compared her with the ancestors of the animals she tends. She has a vision in which she sees "whole companies of White-trash, clean for the first time in their lives, and of Black niggers in white robes, and battalions of freaks an lunatics shouting and clapping and leaping like frogs. And bringing up the end of the procession was a tribe of people whom she recognized at once as those who, like herself and Claud, had always had a little of everything and the God-given wit to use it right" (O'Connor 1989a, 955).

Although she envisioned the great dignity and respectability of those like herself, her vision revealed by "their shocked and altered faces that even their virtues were being burned away" (O'Connor 1989a, 955). She seemed to have come to the realization that there was a connection between the plight of Blacks and White trash and virtuous people like Mrs. Turpin. She seemed to sense, however fleetingly, that the "virtue" of people like herself had served to oppress both Blacks and White trash, that is the socio-economically disadvantaged.

Ethics Questions

1. Did the girl have any justification for calling Mrs. Turpin a "wart hog from hell?" Assuming she did, was she justified in striking out in anger? Was her anger moral outrage?
2. What do we learn from the story about our tendency to engage in moral rationalization, that is to excuse our own weakness and to shift blame to others.
3. Does Mrs. Turpin reveal a tendency on her part to blame Blacks and poor Whites for their poverty? Does she confuse inequality of condition with inequality of ability?
4. Are there any ways that Mrs. Turpin is a victim?

Sally Heath - Speech, Community College of Aurora
(Lisman 1992b, *A Participant's Handbook*, 105-9)

This course developed the following role play activity in which students were confronted with a moral dilemma when planning a speech.

Scenarios for "Angel On My Shoulder"

In each scenario your team will be required to complete a rough sketch of a speech. In each situation you will need to decide on your purpose, then decide if a moral dilemma exists, what moral principles are involved, and how you will handle it. Regardless of the situation, you must give your speech. You may not postpone it or cancel it. One team member, the speaker, will write a core statement and will prepare a rough outline of the speech. At each point in the process, he/she will be coached by two "angels" sitting on his/her shoulders. One angel will see only the ethical and moral implications of the issue; the other angel will be concerned only with getting the job done. Side coaching may be done at any point in the process. (Remember that moral dilemmas rarely have definite solutions and that you may have to look at options other than the obvious ones.)

1. You have been hired to advertise a certain product that you really don't like: Andre's Pizza. Andre has said he'll donate 50% of all sales generated by your advertisement to your favorite charity. The charity really needs the money (it's about ready to fold up unless they get more money), and no other business has offered such a good deal, so you say "yes" to the advertisement. How will you ethically "plug" the pizza?

2. Members of your investment firm have just uncovered an alleged case of embezzlement within the firm. Two employees may have embezzled money from one of the client accounts. Neither the press nor the police has gotten wind of this yet. You are scheduled to make a presentation to a prospective client that afternoon and had hoped to get that company's large account. (If you do get it, it could mean a big promotion for you from sales to management, which would mean a large salary increase and would be a jump up the corporate ladder.) The thrust of your presentation and the way you had planned to separate your company from the competition is by stressing the loyalty and honesty of your company's employees. Now, with the gossip of the possible embezzlement floating about your office, what will you say in your presentation?

3. You've been chosen to present a speech in favor of animal rights at a weekend rally to protest the use of animals in medical research experiments. After you complete your preparation for the speech, you find out that a close relative of yours who had a life threatening disease has been declared in remission after treatment with a new drug that had been tested on laboratory animals. Plan a new speech.

4. You are lobbying in Congress for a bill that will permit euthanasia. As you are planning your speech, you discover that your aunt, who has been in a coma for 18 months and who was not expected to live, seems to have improved and is showing signs of a possible recovery.

5. You are planning to give a speech in class today on banning the use of styrofoam containers that contain fluorocarbons and boycotting those establishments that use them. At lunchtime you decide you must eat or you'll faint during your speech, but you discover you have only $1.00 in your pocket. The only two restaurants close to the school are Harry's Hamburgers where you can get a coke and a burger for under $1.00 and the Elegant Inn where a coke and a burger will cost you $5.00. But Harry uses styrofoam containers that contain fluorocarbons. With only a dollar in your pocket you go to Harry's for a burger, then come back to school and deliver your speech. What will you say in your speech?

6. You are lobbying for local gun control. You are to give a speech to promote banning the ownership of handguns within the state. As you are writing your speech, your sister reminds you that your father left you an antique handgun in his will and you treasure it because it is your only memento of him. Banning the ownership of handguns means you will have to turn it over to the police to be destroyed. How will you get around this in your speech?

7. You work for a small mining company in a mountain community that is known for its beauty and serenity. The community is suffering from economic problems and people are moving away because there are no jobs. Your company has decided to risk an expansion venture which will bring a lot of money and jobs into the community if it is successful. The expansion will scar the land for some years and will destroy the beauty and solitude of the town because the company will have to sink all its profits back into the venture before it can repair the land. You have been transferred to another state and have already sold your house. Your last responsibility to the company before you leave is to put together a speech to persuade the town council to agree to the project.

8. You buy a piece of land in the mountains and you plan to build a cabin on it. When you apply for a permit to dig a well, the county water board denies you permission because water is so scarce this year any further drain on the water supply may harm others in the area. More wells would require strict rationing of water in the town. How do you plan to argue against the decision?

9. You have been out of work for three months and are nearly penniless. At last you've found the perfect job. You meet all its requirements but one: years of experience in the field. The job requires a minimum of five years experience, but you have only three. You know you are capable of doing the work, however. You've heard though that the boss is a stickler for accuracy and detail and he never bends. How will you tell him about your qualifications in the interview?

Barbara Fleming - English, Community College of Aurora
(Lisman 1992b, *Participant's Handbook*, 112-3)

A role-play activity, similar to "Angel On My Shoulder," features an Advertising Company, which wanted to set Madison Avenue on fire with its success in selling to entirely new, previously untapped markets. Students were to pretend that they had been informed when hired as writers for the company that this company rated honesty in advertising very highly. They must tell the truth and sell the products. Students were put in groups of three, with one being the copywriter, one a "practical angel" whose job was to sell first, the third, an "ethical angel," whose job was to be truthful. Each had to pressure the copywriter in his/her assigned direction. Each group received a card with a product and a market listed on it, with the task of writing an advertisement for television, magazine, billboard, or newspaper. After 20 minutes, the students were to present the results to the "board of directors," the rest of the class.

The products and markets were as follows: expensive athletic shoes to poor, inner-city youths; a very expensive, gourmet TV dinner to the elderly retired on fixed incomes; toy assault rifles to children, both boys and girls, 6 to 8 years old; feminine cigarettes to teenaged girls; light beer to residents of Salt Lake City; sports cars to the Amish.

Thomas D. Brosh - Basic Music Skills, Community College of Aurora
(Lisman 1992a, *Project Reports*, 31)

I devoted one class period (April 3, 1991) to the discussion of an ethical dilemma in music. At the end of the class prior to April 3rd, I reviewed the terms "ethics" and "ethical." I then distributed the following question (prelude) for each student to answer and bring to the April 3rd session: "Do you believe that it is ethical for a classically trained professional musician to convert to rock music performance?" (If yes, why? If no, why?) Six responses were "yes," two were "no," with one abstaining.

The purpose of the video-taped "ethical dilemma in music" class was to ascertain whether, or not, it is ethical for such a conversion to actually occur. In order to facilitate this purpose, I chose to survey the life and music of two age 20's classically-trained musicians who, in fact, have successfully converted to rock music performance: Dan Gorklo, CCA guitar instructor, and Katherine Thomas ("The Great Kat").

Dan, with an M.A. in classical guitar, has also been involved in rock music for a number of years, most recently with the heavy metal group, Vendetta. I was fortunate to conduct an interview with Dan for the benefit of the class members. During the course of the interview, I played recordings of not only the various rock bands with which Dan has been associated, but recordings from his 1989 graduate recital. Dan's responses to the interview questions were well-received by all those in attendance.

"The Great Kat" is a violin graduate of the prestigious Julliard School. Impressed by a Judas Priest video on MTV in the mid-1980s, she "put down her violin and picked up an electric guitar, and set out to change history." (Tina Clarke: *Music Express Magazine*, Feb. 1990, 31). After referencing numerous reviews of "Kat" and her music, I played several examples from her album, *Beethoven on Speed*. These recordings served to prove that, although Kat's dress, antics, lyrics, and music are nothing short of bizarre, she obviously uses her classical background wisely to generate some of the heaviest metal music today.

At the end of the "ethics" class, I distributed the following question (postlude): "After attending today's class on Dan Gorklo and The Great Kat, do you have any reason(s) to change your mind about the ethics of classical musicians converting to rock?" (If yes, why? If no, why?)

Anne Van Etten - Voice Class, Community College of Aurora
(Lisman 1992a, *Project Reports*, 28-30)

The student in this class discussed the following case studies:

1. A young single mother works two jobs to support herself and her children. She takes voice lessons from a high priced voice teacher in the hope of becoming a famous singer. Although the teacher feels she has no talent, he encourages her to pursue her goal. Is the teacher acting ethically?

2. You and your roommate are musical theater performers. One day you take a telephone message for your roommate from her agent about an audition for "The Phantom of the Opera." This could be a BIG Break! You say nothing to your roommate, and since the audition is "open," do the audition yourself. You get the role! Is there an ethical problem here?

3. You have studied with Mr. Lovelysound for 10 years; he is a fine teacher who lacks a "big" reputation. You are ready to acquire an agent but feel that you don't have enough "big" names on your resume. You decide to put down the famous artist Mr. Wonderful whom you studied with for one week in his Master-Class as your primary teacher. Does the need for "big names" justify the lie?

4. A young opera singer envies the commercial success of pop singers and decides to enter the field, abandoning her long and costly training for the financial rewards of heavy metal music. Does this represent an ethical dilemma?

5. A reputable university music department teaches a class in career development which encourages students to misrepresent their age when they audition; "as many years as you think you can get away with." Is this an ethical problem?

6. Operas frequently present situations that present ethical conflicts on a grand scale. In "Otello" by Verdi (based on Shakespeare's play) the four main characters become entangled in a web of lies, jealousy, and intrigue which leads to the murder of Desdemona, Otello's wife, and the suicide of Otello, as well as the professional destruction of Iago, Otello's ensign, and the young officer Cassio. Iago, jealous of Cassio who has been promoted over himself, is successful in planting in Otello suspicion that Cassio has been courting his wife, bringing him down. Coveting Otello's position as general, Iago proceeds to nourish Otello's jealousy, eventually driving him to madness and murder. Emilia, Iago's wife, is aware of her husband's plans. As Desdemona's lady in waiting, she has the opportunity to reveal what she had observed, but chooses to remain silent. What are the ethical dilemmas, if any, presented?

Kay D. Galvan - Painting Class, Community College of Aurora
(Lisman 1992a, *Project Reports*, 32-36)

The ethics project I designed for this class was a role play in which three students were assigned the roles of artists, two students played museum curators, and the remainder of the students were members of the art-viewing public. Each student was given a brief description of his/her role two days ahead of the scheduled role play. The situation was presented in this manner: The Denver Art Museum had one exhibition slot open for the 1992 season. The curators of the Contemporary Department had narrowed their choice to three artists, at least one of whom was highly controversial. The information was leaked to a local newspaper, which printed a story describing the situation and briefly outlining the purpose and work of each artist. The information was scant enough to reduce the public's interest. As a result, the museum curators formulated a panel discussion. They and the three finalist artists sat on the panel. Museum members were chosen at random to attend and to question the three artists. The curators hoped for enough input to be able to more easily make their decision for the remaining exhibition opening.

The three artist characters were developed using real artists as models. The first, "Henry Oakton," was patterned after Robert Mapplethorpe, a photographer whose work focuses on many subjects ranging from male nude to flower arrangements. His controversial piece, "Portfolio X" depicts images of male sadomasochism juxtaposed with floral pieces in a passive-aggressive manner.

The second, "Pilar Ortiz," was patterned after Frieda Kahlo, a Mexican artist and wife of the muralist Diego Rivera. Kahlo's images are very strong both in color and content. She was involved in a bus accident at an early age and was impaled with a piece of metal, which severely damaged many internal organs and caused her physical and psychological pain throughout her life. Her images are often beautiful at first glance and bitterly painful upon closer inspection.

The third artist, "D. E. McKay," was patterned after Robert Altman, an American impressionistic landscape painter. Prints of his work are on sale (and sell quite well) at high-priced print galleries throughout the country. He has not changed his style or subject matter in many years.

Roles were assigned somewhat randomly but I tried to split up cliques and placed some of the older, more conservative students in all three role-playing categories. We performed the play during a 2½-hour session on December 4, 1991. The curators first met with each other to develop a philosophy which they would uniformly promote for the museum.

Second, the curators met with and interviewed the three artists to get a better idea of what imagery each represented and of how the imagery fit into their museum philosophy.

Finally, the panel was set up with the museum members present. Questioning started off very simply and conservatively. There was a great deal of politeness and little argument. However, when questioning moved to the third artist on the panel, Henry Oakton (Robert Mapplethorpe), there was more activity. Comments ranged from "I don't think this type of work is right for a public museum" to "this work doesn't represent the entire population" to "you are a sick individual." The argument continued, moderated by one of the curators and by me (only to keep the discussion moving and to prevent monopolizing by the more vocal students).

At the end of the role play, students were instructed to write a paragraph indicating their choice of artist and reasons for doing so. Meanwhile, the two curators met and made their final decision. They decided to choose the landscape painter, D. E. McKay, because "they wanted to keep their jobs." They thought they would have the best museum attendance by choosing the least controversial figure and imagery. They added they would give Pilar Ortiz a chance during the next exhibition season.

Character Descriptions

1. Henry Oakton: You are an artist with a blossoming career. Although your name is not yet a household word, you have been "noticed" lately by major galleries in both New York and Los Angeles, some of the more avant garde collectors and several recognized art critics. A one-person show at a city museum such as the Denver Art Museum would be a welcome addition to your exhibition record and probably would acquire more major museum showings in larger cities.

Your work is sometimes controversial in nature and sometimes not. You deal with the nude figure as a symbol, in order to bring before the public glimpses into your lifestyle—one that you freely choose to live by, one that is considered unacceptable to most. You are a homosexual male and participate in sadomasochistic activities. Your work is representative of the lifestyle, sometimes in a graphic way, other times in a suggestive way.

You now have AIDS and are seriously ill. This may be the last show you are personally able to oversee.

2. <u>Pilar Ortiz</u>: You are fairly new on the exhibition scene although you have been producing images for many years—since childhood, in fact. Your images speak of the violent physical pain you experience day to day as a result of an accident you were involved in at the age of 14. You have and continue to suffer from internal injury, repeated surgeries, and you have experienced more than one miscarriage.

In your art, you combine these experiences with your cultural background (you were born and raised in Mexico City). Your images contain bright colors and decorative motifs representative of your Central American heritage but also depict you in your intense relationship with your injury. The pieces are often done in the form of self portraits—beautiful at first glance, excruciatingly painful upon further exploration.

3. <u>D. E. Mckay</u>: You are an artist of some renown. Your work sells well in a large commercial gallery both in the original form and as prints. You hold a full professorship at a major university, as well. This combination allows you time and financial means to travel worldwide to paint. Your preferred subject matter is the public park; your technique somewhat impressionistic; your color light and airy.

Some of your images are of park landscape only, others include suggestions of people participating in park surroundings. This exhibition at the Denver Art Museum would be another in a long list of major exhibitions for you. It would increase sales and allow you to make further trips to yet unexplored parks so that you can paint these new places also.

4. <u>Curator</u>: You are a curator for the Denver Art Museum's contemporary department. There is one exhibition slot open for the coming year and you have narrowed the choice of artists down to three: Henry Oakton, Pilar Ortiz, and D. E. McKay.

Your choice will follow the policy you and your co-curator have set for the department in recent years: to choose art that is on the cutting edge, art which speaks about current issues and the current status of life in this universal place and of life at this particular time.

Because you are a public institution, you also will consider the public's educational welfare in your decision. With that in mind, you and your co-curator have invited a random sampling into your office in order to "get a feel for" that viewpoint. Because of an ambitious newspaper reporter, a brief biographical account of the three artists being considered and summarizations of their works have appeared in the local paper. By bringing together the artists and representatives of the viewing public, you hope to come to the best decision for the museum and for art, in general.

5. <u>Panel Member</u>: You are a member of the general art-viewing public—a member of the Denver Art Museum. You and your fellow panel members have been selected at random from the DAM membership to discuss an exhibition opening in the contemporary gallery for the coming year.

You have received a letter from the curators explaining why this meeting was called. About a month ago, an article appeared in one of the local newspapers describing the backgrounds and works of the three artists being considered for this showing. The article caused some concern among the public, in general, so the curators of the contemporary department decided to include a representative sampling of that viewing public in a discussion with the prospective artists. You are free to question both the artists and the curators and to give them your opinion of what should be shown.

Mark K. Smith - Photography, Community College of Aurora
(Lisman 1992a, *Project Reports*, 37-38)

Ethics was implemented into Art 151-160, Photography I, by the presentation of a one-hour video on the photographer Robert Mapplethorpe. followed by dividing the students up into small groups and allowing them to discuss the ethical dilemma below regarding approving grants to artists from the National Endowment of the Arts and the subsequent funding of the N.E.A. from Congress. Each group shared with the class as a whole what each group came up with as their answer.

Case Study

On April 6, 1990, "Robert Mapplethorpe: The Perfect Moment" opened to the public at the Contemporary Arts Center in Cincinnati, Ohio. That Saturday Dennis Barrie, the director, found himself named in a two-count criminal indictment for exhibiting allegedly sexually explicit photographs. The majority of the 175 pieces were devoted to flower studies, celebrity portraits, and classically posed nudes. Seven of these pictures brought the indictment. Two, "Honey" and "Rosie" involved nude or semi-nude children. The other five involved sadomasochistic behavior. One was entitled "Helmut-fist fuck" which had hands in an anus. Another had a dildo in an anus and one had a man peeing in a mouth. Robert himself was in one with a whip in his anus. The show had been shown in several cities prior to this without incident and Barrie was eventually found not guilty. The National Endowment of the Arts (NEA) is a federal agency set up in 1965 to help support the arts. It works on a grant system, giving financial support based on artistic merit to artists and art groups. In its handbook, the Endowment claims that it "does not direct or interfere with the creative activities of individual artists." The NEA is reauthorized periodically by Congress. Because of controversial artists, such as Mapplethorpe and Andres Serrano, whose photograph "Piss Christ", depicted a crucifix submerged in urine, expressing the artist's stand against the commercialization of religion, legislation was passed forcing grant applicants to sign a "loyalty oath" saying their art would not be obscene. This was later found to be unconstitutional. Senator Jesse Helms was instrumental in attaching two provisions to the latest reauthorization of the NEA, one that the advisory panel "take into consideration general standards of decency and respect for the diverse beliefs and values of the American public," and the second that if a funded artist is found guilty by the courts on obscenity charges, he or she will be punished by the endowment and would have to return all grant money. It is the feeling of some that the NEA shies away from funding artists whose work might be controversial to avoid problems with any reauthorization from Congress. The question of "What is art?" and certainly the First Amendment come into play during any discussion.

What you have to decide is: Does the NEA have the right to fund only or mainly non-controversial artists or should it include all artists and state your reasons why.

Case Study for a History Class
(Lockwood and Harris 1985, 251-261)

This two-volume work presents many history case studies and guidelines for ethics discussions of these cases.   One of their examples is "What a Waste, My Lai, Vietnam," that presents the incident of twenty-four-year-old Lieutenant William Calley, who was convicted of ordering a massacre of villagers in My Lai, Vietnam. Information is provided about the background of the Vietnam War and the war protests and the nature of the difficulty that the United States was having in waging this war under the circumstances and restraints of the war effort. The students are invited to consider a variety of ethical questions about this incident. Activities that are suggested for a discussion of this history case study include having students discuss specific points concerning the history of the Vietnam War, the facts of the case, and the ethical issues. About the latter, they state:

1. Americans disagreed about whether Lieutenant William Calley and others should have been brought to trial for what happened at My Lai.   Should Calley have been tried? Why or why not?

2. Ronald Ridenhour heard about what happened at My Lai. He decided to report what happened. Was he right in what he did? Write a paragraph expressing your answer to this question. Give reasons for your opinion.

3. *Seeking Additional Information*. In making decisions about such questions as those above, we often feel we need more information before we are satisfied with our judgments. Choose one of the above questions about which you would want more information than is presented in the story. What additional information would you like? Why would that information help you make a more satisfactory decision?

Other examples from this work from Colonial times to the present include the Salem Witch Trials, Benedict Arnold, Thomas Jefferson and Slavery, an Unconquered Indian (Osceola), Pioneer Suffragist, Stealing North (Richard Wright), Rebel Without a Pause (Zelda Fitzgerald), Japanese Relocation during World War II, the U-2 Episode, and the Bakke Decision. While intended for high school use, this work can be been adapted for use by college instructors.

13

Business and Professional Ethics

Business and professional ethics is one area of the curricular integration of ethics that needs little justification. Business textbooks are now including ethics cases as part of a regular course of study. Business ethics topics include justice and economic distribution in relation to capitalism, social and environmental responsibility and economic efficiency, ethical issues in plant relocation, civil liberties in the workplace, whistle blowing, job discrimination, and responsibility to consumers. Also there is a growing literature on professional ethics, featuring ideas such as professional responsibility and professional ethics codes. In this chapter, I discuss selected aspects of business, occupational and professional ethics. I first comment on how one might construct a discussion of a business ethics issue and then discuss the framework for occupational and professional ethics, which in many cases involve ethics codes. I then offer a variety of case studies that business and accounting faculties have used in their courses and the Community College of Aurora.

BUSINESS ETHICS

A Case Study: Honesty Tests

Imagine that you are unemployed and homeless and come to the Salvation Army to find a place to sleep and employment as a kettler, one who collects money for the Army during the Christmas season. You discover that to get the job, you must take an honesty-test. You must answer a battery of questions such as: "'How strong is your conscience?' 'How often do you feel guilty?' ' Do you always tell the truth?' 'Do you occasionally have thoughts you wouldn't want made public?' 'Does everyone steal a little?' 'Do you enjoy stories of successful crimes?' 'Have you ever been so intrigued by the cleverness of a thief that you hoped the person would escape detection?'" (Shaw & Barry 1989, 268). In addition, you may be asked to reveal the nature, frequency, and quantity of drug use, whether you have engaged in drunk driving, illegal gambling, selling or using marijuana, traffic violations, forgery, and vandalism. Companies such as the London House's Personnel Selection Inventory (PSI) administer this type of test for the Salvation Army and other business organizations. Shaw and Barry report that in one city, potential employees for the Salvation Army were screened by the PSI and then hired without consideration of their test scores. After the collections were completed, the company reviewed the amount collected by each individual against whether the individuals were marked as recommended or not recommended for hiring based on the test scores. The Army discovered that the not-recommended individuals turned in on the average seventeen dollars per day less than those the PSI had recommended (Shaw & Barry 1989, 268). It was estimated that there was a loss of $20,000 as a result of not turning away the not-recommended people.

Is it ethical for the Salvation Army to use pre-employment honesty tests? This is similar to issues as to whether companies should screen potential employees with lie detectors or use forms of electronic monitoring, such as listening in on phone calls and keeping track of the amount of time spent on line on a computer, to ensure that employees are working at maximum quality production. The dilemma in the Salvation Army cases and other similar cases concerns whether the privacy rights of individuals are being violated in the interest of protecting the company's interest of ensuring quality production. A company might argue that because of the high amount of theft and abuse of time, they must institute various monitoring mechanisms, or they face the prospect of reduced quality production or profits. On the other hand, one might argue that honesty tests represent an unwarranted intrusion into the private lives of individuals. In the case of the Salvation Army use of the honesty tests, it could be argued that the tests take advantage of street people for whom whether to try to get a job as a kettler is really not much of an option. Against the Salvation Army Policy, one former American Civil Liberties Union official contended: "Given the unequal bargaining power...the ability to refuse to take a test is one of theory rather than choice—if one really wants a job" (Shaw & Barry 1989, 269).

In discussing cases such as this, it is important to identify the stake-holders involved in the case, the norms in conflict, and what business and legal knowledge are relevant to effectively determine what one would recommend is the morally justified course of action. Cases like this, then, provide an excellent stimulus for students both to attain a deeper understanding of the ethical issues in business and to realize the importance of academic knowledge to make thoughtful recommendations.

PROFESSIONAL ETHICS

Bayles (1989) points out that while there is no generally accepted definition of the term "profession," a working definition of the concept can be provided that states several characteristics that most professions share in common: extensive training, a significant intellectual component to practice, the provision of an important service, and possibly credentialing.

A fairly substantial amount of training is required to practice a profession. For example, lawyers generally must attend law school for three years, and public school teachers must now enroll in a one to three year graduate program in teaching education. Many, if not most, professionals have advanced academic degrees, and one author has contended that at least a college baccalaureate is necessary to be a professional (Bayles 1989, 8).

Second, professional training involves a significant intellectual component. Non-professional training for occupations, such as bricklayers, barbers, and craftspeople primarily involves physical skills. On the other hand, the training of professionals, such as accountants, teachers, engineers, lawyers, physicians, and nurses, involve intellectual tasks and skills. Although some professions involve training in physical skills, e.g., surgery and dentistry, intellectual training is predominant.

Third, professionals generally provide a service to society. Physicians, lawyers, teachers, accountants, engineers, and architects provide vital services to society, while chess experts do not. The technological advances in our society and the associated need of technological experts have accounted for much of the development of new professions, as well as the growth of older ones.

A final feature is credentialing. Most professions must obtain a certificate or license to practice. Having a license is not sufficient to make one a professional. For example, one must be licensed to drive a motor vehicle, but having a driver's license does not make one a professional driver. Also, many professions do not require a license. One does not need a license to be a college instructor or to be an accountant. However, if one does not have to have a license to practice a profession, usually one is required to have at least one college degree. Almost all college teachers have advanced degrees in their field, and accountants are distinguished from bookkeepers by their college education (Bayles 1989, 8).

We might conclude by defining a profession as an occupation that requires extensive intellectual training, including usually a college degree and/or specialized training, and which provides an important public service. Occupations are vocations that require training, though not necessarily intellectual training, often a license, and usually provide an important service to society.

A Case Study: The Challenger Disaster

On the night of January 27, 1986, Robert Lund, as vice-president for engineering at Morton Thiokol, met with engineers who had unanimously recommended against launching the Challenger. Lund was concerned that the "O-rings" might not function at low temperatures. Research had demonstrated that the "O-rings" tended to erode in flight with the worst erosion occurring in the cold preceding lift-off. Although the Space Center wanted to launch, they would not do so without Thiokol's approval. They urged Lund's boss, Jerald Mason, to reconsider. Mason subsequently decided that the rings should hold at the expected temperature. Lund was the only one standing in the way of launching. Mason told Lund "to think like a manager rather than an engineer." Lund agreed to the launch, and the shuttle exploded during lift-off, killing all aboard. An O-ring failed (Davis 1991, 150-51).

Justification of Ethics Codes

If Lund had turned to his engineering code of ethics as a basis for determining what decision to make, he might be guided by two canons. One, engineers should hold paramount the safety, health, and welfare of the public. Two, engineers should act in professional matters for each employer or client as faithful agents or trustees. But the problem that Lund faced was that the two canons were in conflict in the case of the O-rings. Lund felt that the first canon should take priority, while his manager thought that the second canon should be preeminent. His manager was advocating that Lund cut corners to save costs that involved risking the safety of the Challenger crew. How does one justify upholding the public safety as having greater priority than fidelity to the company?

A Modified Social Contract Theory of Justification

Dealing with conflicts of professional codes of ethics invites the more basic question concerning the derivability and justifiability of these codes. There are two prominent views regarding this issue. Davis (1991) reflects one view, a modified social contract view, and Bayles (1989) provides the framework for the derivability and justification of professional codes as founded on the broader moral framework of society. Under this view, professional ethics codes are justified as specific applications of more fundamental moral principles or as institutionally specific rules that enable a profession or occupation to serve professional needs in a way that conforms to the broader moral norms. I first take up Davis' view.

Davis claims that a code of ethics is primarily a convention between professionals. He claims that a profession is a group of persons who want to cooperate in serving the same ideal better than they could if they do not cooperate. Engineers, for example, might be thought to serve the ideal of efficient design, construction, and maintenance of safe and useful objects. A code of ethics would then prescribe how professionals are to pursue their common ideal so that each may do the best one can at minimal cost to oneself and those one cares about, including the public.

Davis (1991, 155) maintains that a code protects professionals from certain pressures, such as cutting corners to save money, by making it reasonably likely that most other members of the profession will not take advantage of one's ethical conduct. Thus, a code protects members of a profession from certain consequences of competition. As a convention, then, a code "provides a guide to what engineers may reasonably expect of one another, what 'the rules of the game' are." A code also provides a guide to what a professional may expect other members of their profession to help them do. If, for example, part of being an engineer is putting safety first, engineers have a right to expect support from other engineers if this commitment is challenged by managers in a company pressuring the engineer to "cut corners" to save money. Then Lund's engineers had a right to expect his support.

So why should a professional abide by one's code of ethics? Davis claims that without a professional code an engineer could not object, as an engineer, when asked to do something objectionable, such as cut corners, although he or she might object on personal grounds. If one did object on personal grounds, without a code one would risk being replaced by an engineer who would not object. An employer or client might rightly treat an engineer's personal qualms as a disability, much like a tendency to make errors. The engineer would be under tremendous pressure to keep "personal opinions" to oneself and get on with the job. Thus a given engineer benefits from other engineers acting as their common code requires. A code of ethics, then, is necessary in part because, without it, the self-interest of individual engineers, or even their selfless devotion to their employer, could lead them to harm everyone.

Davis believes that the moral principle on which this argument primarily relies is the principle of fairness. Since an individual professional voluntarily accepts the benefits of being an engineer (by claiming to be an engineer), he or she is morally obliged to follow the morally permissible convention that helps to make those benefits possible. The convention makes the benefits possible by providing a common standard that "prevents" people from being pressured to cut costs, etc. or put their company ahead of safety.

Davis concludes that when Lund's boss asked him to think like a manager rather than an engineer, he was in effect asking Lund to think in a way that Lund must consider unjustified for engineers generally and for which Lund can give no morally defensible principle for making himself an exception. When Lund did as his boss asked, he in effect betrayed all those engineers who helped to establish the practice that today allows engineers to say "no" in such circumstances with the reasonable hope that the client or employer will defer to their professional judgment, and that other engineers will come to their aid if the client or employer does not defer.

There are two difficulties with Davis' (1991) enlightened self-interest argument. The first difficulty is similar to social-contractarian ethical theory in general, namely that is that such arguments lose their appeal when others begin to break the rules. This is a particular problem for small engineering companies. They compete with other companies in bidding on jobs. A company who holds to a certain cost partly out of a desire to do a job safely finds itself underbid by another company who is willing to "cut corners" in order keep costs down. The appeal to mutual self-interest is ignored in such situations.

The second problem with Davis' view concerns that of dealing with conflicting rules in a code of ethics. In response to the conflict of whether to uphold the canon of holding paramount the safety, health, and welfare of the public, or whether to disregard this canon in favor of showing loyalty to the company, Davis argues that it is reasonable to suppose that the framers of the code intended that the first would be the most fundamental principle. Allegiance to the company requires that one would never endorse doing anything immoral.

While I believe this is a reasonable line of argument, it reflects that there is some deeper ground of moral appeal involved in justifying a code of ethics. Davis' enlightened self-interest argument provides no warrant for the kind of appeal he is suggesting to the lexical priority of the interests of public safety. What this type of appeal suggests is that the interest of public safety outweighs company loyalty, because a code of ethics is a derivation of general moral principles in which the principle of non malfeasance generally outweighs considerations of loyalty. Generally, it is not justified to harm someone to promote fairness or to remain loyal.

Deriving Ethics Codes from Moral Principles

The view suggested by Bayles attempts to articulate the relationship of professional codes of ethics to the broader moral framework. According to Bayles, professional ethics includes those moral principles or rules that guide one in their professional conduct. These principles include fundamental moral principles, e.g., principles of beneficence, equality, autonomy, non malfeasance, promise keeping, etc., because they apply to everyone, including professionals. Second, other rules are specifications of these basic principles that specify types of situations that frequently arise in professional practice. Finally some principles are institutionally derived and are justified by the special function of the profession. I want to take up each of these points.

Fundamental Moral Principles. Since professionals are human beings, fundamental principles apply to professionals. For example, professionals generally should not assault or defraud others; they should also be generally trustworthy and not treat others in degrading ways. Teachers are under an obligation not to treat students abusively and to be honest in daily transactions with students.

Professionally Specific Moral Rules. Some ethical principles of a profession are specifications of these fundamental principles. For example, the principle that a lawyer should "not knowingly...make a false statement of material fact or law to a tribunal," specifies one type of situation in which one should not lie. Teachers, at least according to the Ethics Code of the National Education Association, are prohibited from granting "any advantage to any student" and from using "professional relationships with students for private advantage." The first prohibition is an application of the principle of fairness or justice, while the second might be considered an application of the principle of autonomy, namely that we should not coerce others into doing things. Moral principles that are specifications make these more general principles concrete by showing a type of situation a professional encounters.

Bayles claims that some professionally specific moral principles apply to professionals because the features that make conduct wrong for anyone is usually present in professional conduct. For example, the prohibition of sexual activity with a client in a psychiatrist-client situation is an application of the general prohibition against having sexual intercourse without the free consent of both parties, which could be justified by the principles of beneficence and autonomy. It would be wrong for the psychiatrist to engage in sexual intercourse with a client because the psychiatrist would be, in all likelihood, taking advantage of his or her position of trust and imposing him or herself on the client. Also, because sexual conduct between psychotherapists and clients is detrimental to the therapy, non malfeasance would also specify that the conduct is wrong. The same point applies to the employer-employee relation and is the basis for the prohibition of sexual harassment.

Institutionally Derived Rules. Bayles points out that one major issue in professional ethics is whether justifiable institutionally derived rules can require conduct different from that required by fundamental moral principles. Professionals often have additional duties because they are professionals. Professionally specific principles, however, cannot require a departure from fundamental principles because they only apply fundamental principles to particular types of professional situations. However, unlike professional specific principles, institutionally derived rules might differ from fundamental principles in two ways: (1) Fundamental principles might require acts that institutionally derived norms allow or prohibit; (2) Fundamental principles might prohibit acts that institutionally related rules allow or require. In both (1) and (2), institutionally derived rules allow or require conduct that is wrong by fundamental principles (Bayles 1989, 23).

An example of (2) as applied to attorneys is the norm of attorney-client confidentiality. Attorneys are under a moral and legal obligation not to betray the confidence of their client unless the client reveals an intention to commit a crime. This generates what may appear to be a paradox when it contrasts with our duties as a citizen. If I were walking down the street and witnessed a homicide, I have a duty to report this, including a description of the murderer. However, if a murderer retains an attorney and tells the attorney that he has committed a murder, the attorney has an obligation not to reveal this information to anyone. Here we have an example of a legal course of action that seems to involve the refusal to do what is required by more general moral principles. How, one might wonder, could an attorney be morally justified in not telling the police that his or her client has admitted to commiting the crime?

The reason why we have a legally enforceable client/attorney confidentiality is that such a practice serves the needs of our judicial process. Our judicial process requires that people who are convicted of a crime must be found guilty beyond a reasonable doubt. If the client is not assured that what he or she tells his or her attorney is confidential, the attorney may not be able to obtain all of the information necessary to defend the client. So we see that the attorney/client privilege is an institutionally-derived norm that serves the purpose of the judicial process. It would be possible to change the judicial process to eliminate the attorney-client privilege, but from a moral point-of-view, there would have to be justification for this. One would have to show how eliminating this kind of privileged relationship would better serve the interests of justice in a democratic society. However, this privileged relationship remains justified in terms of the nature of the current judicial process.

Although I have only raised some of the theoretical issues of justification of ethics codes for professions and occupations, it is clear that a code of ethics provides the central framework for the moral orientation of a profession or an occupation. Discussing the code of ethics in an occupation is an excellent way to introduce ethical deliberation in occupational courses.

CASE STUDIES AND CLASS ACTIVITIES

Sandra Richtermeyer - Integrated Accounting on Microcomputers II, Community College of Aurora
(Lisman 1992a, *Project Reports*, 16-17)

Case #1

Tom is an accountant at Nelson & Company. He works closely with the controller, Steve, in preparing the monthly financial statements. During the preparation of the June financial statements, Tom uncovered an inventory error that was made by Steve in a previous month. The correction of this error would materially affect net income for the quarter ending June 30, 1991. The company is profitable but is experiencing severe cash flow problems and is currently trying to obtain a bank loan. The bank is requiring financial statements for the period ending June 30, 1991, before they will grant a loan. Tom prepared the necessary journal entry to correct the inventory error. As Steve was reviewing Tom's work, he insisted that Tom delete the correcting entry. Steve told Tom that they would catch up with the correction and make an adjustment before the end of the fiscal year. Tom does not feel that this action is appropriate. What should he do?

Case #2

Sam is the accounting manager for a Snowster snowmobile dealership in Iceberg, Alaska. The dealership is owned by Jack and Marie who are both active in the management of the company and who also own seven other dealerships in the region. Sam was recently responsible for acquiring a new microcomputer accounting software package that is designed specifically for Snowster dealerships. After reviewing several packages, Sam found this package to be the only one suitable for the dealership. The accounting package cost $3,000 and would not be suited for any other type of business. Sam is the only employee at the company who knows how to use the software and effectively operate a microcomputer. Sam has been very successful in quickly learning how to use the software and has completely implemented the software into all aspects of the accounting system.

Jack has a sister, Joan, who owns a Snowster dealership in a small neighboring town. Joan's dealership is experiencing severe financial difficulties and her accounting manger was forced to quit last month due to illness. After a great deal of difficulty in trying to find a qualified accountant in her small town, Joan has recently hired a new accountant. The new accountant insists on working only with an automated system. Joan's dealership has always used a completely manual accounting system. Joan has a personal computer at her home and has considered bringing the computer to her dealership.

In an effort to help Joan, Jack and Marie would like to give her a copy of the accounting software that Sam recently implemented. Jack and Marie feel that the software will help Joan a great deal and her new accountant could start right away with a good accounting system. Marie, who has never even turned the power switch of a computer, has asked Sam to copy the software onto Joan's computer. Sam explained to Marie that the software came with a license agreement that stated the software could not be duplicated after one backup copy was made. Sam is reluctant to copy the software as Marie has asked. What should he do?

Tracy Wilson - Computerized/Fast Track Accounting, Community College of Aurora
(Lisman 1992a, *Project Reports*, 63-64)

Case #1

An accountant was doing all of the books for a business. Sales taxes were due and the accountant sent in his check in the amount of $144.84. His client then sent him a check for reimbursement of these taxes. The accountant's check did not clear the bank and the State of Colorado started collection action against the client. The client was then forced to pay the sales taxes again in order to stop collection action against himself.

The accountant paid the client $800 against the above amount and claimed that the balance owed to him for accounting fees. The client disagreed with this, stating he owed only $97.00 for back fees.

The above information was furnished by the client.

Accountant's response:

He and the client had been in the restaurant business together for years and had been very close friends, this is why he sent his check in for the sales tax. He presented evidence that the client in fact owed him an additional $160 after the sales tax amounts had been deducted.

Case #2

Client complains that her accountant was wearing two hats, that of accountant and also a securities dealer. Client was sold securities by the accountant and was also sold an interest in a partnership by the accountant. The accountant was also a partner in the same partnership. Client was not happy with the work done on her tax returns by the accountant. She also just wanted the complaint put on record.

Case #3

Client owes accountant $2,000. Accountant is refusing to turn over client's records until this amount is paid. IRS is auditing one of the years for which the records are being held by the accountant. Client cannot address the audit without his records.

Constance C. Seiden Computer - Logic & Design,
Community College of Aurora
(Lisman 1992a, *Project Reports*, 71-72)

Case #1

Acme Software, Inc. developed a computerized medical diagnosis system for hospitals. Sales representatives explained the benefits of the system, and also mentioned its limitations, never claiming the system was 100 percent accurate. General Hospital purchased the system, making it available to all physicians and staff. One of the doctors used the system in diagnosing Peter Smith. The computerized system diagnosed Mr. Smith as having renal failure, and the doctor prescribed the appropriate treatment. The treatment failed. After several months, the physician conducted more tests and determined that Mr. Smith was not suffering from renal failure, but from something else. Meanwhile, Mr. Smith developed a serious infection as a result of the treatment he had received. He lost a lot of days at work because of the treatment and his infection. Mr. Smith's kidney function also appeared to have weakened from the treatment. Mr. Smith wants to sue for compensation and damages. What does this situation imply for all phases of design, manufacture, and distribution of this software? What would you do, if you were a computer software designer in such a situation as this and you believed the company was unethically rushing to producing? (Adapted from *Ethical Issues in the Use of Computers*, by D.G. Johnson & J.W. Snapper)

Donna M. Barr - Introduction to Paralegal,
Community College of Aurora
(Lisman 1992a, *Project Reports*, 42-44)

Attorneys' conduct is guided by the Code of Professional Conduct in Colorado. The Code applies to paralegals as well, even though their attorney employers remain responsible under the Code for a paralegal's actions during their employment. There are nine canons of ethics in the Code. On the second night of class we talked generally about ethics and regulation for the paralegal profession. During nine successive classes we discussed each of the canons generally and by use of case studies. We also discussed the application of each canon to paralegals. I used *Ethics for the Legal Assistant*, by Deborah K. Orlik, for my presentation material and case studies. The case studies in the book all involve paralegals. I also designed an advance organizer for the students to use in taking notes for the ethics topics.

Case #1

Jane, a legal assistant with a law firm specializing in criminal defense, has been working on the criminal defense of Robert Smith, an inmate at Santa Ramos penitentiary. Jane frequently visits Mr. Smith at the prison. Jane's firm also is representing Mr. Smith in a civil matter. During a trial in that matter, Jane is asked to testify concerning what Mr. Smith told her about a business transaction in which he engaged before he was incarcerated. Mr. Smith's attorney (Jane's employer) objects. How should the judge rule on the objection and why?

Case #2

Sam, a probate paralegal, often confides in his wife about the estates with which he is involved at work. Sam believes that as long as he doesn't tell his wife the names of his clients, he has not divulged any secrets. Is Sam right about this?

Case #3

George, a civil litigation paralegal, is seeking to relocate with another firm. During his job interviews, George discussed the cases he works to avoid a potential conflict-of-interest problem with his new employment. Should George tell prospective employers about his clients who are contemplating civil litigation but who have not yet filed a complaint?

Linda Duncan-Berry - Introduction to Business, Community College of Aurora
(Lisman 1992a, *Project Reports*, 49-52)

Case #1

You are aware of fellow workers in your office who are taking pencils, paper, tape, and other such items home for their own personal use. It probably amounts to less than $50 per year for each employee, but about 50 percent of the office workers are doing it. Should you inform management about this situation? Are you cheating the stockholders if you don't bring this to management's attention? How are you likely to be treated by the other employees if you do inform on them and they find out it was you who did so? What are you going to do?

Case #2

You are the production manager for a regional chemical company and have just received a report indicating that one of the company's major products, representing 30 percent of the company's business, could cause cancer for the production workers as a result of exposure to the chemical over an extended period of time. If you stop production of the chemical until safety precautions can be instituted, estimated to take two years, it will require laying off 80 percent of the work force and will cost the company approximately 40 percent of its profits. If you continue with production and work on safety precautions, no layoffs or losses will be incurred, but some workers might contract cancer. What are you going to do? Justify your decision from both the employees' and the investors' perspective.

Case #3

You are a sales representative for a manufacturer of electric power drills, and you have an opportunity to close a big order, one that would put you 15 percent over quota and win you a big bonus. However, the purchasing agent is still wavering between your product and that of a competitor. Your marketing manager has suggested that you send the purchasing agent a stereo system as a gift. What would you do? Why? How would you justify your decision to your boss?

Case #4

You are interviewing applicants for a position on the sales force. You have narrowed down the applicants to two: a female and a male. The female applicant is more qualified than the male applicant and has had a higher degree of success. However, the rest of the sales force is male. They would probably resent having a female work with them, and her presence might hurt morale. You also know that the customers are prejudiced against females and are not likely to buy from her. The male applicant, although not as good as the female, would probably do an adequate job. Which applicant would you hire? Why? How would you justify your decision to your boss?

Case #5

Your company has just developed a new facial cream which needs to be applied only once a day, rather than twice as is customary. Because consumers are in the habit of applying similar products twice a day, they will use two applications unless specifically told otherwise. Thus, if you omit the relevant instructions, consumers will use twice as much of your product as they need to. Would you inform consumers? Why? How do you justify your decision to your boss?

Works Cited

Amott, T., and J.A. Matthaei. 1991. *Race, gender and work: A multicultural economic history of women in the United States.* Boston: South End Press.

Ashmore, R.B., and W.C. Starr. 1991. *Ethics across the curriculum: The Marquette experience.* Milwaukee, WI: Marquette University Press.

Atwood, M. 1988. *The handmaid's tale.* New York: Doubleday.

Ballantine, J.H. 1989. *The sociology of education: A systematic analysis.* Englewood Cliffs, NJ: Prentice Hall.

Bambara, T.C. 1989. The lesson, in *Fictions,* ed. J. F. Trimmer & C. W. Jennings. New York: Harcourt Brace Jovanovich, 69-75.

Barclow, M. 1994. *Moral philosophy: Theory and issues.* Belmont, CA: Wadsworth Publishing.

Barrow, R., and R. Woods. 1988. *An introduction to philosophy of education.* 3d ed. New York: Routledge.

Baxter, W.F. 1983. People or penguins, in *People, penguins, and plastic trees: Basic issues in environmental ethics,* ed. D. VanDeVeer and C. Pierce. Belmont, CA: Wadsworth Publishing, 214-217.

Bayles, M.D. 1989. *Professional ethics.* Belmont, CA: Wadsworth Publishing.

Beauchamp, T.L. 1989. *Case studies in business, society, and ethics.* Englewood Cliffs, NJ: Prentice Hall.

Beauchamp, T.L., and L. Walters, eds. 1982. *Contemporary issues in bioethics.* Belmont, CA: Wadsworth Publishing.

Belenky, M.F., B.M. Clinchy, N. R. Goldberger, & J.M. Tarule. 1986. *Women's ways of knowing: The development of self, voice, and mind.* New York: Basic Books, Inc.

Bellah, R.N. 1976. The ethical aims of social inquiry, in *The social function of social science,* ed. D. MacRae. New Haven: Yale University Press.

Bellah, R.N., R. Madsen, W.M. Sullivan, A. Swidler, & S.M. Tipton. 1985. *Habits of the heart: Individualism and commitment in American life.* New York: Harper & Row.

Benedict, R. 1959. *Patterns of culture.* Boston: Houghton Mifflin.

Bentham, J. 1967. An introduction to the principles of morals and legislation, *The Utilitarians.* New York: Dolphin Books.

Berger, P.L., & T. Luckmann. 1967. *The social construction of reality: A treatise in the sociology of knowledge.* New York: Doubleday & Company, Inc.

Bloom, A. 1987. *The closing of the American mind: How higher education has failed democracy and impoverished the souls of today's student.* New York: Simon and Schuster.

Bok, D. 1988. Can ethics be taught? *Ethics: Easier said than done, 1*(1): 9-15.

Booth, W.C. 1988. *The company we keep: An ethics of fiction.* Berkeley: University of

California Press.

Bricker, D.C. 1989. *Classroom life as civic education: Individual achievement and student cooperation in schools.* New York: Teachers College Press.

Brookfield, S.D. 1991. *The skillful teacher: On technique, trust, and responsiveness in the classroom.* San Francisco: Jossey-Bass Publishers.

Brower, K. 1989. The destruction of dolphins. *Atlantic Monthly,* July: 35-58.

Brown, M.T. 1990. *Working ethics: Strategies for decision making and organizational responsibility.* San Francisco: Jossey-Bass Publishers.

Bultmann, R. 1961. *Kerygma and myth.* New York: Harper and Brothers.

Callicott, J.B. 1989. *In defense of the land ethic: Essays in environmental philosophy.* Albany, NY: State University of New York Press.

Carr, D. 1991. *Educating the virtues: An essay on the philosophical psychology of moral development and education.* London: Routledge.

Catalyst. 1991. Case studies in research ethics psychology case unit 3: The ethics of deception in research. Bloomington, IN: The Poynter Center for the Study of Ethics and American Institutions.

Christian-Smith, L. 1990. *Becoming a woman through romance.* New York: Routledge.

Coleman, J.W., & D.R. Cressey. 1992. *Social problems.* New York: Harper Collins College Publishers.

Coles, R. 1989. *The call of stories: Teaching and the moral imagination.* Boston: Houghton Mifflin.

Cortazar, J. 1989. Press clippings, in *Fictions.* ed. J. F. Trimmer & C. W. Jennings. New York: Harcourt Brace Jovanovich.

Cortese, A. 1990. *Ethnic ethics: The restructuring of moral theory.* Albany, NY: State University of New York Press.

Cunningham, S. 1992. The teaching of ethics: A research paper. Program Officer, Colorado Commission on Higher Education.

Davis, A. 1992. Can we save marine mammals? The deadly decline of the Marine Mammal Protection Act, in *Ethics: Social issues resources series,* ed. E. Goldstein. Boca Raton, FL.

Davis, M. 1991. Thinking like an engineer: The place of a code of ethics in the practice of a profession. *Philosophy and public policy,* Spring: 150-67.

Derrida, J. 1976. *Of grammatology,* trans. G.C. Spivak. Baltimore: University of Maryland Press.

——. 1981. *Dissemination,* trans. B. Johnson. Chicago: University of Chicago Press.

DesJardins, J.R., & J.J. McCall. 1990. *Contemporary issues in business ethics.* Belmont, CA: Wadsworth Publishing.

Dubos, R. 1971. *Mirage of health.* New York: Harper & Row.

Dworkin, G. 1990. The good, the bad, and the uncertain. *U of I Chicagoan,* May: 6-7.

Earley, S. 1987. Protest spawns ethical fight, in *Ethics: Social issues resources series,* ed. E. Goldstein. Boca Raton, FL.

Elmer-Dewitt, P. 1994. Cloning: Where do we draw the line? in *Ethics: Social issues resources series,* ed. E. Goldstein. Boca Raton, FL.

Elms, A.C. 1982. Keeping deception honest: Conditions for social scientific research stratagems, in *Ethical issues in social science research,* ed. T.L. Beauchamp, R.R. Faden, R.J. Wallace, Jr., & L. Walters. Baltimore: The Johns Hopkins University Press, 224-45.

Fenstermacher, G.D. 1990. Some moral considerations on teaching as profession, in *The moral dimensions of teaching,* ed. J.I. Goodlad, R. Soder, & K.A. Sirotnik. San Francisco, CA: Jossey-Bass, 130-54.

Fish, S.E. 1980. *Is there a text in this class? The authority of interpretive communities.* Cambridge: Harvard University Press.

Frankfort-Nachmias, C., & D. Nachmias. 1992. *Research methods in the social sciences.* New York: St. Martin's Press.

Frazer, M. J. & A. K. Kornhauser. 1986. Ethics and social responsibility in science education: An overview, in *Ethics and social responsibility in science education*, ed. M. J. Frazer & A. Kornhauser. Oxford: ICSU Press by Pergamon Press.

Gilligan, C. 1982. *In a different voice: Psychological theory and women's development.* Cambridge: Harvard University Press.

Gilligan, C., J.V. Ward, J.M. Taylor & B. Bardige. 1988. *Mapping the moral domain.* Cambridge: Center for the Study of Gender Education and Human Development, Harvard University Graduate School of Education.

Giroux, H.A. 1988. *Teachers as intellectuals: Toward a critical pedagogy of learning.* New York: Bergin & Garvey Publishers.

Goldberg, H. 1982. Feminism and male liberation, in *Social ethics: Morality and social policy*, ed. T. Mapes A. & J. S. Zembaty. New York: McGraw-Hill Books, 136-39.

Goldston, L. & K. Hendrix. 1994. Date rape: Beyond violence, a battle of words, in *Ethics: Social issues resources series*, ed. E. Goldstein. Boca Raton, FL.

Goodlad, J. I. 1990. The occupation of teaching in schools, in *The moral dimensions of teaching*, ed. J. I. Goodlad, R. Soder, & K.A. Sirotnik. San Francisco, CA: Jossey-Bass, 3-34.

Gosling, D., & B. Musschenga, 1985. *Science education and ethical values: Introducing ethics and religion into the classroom and laboratory.* Washington, D.C.: Georgetown University Press.

Greene, M. 1978. *Landscapes of learning.* New York: Teachers College Press.

—. 1988. *The dialectic of freedom.* New York: Teachers College Press.

hooks, b. 1990. *Yearning: race, gender, and cultural politics.* Boston: South End Press.

Hoschild, A. 1989. *The Second shift: Working parents, the revolution at home.* New York: Viking.

Houston, B. 1989. Prolegomena to future caring, in *Who cares? Theory, research, and educational implications of the ethic of care*, ed. M. M. Brabeck. New York: Praeger.

Humphreys, L. 1975. *Tearoom trade: Impersonal sex in public places.* New York: Aldine Publishing.

Jennings, B., K. Nolan, S.C. Camp, & S. Donnelley. 1990. *New choices, new responsibilities: Ethical issues in the life sciences. A teaching resource on bioethics for high school biology courses.* New York: The Hastings Center.

Kant, I. 1964. *Groundwork of the metaphysics of morals*, trans. H. J. Paton. New York: Harper Torchbooks.

Kenny, A. 1963. *Action, emotion and will.* New York: Humanities Press.

Kohlberg, L. 1971. Stages of moral development as a basis to moral education, in *Moral education*, ed. C.M. Beck, B.S. Critenden, & E.V. Sullivan. New York: Newman Press, 30-41.

Leopold, A. 1983. The land ethics, in *People, penguins, and plastic trees: Basic isues in environmental ethics*, ed. D. VanDeVeer & C. Pierce. Belmont, CA: Wadsworth Publishing, 6-8.

Lisman, C.D. 1984. *The morally educative value of literature.* PhD Diss. Madison: University of Wisconsin.

—. 1988. Marxist literary theory: A critique. *Journal of Aesthetic Education*, 22:2.

—. 1989. Yes, Holden should read these books. *The English Journal*, 78:4.

—. 1991. A critical review of the moral dimensions of teaching. *Educational Theory*, *41* (2): 227-34.

—. 1992a. *Project reports: A resource handbook for integrating ethics into the curriculum*. Aurora, CO: Community College of Aurora.

—. 1992b. *A participant's handbook for integrating ethics into the curriculum*. Aurora, CO: Community College of Aurora.

—. 1992c. Final report. Fund for the Improvement of Post-Secondary Education Ethics-Across-the-Curriculum Project, Community College of Aurora, Aurora, Colorado.

Lockwood, A.L., & David E. Harris. 1985. *Reasoning with democratic values: Ethical problems in United States history*. Vols I and II. New York: Teachers College Press.

McCollough, C.R. 1977. *Morality of power: A notebook on Christian education for social change*. Philadelphia: The United Church Press

McInerney, J.D. 1986. Ethical values in biology education, in *Ethics and social responsibility in science education*, ed. M. J. Frazer & A. Kornhauser. Oxford: ICSU Press by Pergamon Press.

MacIntyre, A. 1981. *After virtue*. Notre Dame, IN: Notre Dame University Press.

Macklin, R. 1982. The problem of adequate disclosure in social science research, in *Ethical issues in social science research*, ed. T. L. Beauchamp, R. R. Faden, R. J. Wallace, Jr., & L. Walters. Baltimore: The Johns Hopkins University Press, 193-214.

Mapes, T.A., & J.S. Zembaty, eds. 1992. *Social ethics: Morality and social policy*. New York: McGraw-Hill Books.

Marquez, G.G. 1988. *Love in the time of cholera*. New York: Alfred A. Knopf.

Milgram, S. 1974. *Obedience to authority: An experimental view*. New York: Harper & Row.

Mill, J.S. 1967. Utilitarianism, in *The utilitarians*. New York: Dolphin Books.

Murray, C. 1984. *Losing ground: American social policy, 1950-1980*. New York: Basic Books.

Nietzsche, F. 1969. *On the genealogy of morals and ecce homo*. trans. W. Kaufmann. NewYork: Vintage Books.

Noddings, N. 1984. *Caring: A feminine approach to ethics and moral education*. Berkeley: University of California Press.

O'Connor, F. 1989a. Revelation, in *Fictions*, ed. J. F. Trimmer & C. W. Jennings. New York: Harcourt Brace Jovanovich, 941-55.

—. 1989b. Everything that rises must converge, in *Fictions*, ed. J. F. Trimmer & C. W. Jennings. New York: Harcourt Brace Jovanovich, 956-67.

Ogbu, J.U. 1988. Class stratification, racial stratification, and schooling, in *Class, race, & gender in American education*, ed. L. Weis. Albany, NY: State University of New York Press.

Okin, S.M. 1989. *Justice, gender, and the family*. New York: Basic Books.

Olen, J.O. & V. Barry. 1989. *Applying ethics: A text with readings*. 3d Ed. New York: Wadsworth Publishing.

O'Neil, E. 1990. The liberal tradition of civic education, in *Combining service and learning: A resource book for community and public service*, ed. Janice C. Kendall and Associates. Vol. 1: National Society for Internships and Experiential Education.

Ortiz, F.I. 1988. Hispanic-American children's experiences in classrooms: A comparison between Hispanic and non-Hispanic children, in *Class, race, & gender in American education*, ed. L.Weis. Albany, NY: State University of New York Press, 163-86.

Orwell, G . 1949. *Nineteen eighty-four*. New York: Harcourt, Brace and Company.

Peters, R.S. 1981. *Moral development and moral education*. Boston: George Allen & Unwin.

Puka, B. 1989. *Who cares? Theory, research, and educational implications of the ethic of care*, ed. M.M. Brabeck. New York: Praeger.

Rachels, J., ed. 1986. *The elements of moral philosophy*. Philadelphia: Temple University Press.

—. 1989. *The right thing to do: Basic readings in moral philosophy*. New York: Pantheon House.

Rawls, J. 1971. *A theory of justice*. Cambridge: The Belknap Press of Harvard University Press.

—. 1985. Justice as fairness: Political not metaphysical. *Philosophy in Public Affairs*, Summer: 230.

Restak, Richard. 1987. The AIDS virus has no 'civil rights', in *Ethics: Social issues resources series*, ed. E. Goldstein. Boca Raton, FL.

Robertson, I.R. 1987. *Sociology*. New York: Worth Publishers, Inc.

Rolston, H. 1988. *Environmental ethics: Duties to and values in the natural world*. Philadelpha: Temple University Press.

Sandel, M. 1982. *Liberalism and the limits of justice*. Cambridge: Cambridge University Press.

Seigfried, C.H. 1989. Pragmatism, feminism, and sensitivity to context, in *Who cares? Theory, research, and educational implications of the ethic of care*, ed. M.M. Brabeck. New York: Praeger.

Selznick, P. 1992. *The Moral commonwealth: Social theory and the promise of community*. Berkeley: University of California Press.

Shaw, W. & V. Barry, 1989. *Moral issues in business*. Belmont, CA: Wadsworth Publishing.

Sheehan,T.C. 1986. *The first coming: How the kingdom of god became christianity*. New York: Random House.

Singer, P.S. 1993. Animals and the value of life, in *Matters of life and death: New introductory essays in moral philosophy*, ed. R. Regan. New York: McGraw-Hill, Inc., 280-318.

Solomon, R. 1976. *The passions: The myth and nature of human emotion*. Notre Dame, IN: University of Notre Dame Press.

Spring, J. 1991. *American education: An introduction to social and political aspects*. New York: Longman.

Stone, L. 1990. Who cares?: Theory, research, and educational implications of the ethic of care, in *Educational Studies: A Journal in the Foundations of Education*, 21:4.

Strike, K.A. 1982. *Liberty and learning*. New York: St. Martin's Press.

—. 1990a. *Liberal justice and the marxist critique of education: A study of conflicting research programs*. New York: Routledge.

—. 1990b. The legal and moral responsibility of teachers, in *The moral dimensions of teaching*, ed. J.I. Goodlad, R. Soder, & K.A. Sirotnik. San Francisco: Jossey-Bass, 188-223.

Sullivan, W.M. 1982. *Reconstructing public philosophy*. Berkeley: University of California Press.

Tappan, M.B. 1991. Narrative, language and moral experience. *Journal of Moral Education*, 20:3.

Tappan, M.B. & M.J. Packer, 1991. Narrative and storytelling: Implications for understanding moral development. *New Directions for Child Development*, Winter.

Taylor, P.W. 1991. The ethics of respect for nature in *Morality and practice*, ed. J. P. Sterba. Belmont, CA: Wadsworth Publishing, 443-54.

Thio, A. 1992. *Sociology: An introduction*. New York: Harper Collins Publishers.

Trebilcot, J. 1982. *Social ethics: Morality and social policy*, ed. T.A. Mapes & J. S. Zembaty.

New York: McGraw-Hill Books, 140-45.

Updike, J. 1990. *Rabbit at rest*. New York: Alfred A. Knopf.

Vuillemot, L. 1992. The fate of baby Amy, in *Ethics: Social issues resources series*, ed. E. Goldstein. Boca Raton, FL.

Weiler, K. 1988. *Women teaching for change: Gender, class and power*. New York: Bergin & Garvey.

Weis, L. 1988. High school girls in a de-industrializing economy, in *Class, race, & gender in American education*, ed. L. Weis. Albany, NY: State University of New York Press.

White, J.E. 1991. *Contemporary moral problems*. Minneapolis/St. Paul: West Publishing.

——. 1994. *Contemporary moral problems*. Minneapolis/St. Paul: West Publishing.

Whitley, G. 1987. A Rape in New Bedford: Living with the backlash, in *Ethics: Social issues resources series*, ed. E. Goldstein. Boca Raton, FL.

Wilson, J.W. 1987. *The truly disadvantaged: The inner city, the underclass, and public policy*. Chicago: The University of Chicago Press.

Index

About the Author

C. DAVID LISMAN is Director of the Community Involvement Program and Chair of the Philosophy Department of the Community College of Aurora in Colorado. He is co-editor of *Community Colleges: A Catalyst for Civic Change.*

ISBN 0-275-95304-1

HARDCOVER BAR CODE